Maggie's Brood

Maggie's Brood

An Irish Immigrant's Tale of Tragedy, Trauma and Triumph

Elizabeth Osta

Other books by this Author:

Jeremiah's Hunger
Saving Faith
Life Shifts: Essays of Hope

www.elizabethosta.com

Table of Contents

Dedication

For Margaret Buckley Donegan
Who somehow always got on with it.

And to my husband, Dave Van Arsdale
Who astounds me with his love.

Acknowledgments

xi

With gratitude for the guidance and wisdom of family:

Maggie's daughter, *Aunt Veronica,* who made it possible for so many of us to visit the farm and be touched by its magic.

To Matriarchal cousins Margaret *Mary Donegan Celano* and Maureen *Donegan Mirucki, Betty Donegan Keenan, Ruth Donegan Delaney, Cecilia Donegan Payne,* their brothers, and cousins *Terry Payne* and Kevin Celano whose research and love of family was priceless.

To the Fennelly and Richards families who have brought the Galenas and Kerrigans alive for us all.

To my siblings, *Mary Jean,* John, *Jim,* Tom, Donald Mark, and Kathleen who love these stories. A forever thanks to my nieces and nephews, Kathleen Mary, Mark Francis, David Michael, Jean Elizabeth, Timothy Matthew, and their children whose lives bring hope for continued healing and triumph.

Kudos to the Village who has supported this publication: Lima Historical Society, Livingston County Historical Society, and Ontario Historical Museum, Patrick, and Rose Reynolds of The American Hotel in Lima where many of these stories originated, Tom Tryniski of *Fulton Postcards* that hosts the largest on-line collection of Newspapers in New York State, the *Lima Recorder* key to research for this book.

To Dennis Hogan, genealogist extraordinaire who unlocked the pathway to the *Lima Recorder* and Kathy Urbanic at Sisters of St. Joseph Archives whose assistance was invaluable.

Many thanks to the Mentors and Writers:

To *Finvola Drury* whose class *Writing Your Life* at Writers&Books so many years ago, changed my life forever.

To gifted editor and author Julianna Ricci, who brought order and care to this story, Evie Brady who brought promise and Sarah Itkin who brought vision.

To beloved writers: Marge Reading Brown, Betsy Campbell, Jane Shoston, Maxine Simon, Kathleen Stoddard, Pamela Pepper, Jenny Lloyd, Lee McAvoy, Sonja Livingston, Greg Gerard, Rosita Caridi Miller, Patricia Hart, and Kitty Forbush.

And to Luann Pollock from the Publishing Services division of Story & Song Bookstore Bistro, for assistance with publishing and Caroline Blochlinger for the layout of this second edition.

Special Kudos to Book Cover Designer, Patrice McPeak, @pmmcpeak/ www.patricemcpeak.com

Names in italics are deceased

A Note to the Reader

Dear Reader,

I began to think about writing my Grandmother Maggie's story when I was a young child. The sound of the crushed stones of her driveway as our Chevy station wagon rolled into her home in Lima, New York was my opening description.

All seven of us along with our parents piled out into the rural landscape, a cream-colored barn with big red doors, gardens everywhere and Grandmother, aproned, and hands on her hips, watching us as we roamed about.

The side porch with its chaise lounge; the front porch with white rocking chairs and a green metal glider; the parlor with the piano, the ukulele, the Skunk game; the kitchen and its little metal cupboard that held jelly jar glasses. To me, all of it was magical.

By age fifteen, I awaited my turn for the 'visit' with Grandmother. She was 'holding court' with each of us. I sat on the green corduroy-covered daybed where I would sleep that night. As she sat next to me, she smoothed her apron and said, "I imagine at your age you're beginning to date boys." With her white hair and piercing blue eyes, she studied me. I felt shy, this spotlight of attention not familiar as the fifth child of seven.

That moment in time never left me. Who was this grandmother who wanted to know more about me? I wanted to know more about her.

Over the years, I asked questions that were never fully answered. I longed to know the stories of my mother's two oldest brothers, tall and red-haired, but the stories never came.

It wasn't until I was in college that I learned the first story. After that, I prowled into the dark corners, read newspapers, talked to older cousins and lifted the covers to find the full story. It is a compelling one.

As I write this note, a full moon has stirred me from sleep, just as it once disturbed Maggie's oldest boy. I am aware anew of the importance of Maggie's story. Its power resides in the tales of intergenerational trauma that are collected here. It is my hope that this novel will illuminate the bits and pieces that have been passed down for more than one hundred years. It is also my hope that the light will help obliterate the dark corners and bring healing and authentic pride to what has been goodness.

"…my task is to lift the veil of common knowledge and received wisdom, considering what science and watchful observation tell us, with the aim of unfastening the myths that keep the status quo locked in place."

Gabor Maté, The Myth of Normal

Thank you,

Elizabeth

Chapter 1
Where Would He Take Her?

Maggie sat at the vanity dressing table, the mirror reflecting her satisfied countenance. She unpinned her red hair, watching it fall over her shoulders. She smiled, pleased as she'd ever been. She was in a fine new house with fields of land and a brood of children, healthy and growing faster than a flash. Her blue eyes smiled back at her as she thought of her good fortune.

She had come across an ocean and left a city to find her dream. It seemed like only yesterday, with an infant son and another child on the way, John promised to take her away from the fetid air of New York City. She trusted him. She was eighteen years old.

John was as fed up as she was with the noise of the streets, the poor sanitation, and the lack of meaningful work. Sure enough, they missed Ireland, the clear air, the babbling brooks, the misty hillsides, and the call of the mockingbirds. In their meeting, they discovered they had left Ireland in search of something neither could define, but New York City wasn't it.

Meeting John had been magical. As a child, divinations and folklore intrigued Maggie. A snail placed on a slate could spell out the initials of a future husband. She'd seen the initials J.D. when she had tried it, not giving any serious thought, yet always remembering. When she met John Donegan, all that changed; he seemed as smitten as she. She never doubted him for a second; this was the man she would marry. Even the pastor at the Church of the Holy Innocents encouraged her belief. "Ye never know what the fates have in store for ye."

Maggie had met him at the church through his sister Annie. Maggie's innocence as one newly arrived gave Annie an opening to offer help in the way of her handsome brother, who was living with her and her husband, Hugh. It didn't take long for the sparks to ignite. It was Father John Larkin, the pastor, who married them in a simple ceremony.

It was Father Larkin, from Galway, whose reputation became a legend among his largely Irish congregation. His parish in the area known as the Tenderloin was noted in newspapers worldwide reporting on Queen Victoria's Jubilee in New York City in 1887, the year before Maggie arrived. Stories of the festivities – parades, fireworks, and elaborate receptions were all reported, along with the fact that on the very same day, a solemn Requiem Mass was celebrated in the Church of Holy Innocents for the repose of the souls of 150,000 Irish who died of starvation during Queen Victoria's reign.

The *Ottawa Free Trader*, an Illinois newspaper, wrote: *"In New York while the Englishmen and their friends were drinking toasts with the liveliest felicitations, at the Church of the Holy Innocents a 'Mass for the repose of the souls of Irish victims of Victoria's reign was held and while the jubilee anthem peeled forth at Metropolitan Opera House, the Dies Irae, Dies Illa was sung in the church!"* The celebrant was their own Rev. Dr. John Larkin.

It was the same Father Larkin who baptized their first child, Hugh Michael, born November 19, 1890, and blessed their lives with his sage advice, "Follow your dreams." His encouragement helped them realize they needn't stay any longer in this mishmash of humanity, where it seemed everyone was going somewhere.

They certainly didn't need to stay for the money. Maggie's pay as a housekeeper wasn't much, and now, with an infant boy, it seemed unlikely she could continue to hold the job. John also knew the money he was earning wasn't enough now that there would be another child.

Staying with Annie and Hugh had been a miracle when it happened. Annie was as generous and grand as one of her own, maybe, in fact, better than one of her own. Maggie was not about to ask her sister Mary to keep them when she and her husband Paddy had their own house full of their own woes. It was Annie and Hugh, with two little girls of their own, who were there and helped Maggie when her time came. Their first son, Hugh, with red hair and blue eyes, was named after Annie's generous husband.

John's constant dream included green fields somewhere west in the state, as lush as the ones in Ireland. Fields that stretched out as far as the eye could see, enough rain for strong crops, enough to feed a family of ten. He painted a scene of small communities and picturesque churches, with statues and stained glass, just like home.

Together, they continued to follow their shared dream, and it had come true. With a little more than a dozen years having passed, they were in their own home in the hills of New York State, with forty acres of farmland in a small town named Lima, thanks to widow Flaville Lays and her reasonable price for the land. It had taken faith and the fullness of time to create this roof over their heads that would ever be their own.

Maggie drew a deep breath and smiled as she put down the brush, remembering. At forty-two years of age, with ten healthy children, she was tired but felt so very blessed. Hers was a legacy of mostly joy. The children were, in her estimation, handsome and intelligent, a good combination. Some favored her people, the Buckleys, with red hair and blue eyes, putting her in mind of her own brothers and sisters. The others had dark hair and hazel eyes like John's people, the Donegans.

Since her childhood days in Ireland, she'd known great joy to rival the trials and tragedies that befell her, hers a family of love, laughter, music, and a spirit that believed beyond what the eye could see. She recalled the Irish adage with hope:

May the saddest day of your future
be no worse than the happiest day of your past.

So began her life in upstate New York.

Chapter 2
West Bloomfield, New York

In those early days in upstate New York, Maggie found herself enjoying motherhood. Hugh was an easy baby, and before long, Jerome became one too. Born in the little town of West Bloomfield, just East of Lima, this second son brought another level of joy.

Maggie's memories of her twin siblings, Jeremiah and Elizabeth, came to mind as she watched her own sons kicking their feet about, discovering their fists, soon enough able to babble and talk. Thanks to Annie's little ones, Elizabeth, age 8, and Frances, born in January just ahead of Hugh, she'd had a refresher in how infants grew and changed.

She learned that picking babies up when they cried wasn't always a bad idea, the cry often indicating some discomfort. Soon enough, she learned when to hold them and when to let them cry for a bit because soon Loring Francis and then John Victor were born. Four boys. Thankfully, her longing for a girl was fulfilled within the next few years with the birth of Margaret Mary Josephine and Veronica. A fine lot of six children within ten years.

John was happy for the boys but ecstatic when he became the father of girls. What was it about men and their daughters? Maggie had a close relationship with her own da, Jeremiah, whom she missed with her heart and soul. He'd taught her so much without saying a word.

Maggie knew well her father's loyalty to Ireland, never once giving an inch to the 'bloody Brits.' He listened to the priest who spoke from the altar about Ireland's destiny to become a nation. He sang in the pubs, *"And Ireland long a province, be a Nation Onc Again."* She learned from the Da that it was the Revolution of 1798 that had led to the devastating Acts of Union in 1800. The Irish parliament had been dissolved, and everything came crashing down, a massive loss on the road to freedom.

It was America's revolution that won the Yanks their freedom, and Maggie knew, though her father hated the thought of her leaving, that he greatly admired the American spirit she was going toward.

Maggie knew that while leaving New York City was necessary, its one big downside was leaving Annie and Hugh and their two girls. Letters back and forth and more children for them both kept them in touch.

Then the unthinkable happened.

Annie, pregnant with her fifth child, lost her beloved husband, Hugh. A finer man, the priest said of him at the funeral service, would be hard to find. It was a sudden death, a heart attack, most likely. Hugh's passing called on every ounce of strength and faith that Annie had. Within a few months of his death, her fifth girl, named Hughberta in his memory, was born.

Whether it was the providence of God or the blessings of the Universe, a pal of Hugh's, Bryan Kerrigan, was introduced and took a shine to Annie. Miracle or not, she, with five children ranging from 14 years to 6 months old, struck up a fine relationship. Within the year, Bryan and Annie were married.

It astounded Maggie that by the time her John Victor was but one-year-old, Annie had a sixth child, the first boy, named John, after her brother. The angels and archangels be praised! Maggie said daily rosaries for Annie. And soon enough, two more Kerrigan were born, Catherine and Anna, a total of eight now in the family. Maggie kept pace with four more: Tom, Bernard, Genevieve, and Elizabeth, for a total of ten.

Both families, the Galena/Kerrigans and Donegans, were strong ones and, Maggie prayed, would be destined to do good all their days.

Chapter 3
The Children

Early 1914

After ten pregnancies, Maggie was unprepared for the exhaustion that accompanied this latest one. She found her feet swelled early, her energy gone by mid-afternoon, leaving her tired and cranky. She relied on the older girls for their help with the younger children and household chores, the boys giving a hand with the farm work.

Her two oldest boys, Hugh and Jerome, were already making their way into the world. Handsome young men, Maggie thought. At age twenty-four, Hugh was traveling about the country, finding his way in the Ford auto industry. Ford's recent announcement of an eight-hour day for five dollars pay seemed to give him an incentive, his resolve strong.

"You'll find me," he'd boast to his mother on his sporadic times at home, "one day with my own company." His visits thrilled Maggie. As she peeled potatoes, she'd glance over to see his eyes gleaming as he told of all he would do.

"I'll start something in Columbus," he said as he walked back and forth in the kitchen, tapping the white pump in front of the window each time he came to it, agitated with his new ideas. "There's lots happening these days with the new assembly plant they put up. It's a logical conclusion to land myself right there."

Maggie listened and smiled. Hugh had been as far west as Salem, Oregon, and even found his way to Windsor, Canada. His vocabulary had become a focus for him, using words that he hoped made him sound cultured and intelligent. Such a sensitive child and a determined one, he'd be successful, she was sure. Always a good student, his certificate from the 1905 eighth-grade class of Genesee Wesleyan Seminary was a special source of pride. Hugh was a hard worker and eager to please.

Jerome, just two years younger, had an entirely different nature. He was a good fellow for earning money and working on local farms to bring in cash. In recent months, Maggie also noted, he was attracting young women.

Something that piqued Jerome's interest for a time was the talk of getting a good seed. He'd seen his father test the quality of their seed by doing germination tests, placing one hundred seeds between pieces of blotting paper, and keeping it moist while waiting to count and record his daily results. Cabbage, lettuce, and tomatoes were essential to their prosperity, so his father was taking no risks. Maybe the science of it intrigued Jerome, or the temptation to be off the tractor and learning, dreaming of blossoms that were to come from these seedlings. He was satisfied to bide his time, hoping to learn how to plant his own life.

Meantime, cleaning, laundry, and some of the cooking fell to the two older girls, Josephine and Veronica.

Dark-haired Josephine's defined jawline and deep-set eyes gave her an aristocratic look. She became a whiz at cooking and baking; her meals, as directed by her mother, always included meat, potato, and a vegetable. When there was time, she'd make flaky biscuits that the boys loved.

Veronica, red-haired and freckled, with a diminutive stature, was a great laundress. Maggie heralded her skill at getting stains out as her special gift. Proudly positioned at her steel tub and ribbed washboard when washday came around, she also had a way with the 'boys' and was able to get her brothers to lift the baskets of wet clothes and help her hang the sheets, a mighty task for someone who stood just five feet two inches.

The older boys, Vic, christened John Victor, eighteen, and Loring Francis, at twenty, had romance and adventure on their minds, leaving the 'kids' as they called their younger sisters and brothers to help at home. Schoolwork was a top priority, but chores on the farm were equally important and shared by Tom and Bernard.

Maggie glanced out to the front room from the dining room as she set the table for the farmhands' noon-day meal. Her four youngest, ages ten to three years, were happily engaged, Tommy and Bernard, playing checkers, the talk of the impending war yet to enter their play. Gene (her name shortened from Genevieve to circumvent her being called Jenny, the horse's name) was reading a story to her three-year-old sister Betty. Soon, it would be fall. The school would change the day's rhythm, leaving Betty home with Maggie and the new baby.

Maggie looked forward to the children bringing their lessons, happy to learn what she could beyond her own eighth-grade schooling. She was forever reminding the children of the privilege they had in being able to walk right up Rochester Road to their own St. Rose of Lima school.

It was Rochester's first bishop, Bernard McQuaid, who established the parochial school system. Father FitzSimons, St. Rose of Lima's beloved pastor whose twenty-eight-year tenure had just ended a year or so ago, said that Sisters of St. Joseph had been a blessing in accepting the offer to staff St. Rose of Lima over forty years ago, a request made by then pastor Father Mulheron. "One of their first missions," he was proud to say. "And they have faithfully served ever since."

Bishop McQuaid's leadership of the Rochester Diocese was highlighted not only by his creation of a strong parochial school system but also by a seminary for young boys, St. Andrews, and in 1893, St. Bernard's seminary. The burnt-red Medina stone structure has been educating priests of the Rochester Diocese ever since.

St. Rose of Lima school was a tribute, many said, to the ambition of the families of the congregation, like Maggie and John, Irish mostly, who, even in their own poverty, were anxious to provide educational advantages that they themselves had been denied in the land of their birth.

Chapter 4
Mary

August 21, 1914

As Maggie's days drew closer to her time, she savored moments of stillness. After the younger children had gone to bed and the older ones listened to her play her accordion, she'd often sit alone in the small front parlor just outside her bedroom. She'd recall the day, the difficult moments, and the blessings. Tonight, she savored the memory of dark-haired Josephine, whose birthday they had celebrated earlier. With regal bearing, Josephine read aloud from President Wilson's speech to Congress, declaring neutrality:

> *The United States must be neutral in fact as well as in name during these days that are to try men's souls.*

It was reassuring to have this first-born daughter well-versed in the politics of the day, a new generation helping to sort things out. Maggie prayed the country would remain safe as she prepared to bring new life into it. She felt safe with their St. Rose of Lima pastor, Father Farrell, and the politics he brought to the pulpit, petitioning prayers this last Sunday for thousands of Irish lads fighting in the escalating World War.

Listening to Father Farrell, Maggie was reminded of times as a young girl in Ireland when the priest in the pulpit would wax forth with politics to rile her father, Jeremiah. He'd rant after the Mass, vowing not to go back if he had to listen to such poppycock each Sunday.

"Does he really think he's got a notion of what the good Lord thinks about Home Rule or the dynamite that's blowing up Westminster Hall? He's nosing into men's lives too much and forgetting to keep their souls in his care, not their politics."

Maggie didn't always agree with her father. She loved him but thought him old-fashioned when he initially resisted her coming to America. Yet she cherished the memory of him, once he relented, holding her in his arms for a last dance the night before she left.

Thinking of him now and of Ireland made Maggie miss her sister Mary. As children, Mary had been special to her, teaming up against their cranky sister, who was forever making Maggie feel small. They'd nicknamed her *'Julia Rulia.'*

"That's too much for a little red-haired one like you, Mags," Julia would say in her bossy way, her dark hair and eyes making her look sterner. Mary, whose soft green eyes and easy smile made Maggie feel safe, often spoke the right words to placate Julia.

"She can manage it, Jules," Mary would intervene. "She's spunkier than you think." Mary would wink, making Maggie glow inside.

It was Mary who was first brave enough to come to America. Maggie thought she'd lost her forever. When Mary changed her name to Molly, it seemed official that she'd become a Yank and would never come home.

Maggie remembered both the joy and tears that filled her when she fell into Mary's arms after the three long years it took to save enough for the ship's fare. She'd finally arrived at New York City's Castle Garden, not knowing a soul there except Mary. Their dear Father Riordan, who ran Our Lady of the Rosary Mission for Irish girls, had died suddenly the season before, pneumonia from overwork said to be the cause. Maggie had sobbed at the thought that she might never get to America, but come she did, and she never forgot Mary's welcoming embrace on seeing someone from home who knew what she had left and what she risked in making the voyage.

All of this had been twenty-five years ago. The inevitable misunderstandings between them over the years seemed minor now, especially the hurt Maggie unintentionally caused when she and John moved in with Annie and Hugh on 37th Street. Maggie tried to help Mary understand the distance from 82nd Street was too far for John to easily get to his gardening work. Oh, how Mary had carried on about Maggie's lack of loyalty. In the end, Mary finally softened, saying, "I suppose it'd been foolish for him to travel half the city when his own sister and brother-in- law could keep him 'til the baby was born.

Maggie had been happy to hear Mary's words and happier still when Mary came to see her after the birth of young Hugh Michael, born just before Thanksgiving, in time for a wonderful season.

Tonight, Maggie's eyes misted up, her back aching no matter if she was sitting, standing, or lying down. She found her way to the desk, sat, and pulled Mary's letters from the little cubby. Mary's home on 82nd Street on the same Street as the glorious Metropolitan Museum of Art, could have been as far away as Ireland for Maggie's chance of getting to see her anytime soon.

She pulled the letters out and opened one:

November 23, 1913

My dear sister,

I suppose you think we are all dead by this time, well, very near it, but it is hard to kill bad things. Jerome is no better; he is a very sensitive poor boy, as I suppose all sick people are. he is a great care and worry to me, but I would not mind that if he pulled through. I do everything I possibly can for him, but if God wants him, we can't keep him. I suppose he knows best what to do...

Maggie paused, holding the letter as she reached her hand back on her spine, hoping to ease the pain that was quickening.

Mary's time in New York City since her arrival hadn't been easy. She had written, "The city is contaminated with every disease although they do everything that possibly can be done to have a healthy one." She'd worked long days and nights, doing laundry and cleaning in fancy houses that weren't her own. Now, at least, she had the comfort of her grown daughter Margaret, a blessing to her. Maggie felt the same blessing from her own brood. She read the closing line with a smile:

How is the baby, or have you had another since?
Your loving sister, Mary.

Maggie straightened herself in the chair, trying to get a stitch of comfort. Soon, she would have something to write about *'another since.'*

Mary's second letter lay on its side on the desk. Maggie fingered it, knowing too well its message:

May 24th, 1914

Dear Sister,

Just a few lines to let you know I buried my lovely boy four weeks ago, just six days short of seventeen years. He suffered long and patiently until our Blessed Lord took him home, where I hope his suffering will cease and he will know sorrow no more but be admitted to that celestial bliss where there is all happiness and glory. He died a beautiful death, and the Blessed Sacrament was the last thing that entered his mouth. I will miss him very much as he was always with me, but there is one consoling thought that he will never be crushed by the rough paths of life. He grew so much while he was sick. He was 5 feet 7 inches. When he died, he took a full-sized casket, and about a year ago, he was only 5 foot 3 inches. I used to think he would be small, but if he lived, he would be as tall as his Uncle Dan, and he had such a lovely disposition, more like a refined lady than a boy. John is so different - more like a boy. I don't think I will ever get over the loss of him. I felt bad after Eugene, but this clapped the climax. Just one day short of the year between him and my mother, his the 24th and mother the 25th of April. Oh, the pity of it all. I could just scream out all the time. It seems there is no comfort for me in this world. The priest says it's because God loves me. I wish his love to come some other way. My dear Jerome had the priest coming 4 months every Monday morning, and he was with him for one hour and a half when he died. I hope you are all well and happy. Love from Mary.

Maggie folded the letters, their black border somber, and returned them to the cubby.

Enough memory for one day.

Chapter 5
Settled In

August 24, 1914

The heat of the summer day seeped into the kitchen. The noon meal finished and laundry sorted, Maggie took time to catch her breath, her back feeling the strain of the day. The humid air sapped any reserve strength she had. Everything felt sticky.

Earlier, seven of the children had been at the table with the two hired field hands from Livonia, ten miles to the south. John and his son Jerome graced each end of the table. Maggie sat next to John, noting his graying hair, his deep-set green eyes, and his graying mustache. He was as handsome as when she met him. As he gave the blessing, she watched with satisfaction as the food she prepared was devoured with relish, sliced ham, and potato salad, along with fresh beans, sliced tomato, and hard- boiled eggs. A sufficient meal in all this heat, she thought.

She'd been up at her usual five o'clock hour to prepare a breakfast of johnnycakes, bacon, eggs, and toast. Leaving the dishes until later, milking the cows came next. There is not much flexibility in their schedule, especially the black and white Bessie. She was their oldest and best milker but could be downright nasty if she was left until last, often kicking out at just the right time. Maggie had not wanted to tangle with those muscular legs and sharp hooves.

Once free from the milking, Maggie went on to churn some cream and put milk out for the barn cats that were multiplying as fast as her children.

"Are you alright, Ma?" Veronica asked as she watched her mother push her gray-flecked red hair back in place and wipe her brow with her slightly soiled apron. Even at age thirteen, she could see Maggie's fatigue around her eyes and in her bent posture.

"I'll be fine enough, but I think I'd best take a little rest before dinner," Maggie said as she lifted her apron over her head and hung it on the hook by the door. With her hand on her back, she ambled off to the south bedroom.

Maggie lay down on the bed, her room barely big enough for the full-sized bed and dressing table, its wild roses wallpaper so like the ones out by the hay barn. The smaller bedroom by the back door had a pattern of white morning glories on a pale green background, matching the ones off the side porch. This was the room that was now Betty's, a small bed by the door, the crib next to the window filled with clothes to be mended. Another task before the next child.

The great dormitory room upstairs kept the older children well-sorted. With Hugh off trying his hand in the car business, there was more room in the large open area, its narrow oblong windows tucked into the dormer of the roof bringing in light. Jerome, Loring, and Vic each had beds of their own, with Bernard and Tommy sharing one. Josephine, Veronica, and Gene were in two adjoining tiny rooms.

Maggie and John had scrimped and saved throughout their twenty-two years in upstate New York and finally were able to afford this forty-acre farm on Rochester Road. Their first house on Clay Road on the Keenan farm off Rte 5 and 20 had been rent-free since their labor counted toward payment. They'd conserved money well, mending clothes that were reused from child to child. Hand-made gifts filled in for birthday celebrations.

Maggie knew John Donegan had farming in his bones, and now she knew he finally felt successful here in Lima, New York.

On their first night in their new home, with its green shingles and little eyebrow windows on the second story giving them light and hope, John shared with Maggie why this purchase meant so much to him.

"As ye know, I came from Kenagh, Longford," John told her, " in the central part of Ireland. It was a place where people took pride in being able to bring life to any land with just a spade, a hoe, and a prayer. We didn't own land, but my father did find love."

His parents' love story intrigued John, and over the years, he became aware of how fragile an existence they had lived.

His mother, Brigid Thompson, lived in the Big House, owned by the landlord in the neighboring town of Ballymahon. John's father, Thomas Donegan, was one of many young men brought in for the harvest. But more than reaping hay and wheat filled Thomas' day. He had his eye set on the forbidden: the landlord's daughter, a dark-haired beauty who oversaw the meals. Before too long, Thomas and Brigid met up for early evening walks and talks, both knowing the danger that could follow in crossing over into the other's world. Yet neither of them faced reality until they found themselves in each other's arms. By then, it was too late.

Brigid, shunned by her own family for carrying on with a tenant farmer's son, soon became a part of Thomas' people. They accepted her with open arms, knowing the two would have burdens to bear beyond banishment.

Thomas, born into the heart of An Gorta Mor, the Great Hunger, had known want beyond material wealth. Brigid, from the landed gentry, never knew such a want. Thomas never scorned her for her fortunate birth; her kindness, compassion, and understanding counted far more than food or money.

Marrying in a small ceremony in Thomas's Catholic Church, Brigid was willing to sacrifice her own Church of Ireland, which wasn't Catholic, her love for Thomas surpassing any religion.

They moved out on their own, with fewer judging eyes to greet them.

Ultimately, they moved from town to town to find work: fence mending, field clearings, - and even doing house repairs. Finally, they settled on the edge of the small town of Kenagh, its single winding main Street lined by a variety of buildings, like many towns in Ireland. This was the closest they'd ever come to putting down roots.

By now, they had three children, John, Anna, and Michael, who had been schooled in the history of their town, learning that Kenagh was from the Irish 'Caonach,' meaning 'Moss.' They also learned that this part of the country fared better than others due to its proximity to the Royal Canal, which gave them the option of fishing during the hungry days.

At age ten, John witnessed a moment in history: a town clock tower dedicated to Lawrence King Harman, "a good landlord and an upright man," the plaque read. The pride of place.

His father counseled him as he left for America, "Remember where you're from and where you're going," And now, in Lima, New York, John found a new place to be, a place he could give to his children and maybe even their children.

Maggie couldn't sleep remembering these old stories. She did rest, though, her back settling down a bit, the pulsing in her tired legs slowing. She looked forward with gratitude for this new life in her belly, even as she sorrowed for Mary's loss of her Jerome.

Four years earlier, her older sister Mary had lost her little Eugene, not even a year old, and now Jerome. How does one handle such loss, she wondered. She recalled Mary's New York City letters and the faith she held onto, but oh, the heartache.

"Do you need anything, Ma?" Veronica peeked in, breaking Maggie's reverie. She was a good one for helping.

"I don't need a thing just now," Maggie answered. "I'll be right as rain in a little while. Just knowing you and your sister are seeing the little ones brings me sweet relief."

Maggie sighed and returned to her memories of this home. They had bought the farm from the Flavia Lays at a fair price, the mortgage high enough but manageable, their family having grown by leaps and bounds. The green-shingled house, its front door adorned with a brass doorbell and a modern thumb turn ringer, gave Maggie a feeling of satisfaction. Her own home in Ireland had been so much simpler. This grand house had two pumps for water, adequate warmth, and light and sat on good soil, all theirs, no landlord involved, a sign to Maggie of new blessings.

The double front parlors were stately, one separated from the dining room by double glass doors and lit by gas sconces on each wall that gave plenty of light. Two double-hung windows on each of the front walls and one on each sidewall provided gentle moments of light throughout the day.

The dining room easily held a table large enough to feed a crowd. One special feature for Maggie was a painting the Lays family had left behind. An oval tiger maple frame held a depiction of two peasants in a field, a basket of potatoes at their feet, heads bowed in prayer, a church on the horizon, a potato fork, sacks, and a wheelbarrow in plain view.

Maggie knew nothing of the artist or the value of Jean Francoise Millet's Angelus. She just knew she loved this reminder to add prayer to each day and acknowledge the root of their blessings.

"The angel of the Lord declared unto Mary,
And she conceived of the Holy Ghost."

As often as she could, when she heard the church bells, she recited the three Hail Marys accompanied by the versicle, counting the nine rings of the bell. With John's help, Maggie had created a little shrine to Our Lady near the window in the dining room, reminding her of a similar window she'd had as a child in Ireland. She had lined the balsam shrine with white linen left over from curtains for the baby's bedroom, painting it white outside and blue inside; the small statue of the Blessed Virgin Mary stood in the center, surrounded by cut-out stars from the pages of the last season's Sears, Roebuck, and Co. catalog. A little jelly jar juice glass served as a vase for the wildflowers.

This chance for daily devotion brought such comfort with the hope that it would be a source of solace through the inevitable heartaches that arise. She'd already seen enough in her forty-three years to know each life is laden with its own sorrow, her own sister Mary's losses a heartbreaking reminder.

Maggie sat up from her rest and went out to her shrine. She smiled at the little forget-me-nots Veronica and Gene had picked for the vase.

She thought of John, who was not always easy, his fiftieth birthday approaching, his aging evident. She'd seen him often pushing his graying hair back from his forehead in exasperation over this or that: a child's toy out of place, a kitten's meowing, or a rainy day. His hope for his sons to join him on this newly purchased farm was fading, his disappointment growing.

She stood silently and deliberately lifted all her woes to the Lady, sending up a prayer for fathers and sons, lost children, and her own coming child. In her new home, with her new shrine, she would let the cares of tomorrow wait 'til this day was done.

Chapter 6
Mrs. Slattery

August 26, 1914

Maggie's little lay down before supper turned out to be more than just needing rest. When John came in to wash for supper, he found her still in bed, more uncomfortable than he'd ever seen her. Her color was pale, her face drawn, her eyes almost glazed. He became alarmed and decided to call the midwife. Maggie's other pregnancies and births had been less difficult, it seemed to John, but he wasn't the one giving birth. He'd never seen her in such distress so early before her time, her breathing irregular, groans accompanying what appeared to be a sharp pain.

John kissed Maggie's forehead and slipped out, going to the black phone sitting on the desk outside the second bedroom. He picked up the handset and listened for the familiar sound of the operator's voice. Mildred was a member of St. Rose of Lima church and a reliable friend. "I need to ring Mrs. Slattery," John said breathlessly. "Just one moment, John," Mildred said and, without delay, connected them. She understood his urgency, for she'd seen Maggie at church looking very uncomfortable and very big.

When John heard Mrs. Slattery's voice, he burst forth hurriedly, "It's John Donegan down here on Rochester Road. 'Tis early for her, but Maggie's in great distress with this one," he said. He listened as Mrs. Slattery told him not to worry. "I'll be there in a flash," she said. John felt a bit of reassurance as he returned the handset to the base of the phone, happy for this modern convenience.

When he came back to Maggie, he found her distress as great as before. Her red hair was still combed back in place, but the blue eyes that looked at him were full of fear. "There's something different now, John, and I mightn't know if things are all right." Her voice broke.

John squared his shoulders, pulled his suspenders into place, and took a deep breath. He bent down and kissed Maggie's cheek, then knelt by the side of the bed and took her clammy hand, noting beads of sweat covering her brow.

She'd been nineteen when their first child was born, Annie and Hugh right by her side, encouraging her and helping her with the birth. That had been in 1890, twenty-four years ago. It'd been rough all right, but hadn't women been bearing the pain of childbirth for centuries? And hadn't Maggie borne ten other children without any such discomfort and misgiving? In the past, when her time came, John saw that the pain was something mighty, her writhing and screaming out beyond anything he could prepare for, yet ultimately, there was the joy of the baby. And didn't Maggie's own mother have six healthy children? Sure, this child would be fine. He avoided thinking about baby Julia, Maggie's oldest sibling, who'd been stillborn. Now was not the time for such thoughts. Instead, John calmed Maggie, reminding her of her strength and hushing her fears.

"Sure, you're as strong as an ox with all you've been doing since first I laid eyes on ye in that garden in Manhattan. Didn't I know when I saw ye that ye were the best one hired in the house? They all said so."

Maggie's eyes stayed steady on him as if the talk of their early days brought relief. He continued, hoping she'd ease into a bit of reverie. Suddenly, she jolted with pain and squeezed his hand with a might that surprised him.

It seemed an eternity, but within the half hour, Mrs. Slattery arrived and shooed John away. She was a large woman with a red face and round dark eyes. Her no-nonsense approach consoled John immediately.

"I'll take her from here. She'll be fine. Send in the two oldest girls in a few minutes with some boiling water and towels, too."

Josephine and Veronica had prepared a supper of corn, beans, and potato, along with a bit of bacon. Bernard and Genevieve were in the front room, a checker match occupying them. Three-year-old Betty clung to Josephine, who alternately held her on her hip and set her down as she went about her chores, sensing her fright not to have her mother about. Tommy stayed outdoors doing, Lord knows what, but the girls knew he'd be there if they needed him. He was like that.

When John finally came into the kitchen, his eyes bloodshot and shoulders slumped, the girls saw worry spilling out of him.

"She'll be fine, but this one's a rough one. Ten times already, she's delivered children, but this one. . ." He paused and ran his hand through his thinning hair.

"Maybe her age is slowing her," Josephine said as she picked Betty up.

"Mrs. Slattery will know best," John said. She wants you girls to go in with towels and hot water."

Veronica indicated a place at the small table by the window for their father and served him a plate of food. Josephine put Betty down, who promptly went over to her father and asked, "Where's Mama, Dada?" before Josephine could hush her.

John bent over to the child and lifted her into his lap. "Mama is working hard to get you the new baby she's been telling you about. Won't you like that?"

Betty's eyes darted to her sisters and back to her father. "Not a baby, Dada; I want a dolly!"

"Well then, it's a dolly you'll have in no time," John laughed as he hugged her to him and looked up at the older girls.

Veronica nodded to Josephine, picked up Betty, and took her into the front room. Josephine gave John a bit of custard and his tea, then followed Veronica.

The two oldest girls were still young for what they were about to do. Veronica, almost thirteen, and Josephine, fifteen, just three days before, were both glad for Mrs. Slattery.

Mrs. Slattery sometimes wished that she could get her hands on that pain-relieving medicine she'd read about in *McClure's Magazine*. The agony she'd witnessed women enduring during childbirth often seared her soul. This new Twilight Sleep was controversial enough, but at least there was a conversation about addressing this pain unique to women. It was first used with wealthy German women who were given a combination of varied doses of morphine and scopolamine. Mrs. Slattery knew enough of medicine to know this to be a rigorous dosage. She'd spoken with Doc Hinman about it, his opinion one she valued.

"It puts the mother in a state of clouded consciousness with complete forgetfulness of the entire birth," the doctor had said. "Some women sleep through their labor; others have uncontrollable hysterics. I wouldn't risk it," he added.

From all Mrs. Slattery could learn, reviews were mixed, yet the demand for Twilight Sleep outstripped the availability of trained physicians. Ultimately, the dangers of the drug, with its accompanying confusion, delirium, and hemorrhaging resulting in fetal death, caused it to lose credibility. The demand subsided, but not before attention was called to the field of obstetrics, and it helped change the face of childbirth around the world. This movement was coming at a time when women were also uniting to get the vote, a major step in being heard.

Maggie didn't know of hospitals, doctors, or anesthesia. She knew only of a new fear of something gone astray that caused her breathing to be more difficult than she'd ever known. Her dizziness and nausea, combined with incredible back pain, lower than it had ever been, alarmed her. *Was she too old? She asked herself. Forty-three didn't need to be, but maybe. Had she worked too hard?* Mrs. Slattery, who'd assisted at her last four deliveries, assured her she'd be fine, but Maggie sensed even Mrs. Slattery was worried. Her time for delivery was several weeks earlier than either of them had estimated.

Maybe it was this house that made things different. Seven of the children had been born on Clay Street, the Noonan Farm they had first rented and then owned, its first-floor bedroom serving as a fine birthing room. Now she was in a smaller, nicer room, she thought, yet things weren't right.

When the girls peeked in, Mrs. Slattery said, "Your ma's getting ready to have her baby. Here's what you can do to help."

Over the next several hours, the girls set about doing whatever Mrs. Slattery directed, bringing clean linens and boiled water and standing back as their mother writhed in pain. Josephine, who'd been talking of becoming a nurse since she was ten and had helped birth the calves, was in her glory, staying close to Mrs. Slattery, ready for instruction, occasionally wiping her mother's face and soothing her.

Veronica, who had no such inclination, closed her eyes so she didn't have to see. She slipped out to see to bedtime for Betty, who was already yawning when she found her with Genevieve just finishing a story from Aesop's Fables, *The Nurse and the Wolf.* John had seen to it that the other children were reassured by his promise to wake them if there was any news. He himself sat in the front room, stroking his chin and staring out the front window.

After an hour, at Mrs. Slattery's suggestion, Josephine and Veronica went out into the yard for a break. As dark settled over the earth, the stars beginning to cluster over the fields, an infant's cry pierced the air. They rushed back just in time. Mrs. Slattery handed Josephine a wriggling young baby boy, and Veronica helped wrap him in the soft cotton blanket they'd set aside. As they snuggled the blanket around the little one, they heard Mrs. Slattery say aloud, "Jesus, Mary, and Joseph. Look what we have here!"

Within minutes, they heard another infant cry, this time from a baby girl.

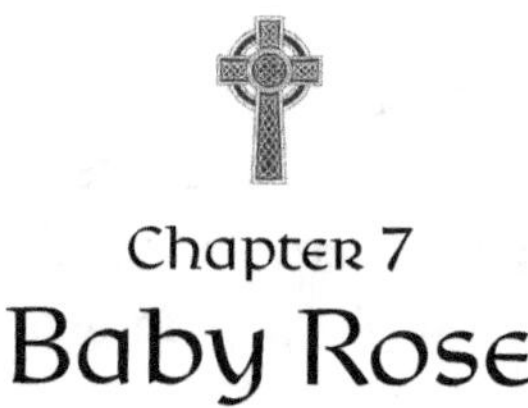

Chapter 7
Baby Rose

November 30, 1914

The household hummed with the birth of the twins. Josephine and Veronica awakened the children, who had barely gone to sleep, telling them they could come for a surprise.

Holding the two babies on her breast, Maggie's fresh pink nightie matched the pinkness of the infants' skin. She wore a wondrous, satisfied look on her face. Though her blue eyes were gauzy, her small lips were pursed in a smile, the weariness and worry gone.

Genevieve and Betty were the first admitted into the room to see their mother and the babies, followed by Bernard and Tom. The children lined up around the bed, their mouths opened in awe to see not one but two tiny babies. They couldn't believe they were ever that small.

"Can they talk?" Betty asked her mother. Her older sisters and brothers giggled.

"For now, all they'll do is squawk when they're hungry, but just like you, one day, they'll start and not stop," Maggie answered with a gleam in her eye.

Mrs. Slattery, her gray hair disheveled and her blue eyes looking weary, was just outside Maggie's bedroom, resting on the platform rocker. She had seen Maggie through the birth of some of these very children who were now witnessing the miracle of the twins. Pleased she could help, despite her now aching back and feet, she knew she'd be right as rain once she got some rest, her own age creeping up towards fifty. But first, she'd see to getting Maggie straightened around for a bit of a rest, the twins having nursed sufficiently. A good night's sleep for them all was definitely in order.

As the children settled down again, Mrs. Slattery told John she'd be back for breakfast. She left Josephine and Veronica in charge of assisting their mother. They agreed to help her in shifts, Veronica taking the first and waking Josephine when she was ready to be relieved.

Veronica opened the door to the bedroom from the parlor, closing the second one that was off the dining room, hoping to soften the sound of any household stirrings that might disturb Maggie. John had gone upstairs to sleep in the dorm room.

Veronica slipped out the front door and stood on the stoop to visit with the moon, sure that the crescent slice was more special because of the birth of the twins. These babies were tinier than any she had ever seen. She was ten when Betty was born and remembered having to use both hands when holding her. These precious little ones fit in the crook of her arm; the tiny fingernails are precise, reminding her of the ones on the dolly she'd gotten for her seventh birthday. Maybe she could give her dolly to the new little baby girl when she got big enough.

Veronica watched the clouds dart across the moon, casting shadows on the illumined lawn, the leaves from the chestnut tree making lace patterns. She thought how surprised her older brothers would be when they learned of the twins. Hugh, traveling now for Ford Motor Company, would try to come home, she suspected. Jerome was off on a fur-buying trip with his pal, Will Wilson. Their plan was to go east to Albany, where the dealers gathered. Loring would be back from New York City, where he'd been visiting the Donegan cousins. Aunt Annie always opened her home to any of the nieces and nephews for a visit.

Veronica went back into the house to the sound of a soft baby's cry. She tiptoed into the bedroom to see Maggie holding the littlest one at her breast, hoping it was just more food she wanted.

"She's so tiny, Ma. Maybe she needs just a little taste at a time," Veronica offered, proud to be giving soothing ideas.

"I'm sure you're right," Maggie said, her lidded eyes near closing again. "We'll hope this one settles down, and tomorrow we'll find names for the two of them."

Once things quieted, Veronica went upstairs to swap places with Josephine, tiptoeing past Tom, Bernard, and her father to her own single bed. She peeked in on Betty, whom Gene had brought up with her for this special night; the two snuggled together in one twin bed. Josephine jumped at Veronica's tap on her shoulder and sat up in bed, startled for a moment. Though she hated to wake her, Veronica was glad that Josephine's short sleep seemed to have been a sound one.

Thursday morning, the sun rose over the fields in a clear sky, hints of autumn in the crispness. Mrs. Slattery, good to her word, was back on duty, looking rested and ready for the day. She not only tended to Maggie and the babies but, to Josephine and Veronica's relief, she helped out with meals and laundry. After his breakfast, John was off to the fields while the girls gathered the eggs, fed the hens, and helped to feed the younger ones.

The house was quiet most of the day, given over to sleep for the twins and their weary mother. The children were allowed to visit at dinnertime, still in awe, the girl's baby even tinier than the boy's. It seemed impossible.

On Friday, the silence continued for the most part, and the children were encouraged to stay outdoors in the far yard beyond the barns and the chicken coop, where their voices wouldn't carry into the bedroom.

Maggie dozed between feeding the little ones, Mrs. Slattery reassuring her often that all was well. Both women hoped that the difficulties of early birth hadn't caused problems. The babies were tiny, true enough, but they seemed to take adequate nourishment. The lungs of the little boy were healthy; his sister sounded more like a tiny bleating lamb.

That same night, Maggie felt strong enough to come out to sit at the supper table. The children and John gathered around. Mrs. Slattery had gone for the night. The excitement of having their mother with them and two new babies was more than Betty could manage. She wrapped her arms around Josephine, who was holding her, and exclaimed: "Isn't it wonderful to have so many babies?"

Her joy spilled over into them all as they clustered around the table. Maggie, whose own color seemed to be returning, held each child so they could face out to their brothers and sisters.

"What will we call them, Ma?" Gene asked as she stood stroking the infants.

"Yes, do we have names for them yet, Margaret, dear?" John asked sheepishly, sitting in his chair opposite Maggie. Their eyes met, and the spark between them lit the room.

"Ah, your lordship," Maggie said in response. "'Tis the names we've been saving up for a little boy or a little girl. Now, we'll use them both."

Little Betty clapped her hands in joy, and the boys sat up straight in their chairs. With a great ceremony, Maggie announced the names, holding each child a bit higher. "This little fellow," she said as she looked down at the bundle in her right arm, will henceforth be known as Donnell." As if on cue, little Donnell wriggled in his mother's embrace. "His middle name will be Gervase, after the saint who was also a twin."

The children were all smiles, waving to Donnell.

"And this little girl," Maggie said, lifting the tiny pink bundle up a bit, "who looks so much like a sweet flower, will be Rose. And she'll also have my middle name given to me by my dear mother. Rose Agnes."

Along with little Betty, the children applauded. With that, Baby Rose made a soft sound, a whimpering. They all listened. Maggie stood and moved toward the bedroom.

"This little lady and gent and their ma are going in for a bit more rest with thanks to each of you for your fine welcome and consideration."

Joy filled the room as they all watched their ma heading back. Josephine put little Betty down to help settle her mother and the babies.

Just after the noonday dinner on Saturday, the doctor came. "'Tis nothing to worry for," he said to Josephine, who answered the door. "We're making sure these little ones are on the right start." Doc Hinman was a familiar face from Church each Sunday morning and an occasional presence to help soothe flu and fever. His own ruddy complexion and spectacles gave him an air of authority, comforting to all he helped.

Mrs. Slattery asked the girls to take the younger children outdoors, the weather cooperating nicely. John went into the bedroom with Maggie and the twins.

Out of earshot of the children, Doc Hinman examined the twins, listening with his stethoscope to their hearts and lungs. Then, with soft eyes, he looked up to Maggie and John and shared his diagnosis.

"This little one mightn't make it," he said of Rose Agnes. It doesn't seem her lungs are giving her enough air. It happens sometimes this way." Maggie's eyes pooled with tears as he continued. "The best you can do is hold her and love her, and when the time comes, let her go."

Both Maggie and Mrs. Slattery had worried for Baby Rose but didn't let on, hoping they were wrong. Now it was sure, the doctor giving confirmation to their worst fears.

Maggie looked up at John, whose face was stone. Then she peered down at the little pink cheeks of Baby Rose, the blue of her eyes every bit as beautiful as the ocean, the tininess of her lips and nose, miraculous beyond belief. She was indeed as sweet as a rose and as delicate. Tears streamed down Maggie's cheeks as Mrs. Slattery lifted Donnell to her, gently placing him on her chest. Seeing the two side by side, it was clear that little Rose was failing.

The doctor left quietly, Josephine seeing him out. Mrs. Slattery helped Maggie as she nursed first Donnell, who ate mightily, his sucking sound productive. When Baby Rose started, she could hardly latch onto the breast. Her whimpers barely amounted to any sound, her color more and more pale. Mrs. Slattery watched as Maggie held her and rocked her, her own heart bursting with sorrow. John came around and sat at her bedside. Mrs. Slattery slipped out.

Leftover pork and potatoes with canned applesauce was the Saturday supper. Mrs. Slattery directed Josephine and Veronica to set the table first and then gather the children. An ominous hush seemed to surround their chores, and Mrs. Slattery said little.

"Keep the little ones still as best you can when you call them. Your Ma's resting, and so are the babies."

Within the hour, John and the children came around the table with little fanfare. Complaints about what was served had never been tolerated. They ate quietly, remembering to finish everything on their plate. They'd been told that many children in Europe were starving. The gelatin and cookie for dessert were served silently as well.

When they all had finished eating, John stood up from the table and waited until the children looked up at him. Veronica nudged Gene and Betty to be still. The boys put down their spoons and waited.

"We've sad news to share with you this day," John said softly. "There's no easy way to tell you that your newest little sister, our baby Rose, is being called back to God very soon to be one of His angels. Your ma would like you to say goodbye this evening, and then we'll all say a rosary together."

One at a time, the children stood at their places and followed their father to the bedroom door. Mrs. Slattery blessed herself as she watched. As they all came out into the front parlor, they knelt in prayer. She knelt with them until they said the last Hail Mary, then quietly let herself out of the house, tears streaming down her cheeks.

Before the next sunrise, on Sunday morning, August 30, 1914, just as they had been told, Baby Rose was returned to God.

Chapter 8
Lasting Memory

August 30, 1914

The sun had gone from the sky, the day too gloomy for the last day of August. The children awoke to the news that Baby Rose had ascended into the glory of heaven.

"Sure, the angels and archangels have a new helper to sing their heavenly song," their father told them over porridge and warm milk. "She was with us almost the whole night, barely whimpering."

Tears streamed down faces that smiled back at their father's imagined scene. They collectively moped about the house, keenly feeling the loss of their newest little sister. Tom slipped away on his own, not making a sound, his face filled with sadness. Bernard caught up with him, the two of them now in the backyard, waiting for their older brothers. They kicked stones, their hazel eyes saddened.

Gene took charge of Betty, "Let's draw a picture of our new angel, Baby Rose," Gene suggested.

John went off to the barn, his place of solace, where he dealt with many a problem, and sorrow.

Veronica and Josephine were glad for Mrs. Slattery's continued presence. They watched her organize the meatloaf and potato dinner, get the laundry in place, and make sandwiches for supper. They helped as she directed, but Mrs. Slattery put no heavy demands on them. She was from Ireland's County Clare; her name, she was proud to say, meant bold and strong. It fit her well.

"You girls are most helpful," she said, her eyes kind. "Don't you worry; I'll see your Ma through this terrible time. You've all lost a precious one, and there's nothing to do but weep and wait."

Father Farrell arrived in the late morning, his mouth drawn downward, his black suit and white collar lending a somber presence. It was then that the family gathered in both doorways of the bedroom. The children held hands, and John stood close to Maggie, who was holding Baby Rose, with little Donnell in his arms. Mrs. Slattery stood by as well. Father Farrell blessed the little one, an angel for God, he declared.

"May the angels open their wings to bring this little one to their heavenly choir where she will sing the songs of peace and love forever and ever. Amen."

The family joined in a decade of the Rosary as Maggie, bleary-eyed with weeping, listened. Her arms held the tiny infant closely as little Donnell slept in his father's arms.

As they finished their prayers, Doc Hinman, his worn black bag in hand, arrived to certify the baby's death. He greeted the priest as he stepped out the door, nodding to John as he went. And just before the noon-day dinner, Mr. O'Connell from the funeral home, his soft blue eyes moist, took the tiny body to be returned that evening in readiness for the wake.

It was after the meal Hugh and Loring arrived home. The children knew these brothers had missed knowing Baby Rose for even that short time. "We have an angel in heaven now," Betty exclaimed to them.

Vic and Jerome came later that night to a somber household, filled only with the occasional cries of little Donnell, who was now without his twin sister. "Your mother will be glad you're all here," John said to the four older ones. "It's been a scourge these last days. I'm glad you're here as well."

Like the younger children, the older boys were led into the south bedroom, their mother holding their newest brother, Donnell. They never even got to see Baby Rose, a sorrow missed.

The excitement of having the four older boys home distracted the rest of the children a bit from their sorrow. They watched their brothers banter with one another, learning bits and pieces about their travels and jobs.

"You're looking a bit stout there, Sandy," Loring said to Jerome. He poked Sandy's stomach, which showed a minuscule bulge of fat. "Where are you getting all the food in these sparse times?"

"While I'm out making a living, riding the countryside, you're not doing too badly down there in the City with Aunt Annie feeding you her home cooking," Jerome retorted.

Hugh joined in, "Aunt Annie sure learned how to cook in Ireland. Not like some of them that came over and can hardly boil a potato."

Vic listened as his brothers talked of their Aunt Annie. He was hoping to hear about his cousin John, who worked for the New York Stock Exchange. Vic hoped one day to catch up with him and learn a thing or two. Vic's thoughts were lofty these days since starting Mechanics Institute in Rochester this past fall, where he'd learn a trade for a lifetime, automobiles the coming wave for them all.

The younger children watched and admired the awe in their older brothers' eyes as they met Donnell, most likely the last baby to grace the family. "He'll be the best of us all," they told their mother. They visited with her only briefly, for they could see the sleep in her eyes was covering the sadness.

Josephine noticed how handsome her brothers were now that she didn't have to clean up after them. Jerome, his blonde- red hair, blue eyes, and fine features, put her in mind of the popular Irish singer John McCormack, whose eyes and hair were similar. No wonder his brothers called him Sandy. And when they sang around the old square piano in the parlor as she played, she even thought he sang like McCormack, his rich tenor voice sending chills through her. She especially liked it when they sang *Macushla*, the Irish for 'darling,' Jerome's tenor voice hitting the high notes beautifully. He might be thinking about a special woman he might sing to one day, Josephine thought.

Sitting that evening over a supper of sandwiches and soup, the ten Donegan children, aged from twenty-four to three years, talked more politely than usual. It was no time for taunting and teasing; they could see that. They chatted more about Aunt Annie and their cousins in New York.

"How did you find them all holding up, Loring?" John asked about his sister and her family.

"They're a busy lot of women," Loring said, taking his cue to bring life into the conversation of this woeful group. "Aunt Annie is proud as can be of the oldest girls, Lizzie and Frankie, both nurses and skilled ones at that. They're working at the German Hospital and Dispensary where they studied. A fine place, they said."

"Imagine Irish girls working in a German hospital," Josephine said. She'd often asked her mother when she could go on her own to visit her New York City cousins. As she heard talk of them, she became more curious than ever. A knock at the front door interrupted the conversation.

"That'd be Mr. O'Connell," John said as he stood, his shoulders rounded, his nearly fifty-year-old frame showing the years.

"You older fellas, Hugh, Jerome, Loring, and Vic, come with me to greet him." The four boys stood, Hugh and Jerome, several inches taller than their brothers and father.

"Tomorrow, we'll have calling hours for our sweet child. 9:00 from the house. 10:00 from the church." He paused and looked at the four older boys. "Mr. O'Connell has asked that you fellas carry the coffin."

Veronica and Josephine stood and cleared the table, noting Mrs. Slattery had left things in order, the laundry folded, and the food ready for tomorrow. The two sisters worked well together, washing, rinsing, and drying the few dishes they'd used for this simple supper. The younger children stayed seated, not certain of what would happen next.

Within minutes, the front door opened. Mr. O'Connell and their father came in, followed by their brothers. The younger children slipped out of their chairs and went towards the front of the house. The older boys lifted the miniature coffin into the front parlor and placed it on the oval oak table under the window that had been cleared of its book and lamp.

Gene let go of Betty's hand and crept into the room to see what was happening. Tom and Bernard came too. Gene already missed the newest little sister, whom she had barely gotten to know. She'd had dreams that she would help dress her and carry her around. She looked up as they opened the lid of the coffin. Soft pink light from the satin lining shone into the room. Her father and Mr. O'Connell stood on either side; her big brothers lined up along the wall.

Gene turned to Tom and Bernard and whispered, "Wouldn't it have been nice if those nurse cousins could have been right here and kept Baby Rose alive?"

Nine-year-old Tom bent down and picked up Betty, who had followed in. "See the special crib for our Baby Rose so people can come and say goodbye to her tomorrow?" He whispered to her. Together, they gazed at the tiny infant, dressed in a white bonnet and long white dress, her eyes closed, her face peaceful.

Tom didn't speak another word but put Betty down next to Bernard, who took her hand. Tom slipped out the door, where he could wipe his eyes.

Josephine and Veronica joined the others as their mother came into the parlor. Maggie handed Donnell to Josephine and stepped toward her little girl, blessing herself and saying the same prayer she'd said only a little while ago.

May the angels open their wings to bring this little one to their heavenly choir, where she will sing the songs of peace and love forever and ever. Amen."

Mr. O'Connell then began the Rosary, this time the Sorrowful Mysteries. Maggie sat in the nursing chair, taking Donnell back into her arms.

As she handed Donnell back to her mother, Josephine thought of Lizzie and Frankie. If I was a nurse, she thought, I might have saved our little Rose.

Margaret and John were glad for the decision to have the wake for little Rose in the morning just before the funeral.

"You'd be too weak for it tonight, Maggie," John had insisted. "Our friends will be there for you in the coming days. For now, let's put this precious child of ours to peaceful rest."

Having the older boys all home, the family saying prayers over the tiny coffin, the priest offering blessings, and Josephine playing Ave Maria was solace enough for a time and a lasting memory for all.

Chapter 9
Talk of War

Autumn, 1914

Maggie wandered out to the barnyard, the day mild, a slight breeze rippling through the autumn leaves of the spent peony bush bordering the driveway. A hazy sun made her glad for her knitted shawl. She stepped over two black and white barn cats sleeping on the stoop and peeked in the side barn where the tractor was kept. The doors were ajar enough for her to see the steel tires and green frame of the machine that gave their work a boost she'd not thought possible.

These tractors with kerosene-powered engines were more and more plentiful. Hugh saw to it his family was among the first to get this Waterloo Boy Model-R tractor. It allowed farmers to put aside the horse-pulled plows first developed by John Deere, whose name had become synonymous with advances in farm machinery, allowing them to put aside steam-powered tractors that so often caused field fires.

Maggie grinned to remember Hugh talking up the advantages of these new machines. His own work with the Ford Motor Company gave him inside information and even a bit of credibility with his father.

She walked up to the big yellow barn, its red doors parted wide, and looked up at the hayloft piled high with this season's bounty. She sighed deeply at the blessing of it, yet still her breath caught up short with the sorrow she carried with her, sorrow that didn't leave her alone these days.

Her baby Donnell was thriving, and for that, she was grateful. He looked like John's people, with the same dark hair and hazel eyes many of the children carried. When Josephine was born, the first girl after four boys, her chestnut brown hair and hazel- green eyes that always seemed to smile brought such joy. John took a special shine to her, though he'd not admit it, saying she put him in mind of his sister Annie.

When Veronica came along, she favored Maggie's siblings: pink cheeks, blue eyes, and wisps of red hair. Then along came Tom, Bernard, Genevieve, Elizabeth, and now baby Donnell and dear Baby Rose, all with the Donegan look, one she was proud to propagate, the handsome lot of them all carrying their father's looks.

Maggie wrapped her arms around her waist and hugged herself as she thought again of little Donnell, who sensed the loss of his sister, his eyes so sad. She cooed at him and stroked his tiny body often, vowing nothing would harm this last child of hers.

Eleven children. She couldn't believe it some days, and other days, she felt every bit of it. How, she wondered, would it all turn out? Her sister Mary had lost not one but two children already. What, Maggie wondered, would she be asked to face in her own lifetime? She prayed that Hugh would not get distracted from his automobile work by thoughts of war.

Talk of war continued over the weeks before the birth of the twins, John recounting details of the news to Maggie. "It began with the assassination of Archduke Ferdinand and his wife Sofie," he said. This past week, the bitter Battle of Tannenberg, where fifty thousand Russians were killed, had been a major victory for Germany. It had taken place on the very day their Baby Rose died.

Maggie minded it all and found herself increasingly frightened. Recent news from Ireland that Germany helped provide arms to the Irish for a possible rebellion added to her anxiety.

"Hush, John," Maggie said, touching his lips with her fingers. "The talk of war isn't good for the wee ones, nor is it doing me any good."

Now, Maggie moved quietly toward the stall where Jenny, their mare who had carried them hither and yon so faithfully through all these years, stood. She reached in and stroked the wide, white blaze that stretched down the middle of Jenny's face. "A fine day to you, Miss Jenny," she said aloud. "With all this nonsensical talk of war, at least we've you to count on, don't we?"

Jenny snorted as if in agreement as Maggie scooped up some hay for her. "Ye won't carry us anywhere we wouldn't want to go now, would ye?" As she fed the horse, she heard the boys above in the loft as they piled the hay high.

"I'd sure enlist if they asked me," Jerome said as he grunted under a pitchfork full of hay.

"They're not looking for runts," Loring said with a laugh. "So, I'd say you won't be going then, will you?" Jerome responded.

Their sparring put Maggie in mind of the Irish boys who had signed up already with the British army. She and John kept up-to-date with Irish politics, thanks to letters from her sister Julia and conversations with Annie and Hugh, who were an embedded part of the Irish immigrant societies in Woodside, where they'd recently moved.

Several acquaintances from church had managed to travel back and forth to their homeland, bringing disturbing news. New York City, at one time, had far more Irish living within it than in Dublin. The most recent news of the suspension of the Irish Home Rule bill because of the impending war was causing major alarm.

"Listen to this now. Redmond's telling the lads to enlist in the British Army," John murmured to Maggie, referring to the speech given by John Redmond, the Irish Parliamentary Party leader. "What is this world coming to?"

Maggie wondered the same thing. Here in America, with their own farm and proper schooling for the children, sometimes Ireland seemed light years away.

Julia's letters were Maggie's main tie to her home in Ireland. Her last one delivered a blow, telling of their mother's death. Neither Maggie, her sister Mary, nor Lizzie or Jer could go 'home' for the funeral, the cost and distance too great. Only Julia would be there.

Margaret Riordan Buckley lived to age eighty-two, her daughter Julia assuring her good care 'til the end. Maggie knew Julia would see to it there was a fine service and that the rituals would be attended to as her mother would have wished: opening the window for two hours to let the spirit fly free, then closing it to prevent the spirit from coming back in; covering the mirrors, stopping the clocks, closing the curtains, all signs of respect for the deceased. Maggie was also certain that Julia would be sure that, as her mother was washed and dressed, Julia would be sure her mother's Rosary would be entwined in her hands.

In late April, as the services in Ireland were held, Maggie took time to kneel by the little dining room shrine and say a Rosary. She knew of wakes and funerals from her childhood, and as she spent time saying a rosary, she remembered with tears the love of her mother, who had sent her forth to America twenty-five years ago, knowing she'd not see her again. Her heart swelled at the thought of the music her mother had given, her accordion, the metal Jew's harp, and melodies for a lifetime.

A rumble from the skies surprised Maggie. She looked out to see a sudden storm filling the ground with puddles. She headed away from the barn, worrying for her Donnell. As she darted the thirty feet back to the house, she pulled the door open by the pump. To her surprise, John stood holding Donnell and soothing him.

"Must have been the sound of the rain or something," John said. "He woke up wailing as if there was no tomorrow." He rocked Donnell in his arms and said, "But once I held him, he calmed right down. There's some power now, wouldn't you say?"

Taking off her wet shawl and shaking herself out, Maggie reached for the baby. "I'd say you've learned the knack after all these years." John handed over the infant and kissed the top of Maggie's head. Another knack he'd learned.

Chapter 10
Hugh's Letters

January 1917

"Will you read us Hugh's letter, Ma?" Tom asked.

It was just after supper, and the most recent letter tantalized the children like candy waiting on the sideboard.

Maggie had read this most recent one herself when it first arrived in yesterday's mail and was pleased that the children cared enough to want to hear Hugh's latest missive. They often asked to hear his other ones again as well. He was a magical figure to them, older, often absent, and revered.

While Gene and Veronica cleared the dishes from the table, except for Maggie and John's teacups, Maggie put Don to bed. Then she pulled six-year-old Betty onto her lap, opened Hugh's letter, and began to read to the children at the table:

December 28, 1916
Baltimore, Maryland

Dear Mother,

"Your letter arrived OK, and I was glad to hear you received your Xmas present."

Maggie paused and said by way of explanation, "He means to say Christmas instead of Xmas," then continued.

"I have been very busy, and that accounts for not sending it sooner. I am going to be in New York on the 6 to 10th of January. Loring wrote and said to see him before I went out to Long Island, so I think I will."

Maggie paused. She was so pleased that her boys were chums, their childhood jealousies not causing ongoing feuds. She remembered her own brothers, Michael and Tims, who often

sniped at each other. Maggie didn't take any credit for the behavior of her boys. They had been easy playmates since they were young. Hugh was the leader and made sure everyone had a turn, whether at stickball, tag, or marbles. As Maggie hung the laundry, she'd been amazed to watch the diplomacy her oldest son exercised.

"You mightn't take two turns, now, Sandy," she heard him, using Jerome's nickname, "'til your younger brothers both get their chance. It's only fair. Besides, Loring and Vic want to play, too!"

Where had he ever learned such a way? John had been gentle enough, but this was a gift. Maggie's musing was interrupted by Tom. "Ma, will you keep on reading, pleeeasee? What else does he say?"

The older girls, Veronica and Gene, were interested, but not half as much as Tom. Hugh's letters were delicious to Tom, and talk of Hugh's travels and work was compelling.

Maggie put little Betty onto the floor next to her to play with her cloth dolly named Rosie. Maggie started reading aloud again, aware that Tom was pining after this older brother, Maggie thought.

I am busy studying the dictionary, and I pity any vocabulary that stretches itself on me. I am fully armed, and if my ammunition doesn't give out, I'll be all OK.

"Would you listen to that, Mother?" Veronica commented. "He sounds supercilious, boasting about being armed by a dictionary."

Maggie smiled. "Since he finished up his certificate from Genesee Wesleyan Seminary, he's been determined to make something of himself, and studying the dictionary is one way he'll do it."

"Let her finish reading, will you?" Tom grumbled.

Veronica sat back in her chair, her red hair curled down her cheeks, smiling. When Hugh was home for his occasional visits,

Tommy was always sitting right next to him. Their fourteen-year age difference made Hugh almost like a father to his younger brother and sisters. He took his role seriously and treated them with genuine affection that made them like him all the more. He'd even bring special candy treats that assured him a hero's status.

"I was only adding a thought," Veronica said to Tom in her own defense.

"Can we go on, Ma?" Tom urged again.

Maggie glanced around and saw Gene and Betty were getting sleepy. She hurried the last part of the letter about his job.

"The weather here is O.K. I had good offers to go back to Michigan this week as Supt (Superintendent) of Sales and Service for Northern Michigan) Ford Branch. I worked in competition with them and put over many a second-hand car where they could have sold a Ford. And I guess they decided I should have seen them before leaving Mich(igan)."

I wrote them a nice letter, and much as I hate to be moving around, if they come across with the right thing, I may travel back to Michigan."

It certainly seemed to Maggie that this oldest boy had landed on his feet.

"Read the last part, Ma. How does he sign it?" Gene perked up to ask. As a fourth-grade student, letter writing was one of her assignments. She listened intently as Maggie read the last lines.

"Well, I must do some more work tonight, so I will close. Wishing you all a Happy New Year; I am Your Loving Son, Hugh.

Gene loved to hear that closing, *"I am Your Loving Son Hugh."* Would she sign her letters, "I am Your Loving Daughter Genevieve?" She liked the sound of it.

Tom listened intently, his chin in his hands, his elbows, now that the meal was over, planted on the table. He loved the part about traveling from Baltimore to New York and then Long Island. What adventures Hugh had going from city to city and then meeting up with his brother Loring, whose nickname, "Lucky," suited him, lucky to have such times with his older brother Hugh.

Tom figured out that he had Hugh's middle name, 'Michael,' as his own first name. Michael Thomas was named after his Uncle Mike and his grandfather, Thomas. Now, he'd remember his brother Hugh Michael, too. He dreamed of one day going off with Hugh in one of his shiny Ford cars.

Maggie read the last lines and smiled within. Her oldest boy seemed to have the world by the tail. She kept his Genesee Wesleyan Seminary achievement certificate in a special drawer. How lucky they were to have the 'Seminary,' as they called it, in town. Started by the Methodist Episcopal denomination, education was a gift for the town.

Hugh's certificate, signed by Principal Lafayette Congdon, signified the beginning of his success. While the others could often be found out running in the fields, Hugh would be off on his own, studying. He'd often entertain his youngest brothers and sisters with stories that he'd made up, never seeming to tire of telling them. His smile warmed Maggie's heart when she watched Hugh carrying young Don around on his shoulders, looking for all the world like a proud parent.

For no reason that she could put her finger on, Maggie worried at times that Hugh would be crushed by the weight of the world. John dismissed her worries.

"You needn't worry for that lad, Maggie," John had said. "He's a head on his shoulders for numbers and words. It's a winning combination; just wait and see."

Maggie listened and hoped John was right.

Tommy looked at the letter after his mother finally finished reading it. The girls had commented on Hugh's penmanship. It had a flourish that was almost artistic. Even with no lines on the paper, the sentences lined up perfectly. It seemed Hugh had inherited his mother's curiosity and love of words. No wonder he was taking on the dictionary.

Maggie noted that Hugh had a look a bit like her older brother Tims, though she prayed he'd not have the same love of the drink. Her sister Julia wrote that Tims still hadn't given up on the drink, and his sweetheart Nora had gone from him on the head of it. Such a sweet girl. If only…

Maggie had a chance now to bring her first son to a much richer outcome. He'd been a fine baby and a strong one who didn't seem a bit bothered by the move to upstate New York when he was just under two years old. He never even caught a cold, the seven-hour train trip to Western New York finding him sleeping through the stops at Albany and again in Syracuse as if he'd been born to travel.

His laughing eyes had kept her heart young as she and John journeyed off to a new adventure. Maybe it was their travel so early in his infancy that gave him a solid start in the automobile business going from place to place. After all, he was about to be Superintendent of Sales. Such success at age twenty-seven! Maybe John was right. Maybe she shouldn't worry.

Chapter II
Women's Suffrage

January 1917

"Sure, shouldn't women have the right to vote?" Maggie said, her blue eyes quizzical. She put down the newspaper, its headline displaying a banner with a message to "Kaiser Wilson" asking, "Have You Forgotten?" The banner was courtesy of Alice Paul and the National Woman's Party, who set up a silent picket at the White House gate. They pledged to have a sentinel on post every day to remind President Wilson of his hypocrisy in supporting the cause of freedom in the First World War, yet not supporting the freedom of women at home to vote.

Maggie looked at her husband and sons as she poured her tea and put the pot in the middle of the table. The supper was ended, and the young ones were scattered for their evening's play, Veronica supervising.

"Ma," Jerome said, his sandy hair pushed back from his forehead in a wave as he leaned back in his chair, "if women start voting, there'll be no peace for us men at all!" He looked at her with a wry smile. "Why, we'll have to believe they have intelligence and wisdom beyond household chores, and if that happens, who'll cook the meals when we come in from the fields?"

"I wouldn't expect you should carry on too much like that," John cautioned his second oldest son. He stroked his gray mustache as he counseled, "You've still a few more months of meals you'll be hoping for before you move up to Livonia."

"Pa is right, Sandy!" Loring chimed in, "Until you've hooked up with your own woman, you'd better not bite the hand that feeds you."

Josephine stood up to clear the remaining few dishes. She looked around the table at her parents and older brothers, measuring her response. She decided not to give one. She was glad to be home for this week off. She'd missed the family terribly. Yet she loved her studies at the German Hospital Training School for Nurses, the same school her cousins Lizzie and Frankie had attended. It was a dream of hers to become a nurse. She knew housewifery was not for her. She'd already had enough of caring for children, making meals, and doing dishes. And enough of her brothers spouting off about women, even if in jest.

Down the road, the Seminary, as they called it, where Josephine had taken classes, the high school in Lima not yet started, – became a place of enlightenment for her. She was quickly enamored with stories of one of the school's famous graduates, Belva Lockwood, who had attended the school as a widow with a young child, not a usual circumstance in the 1850s. Belva had graduated with honors and had gone on to serve as principal in several local schools. Ultimately, Belva met up with Susan B. Anthony, whose concern was that most girls' schools prepared female students primarily for domestic life only.

The idea of including more options for careers with better pay caught Lockwood's interest and Josephine's. Even though Josephine was settled on nursing, she agreed vehemently that the curriculum should be expanded to include the same courses that young men took - public speaking, botany, and gymnastics. Lockwood was encouraged to make changes at her schools and did. She went on to examine her own education and decided to study law rather than continue teaching.

Josephine was attracted to the spunk of Lockwood's story and her groundbreaking run in 1884 and again in 1888 for President of the United States. It was amazing to Josephine and others that, as a woman, Lockwood, a candidate for President, could not cast a vote for herself. How glad Josephine was that times were changing despite her brother's banter.

Women's Suffrage was becoming a more popular conversation despite the conservative nature of Western New York women. Many women traveled to Buffalo to hear local leaders of the Suffrage Movement: artist Evelyn Rumsey Cary whose 1905 Woman Suffrage poster played a key role in the movement; doctors like Sarah Lamb of Lockport and Sarah Morris of Buffalo, who convinced it was a disease, started a clinic to assist women to recover from alcoholism; Helen Rodgers, first woman in a graduating class from Buffalo Law School; Mary Burnett Talbert, the only African-American to hold a vice-principal position thus far. These women inspired and engaged other women to believe and follow. Josephine drank it all in. Her mother was ever encouraging, her mother, who no one could say was subservient to any man.

As the teapot was passed around, Loring told them of the time he and Josephine had spent after Thanksgiving at Aunt Annie's. Loring sat up, his plaid shirt sleeves folded back, his red hair combed with a part, his blue eyes shining as he spoke.

"Did you hear about the 'Suff' Bird Women?" he asked. "It might not have made it to the *Lima Recorder*, but it's a tale worth telling."

"Out with it, lad," Maggie said. "The young ones will be back soon, leaving no time if you don't hurry your telling."

"Is this about the lighting of the Statue of Liberty?" John asked, suddenly remembering something he'd heard.

"Yes, Aunt Annie told us we should go over to watch the lighting of it," Loring continued. By now, Josephine had returned and was glad to hear the story again.

"President Wilson was to light it off with a wireless key that turned on the new floodlights from his luxurious steam yacht, *The Mayflower*. Well, we never did go over, but the next day's Times told us what happened. You've got to hand it to these women, and they're passionate about the vote."

"Will you go on and tell us?" Sandy said, his own impatience building.

"All right, all right, keep your shirt on," Loring replied. He sat forward a bit.

"It seems there was a plan on the Saturday afternoon of the Statue of Liberty lighting to 'bomb' President Wilson on the presidential yacht as it steamed down the Hudson."

Loring paused. Josephine nodded and smiled. Now that he had full attention, he went on. "The 'bombs,' he explained, "were yellow signed petitions from 'women voters of the West' and leaflets in support of the Susan B. Anthony suffrage movement. Ruth Law, a suffrage leader and pilot, was to be the 'bomber.' The trouble was she had accepted an earlier request to fly another plane that had the word Liberty written on the bottom to circle the Statue of Liberty as it was lit."

Loring smiled at his captive audience. "So up comes one Leda Richberg–Hornsby of Chicago, only the eighth woman in the United States to earn a pilot's license, the first woman graduate of the Wright Flying School in Dayton. She becomes the pilot of this intrepid suffrage plane. From what they said, she was something. The *New York Sun* called her 'petite, plucky and brunette'. Ida Blair, another suffrage leader, joined her in the plane that carried a large banner reading "Women Want Liberty Too." Members of the National American Women's Suffrage Association cheered them on their way."

Loring eyed his audience, ready for the close of his story. "Imagine, if you can, these women, prepared as they were with their 'bombs' in place. And just after a 5:45 p.m. take off, a mile in the air, a gale-force wind had no mercy. It forced them to crash land in a Staten Island swamp." He paused and then said, "Their biggest injury was to their spirits."

With that, as Maggie had predicted, the youngsters burst in the door, thirsty, noisy, and soon to be ready for bed.

Veronica and Genevieve got up to tend to the children as Maggie and John quizzed Loring. "Was anyone hurt in the crash? Did the President learn of the plan?"

Before Loring could answer, Josephine replied, "The plan made the news so everyone knew. Not bad publicity at all." "Not bad at all," Loring said, satisfied his tale had similar interest.

Chapter 12
Josephine

January 1917

"Mother," Josephine said, her chestnut hair pulled back and falling softly around her angular face, her tone confidential, "when Loring talked about the Saturday night that Lady Liberty was to be lit, he never told you what we did instead of going to the lighting." Her dark eyes sparkled as she paused.

"Well, it looks as if you're bursting to tell me, and I'm all ears," Maggie said lightly.

"I've been waiting for a chance to talk with you, but with everything that goes on, there never seemed a moment. And soon, I'll be going back." Josephine leaned forward in the brocade chair and poured tea for them.

"There's so much to share, Mother, but one of the things I'd love you to know about that night is that Frankie, Lizzie, Margaret, Loring, and I were all invited to the New Amsterdam Theatre on 42nd Street to see the Ziegfeld Follies!" Josephine practically jumped from her chair, giggling with excitement.

She was so glad to have this time alone to talk with her mother. They were sitting in the front parlor; sheet music opened on the piano, the games and puzzles stacked on the bookshelves.

"Mother, what a thrilling time we had." Sitting on the edge of her chair, she could hardly contain herself. "The glitter of the costumes and the music, and oh, Jerome Kern was divine. I wished so very much you'd been there with us. It's something I'll never forget."

Maggie smiled to see her oldest girl so joyful. She recalled her own time in New York almost thirty years ago, filled with little glamour and plenty of work. Her time as a domestic with the James family was fair enough. Mr. James was a lawyer, and his wife was in charge of the household. Maggie had advanced from doing laundry and dishes to cooking meals and then to serving dinners. John came along in the nick of time, her patience for being 'commanded about' wearing thin. Ah, those were some days, Maggie thought as Josephine continued.

"The work at the hospital is hard, I won't deny that. But it's just wonderful to be learning and helping. I miss you all so much, but I do love New York. It's everything I've dreamt of."

Josephine reached out and held Maggie's hands for a moment, so excited for all she was learning and so grateful to Maggie for advocating on her behalf for nursing school. She didn't know how to thank her except to be a good student and competent nurse.

"It was one of Frankie's patients that got us the tickets. It was so very magical. Oh, Mother, please say you'll come visit sometime, won't you? Little Donnell will soon be old enough to stay on without you. Aunt Annie says he's almost old enough to come with you."

Maggie poured herself another cup of tea. She wasn't about to bring her young son to New York City, or any city for that matter. But there was no need to say that to this daughter, so full of hope and idealism.

"Mother, there's something else I want to tell you," Josephine said cautiously. Her mother, whose red hair had more silver since last fall, straightened her spine, alerted by Josephine's tone. She waited, not sure what was coming.

"Mother, I think you'll be proud. Aunt Annie is."

For Josephine, gone for such a short time, everything seemed so different. She saw things on this Christmas holiday with new eyes. The kids were bigger, the house was smaller, and her parents were older. She'd spent Thanksgiving at Aunt Annie's home in Woodside, a short train ride from the city. Hugh and Loring were frequent visitors due to their business dealings. It was a thrill to visit with their cousins, whose worldly life in New York was so different from their rural farm life.

She looked into her mother's blue eyes and saw the tiredness in them. She saw the heartache, too. She hoped her news would bring her some joy.

"Mother, Frankie, Lizzie, Margaret, and I are all going to be in the Suffragette's Parade in October. It's in the planning stages right now and a bit of a secret, but I wanted to tell you. We'll be marching down Fifth Avenue. We've been asked to go with others from the German Hospital, and we've all agreed. Isn't that wonderful?"

Josephine waited a minute while Maggie absorbed the news, hoping it would please her. "Mother, we're helping to collect signatures now. We're not allowed to ask patients, but we can canvass visitors after hours. The women are more than happy to sign. We're hoping to carry placards telling of over one million signatures of New York women demanding the vote."

Maggie reached for the teapot as she eyed this oldest daughter. "If your enthusiasm counts for anything, dear Josephine, you'll have the signatures in no time." Maggie's eyes gleamed with pride, thinking there seemed to be no bounds to what this child of hers might accomplish.

"I wanted you to know, Mother – because it's so important to me and the others. It's important to all women."

Maggie couldn't agree more. She'd been a supporter of women's right to vote, especially as she watched what was happening in her own homeland, held in bondage far too long. She followed the work of the unusual couple Hannah and Frank Sheehy Skeffington, who founded the Irish Women's Franchise League. So many others, too, who fought for suffrage right alongside English women. Yes, she was proud of Josephine.

As they parted for bed, Maggie thought of Josephine's strength. She'd always been a good student, and now, attending the same nursing school her cousins Frankie, Lizzie, and Hughberta had gone to, she was working for Women's suffrage. There was no telling where she'd end up.

Maggie promised herself she would write a note to Annie to thank her for what she was doing for this child, now most definitely a woman.

Chapter 13
The Draft

June 1917

Maggie sat in the front parlor, alone for a moment as the children finished breakfast and readied themselves for school. She looked across at the little cradle, now filled with cloth doilies and blankets, Donnell well past the stage where he could fit it. She was firm in her determination to honor Baby Rose, and one of her best hopes, besides prayer, was to bring Donnell up strong and bright. She couldn't bring that beautiful pink baby girl back, but she could cuddle and spoil her twin brother. And she did.

Her two oldest daughters sensed it when she wouldn't let him cry for a minute. "Veronica, would you bring him to me," she called from her bedroom when she heard him whimpering. Before she'd even finished gathering herself for the morning, she'd often be soothing him, whatever his problem.

"There you are, little one; see how you like that bouncy big bed while I put me stockings on," Maggie would say as she hoisted him up onto the full-size mattress and put a pillow on either side of him. "Such a big, strong boy you are."

Veronica stood in the doorway, watching as the baby boy looked at his mother as if she were a goddess. She could never compete with that.

The backdrop to Baby Rose's death that hadn't escaped Maggie's attention was the start of World War I. She had no interest in war, the troubles of Europe not reaching into her world except for the occasional news article that John told her about or when Julia's letters made mention of it.

"The Phelan boys down the road are gone to be soldiers in the war," Julia had written. "We've no mind for the Home Rule for now, I suppose, 'til this war's done."

It is impossible to think that Irish boys found work soldiering for the English, but true, Ireland's struggle to be free of British rule was suspended for a time.

Maggie picked up little Donnell and took him to the kitchen for his porridge. She waved the other children off to school as they gathered their schoolbooks and sweaters for their walk up to St. Rose, which was just short of a mile. Sun beamed across the neighboring field, giving it a gold quality. A light breeze was enough to warrant the sweaters the girls wore. Gene, now ten, took charge of seven-year-old Betty. Tom and Bernard were on their own except for Veronica's watchful eye. Maggie missed Josephine. They all did.

The talk of war was becoming a more pressing concern. Even though President Wilson's campaign slogan for his second term in office had been, "He kept us out of war," it wasn't holding true. This past April, Wilson declared war on Germany. And in May, a military draft was enacted for the first time since the Civil War.

As Donnell ate his porridge, Maggie cleaned up the breakfast dishes, thinking about four of her oldest boys. Each one would have to register. A new draft office had been set up in the Livingston County seat of Geneseo where the boys and that's what so many were, mere boys, would fill out draft cards and have their physical health assessed by medical personnel.

Maggie shivered to think of her boys at war. She shivered to think of anyone at war. The talk of it during her childhood had been enough to sour her on soldiering and killing. She'd heard the songs of Roddy McCorley, Boolavogue, and Bold Fenian Men, all making heroes of men who fought for Ireland. She'd take nothing away from them for their heroism, but it didn't mean she had to like war.

Maggie had prayed fervently over the last several years that the United States would not be drawn into this horrid European conflict. She said an extra decade of the rosary each evening to keep America out. But after a German U-boat sank the Cunard luxury passenger ship, the *Lusitania*, and one hundred and twenty-eight Americans drowned, she was unsure. She wasn't alone in her uncertainty.

The German torpedo that struck the *Lusitania* hit the starboard side right behind the bridge. The ship was located off the southern coast of Ireland at Old Head Kinsale. Survivors and those who died were all brought to the small town of Cobh (Cove) aboard the RMS Etruria, an earlier Cunard vessel.

Maggie couldn't imagine what Cobh was like after the ship sank: burying the dead, tending to the survivors, finding them housing and food, helping to contact relatives. A great sorrow for all those whose lives were lost, for all those families who mourned. And for what? How could the Germans close their eyes to all the deaths they were causing? Were they really that blind and selfish?

Maggie gazed out the window at the row of peonies that were growing on the path near the house. Soon enough, her four sons would have to sign up to be soldiers. On June 5, men between the ages of 21 and 31 would be called up. Hugh was 26 last November, Jerome, 23, and Loring, 21. Vic could wait until June 5th the following year, his own age, presently just 20.

Maggie hung the dishtowel on the rung by the stove, lifted off her apron, and scooped Donnell up in her arms. "Praise God, there'll be no war waiting for you, little one." With that, she nestled him down for his morning nap, his hazel eyes looking adoringly at her. Her blue eyes returned the gaze, tears pooling in them.

Chapter 14
The Story of the Dancing Sun

Fall 1917

Once America entered the Great War, talk of it escalated at the dinner table, especially as the draft progressed. Tom's older brothers, Hugh, Jerome, Loring, and Victor, were all eligible to be called up for service. Tom found the notion scary.

Articles about the war from the *Lima Recorder* and the *Democrat and Chronicle* became central topics at dinner, Tom listening and wondering about the fighting and killing. He was much too young to be a part of it and wasn't sure he ever wanted to be.

It was in his eighth-grade class at St. Rose School that Sister Teresita, a stately, stern woman with dark eyes and a brow that was always furrowed, told a tale that captured Tom. Pope Benedict XV, she said, was desperate for world peace, saying he would turn all his efforts over to Our Lady. He urged all Christians to beg the Virgin Mary to bring peace to the world. Tom imagined the Pope from pictures he'd seen of him, his red robe, wire-framed glasses, and tired eyes. Sister read his words:

"Our earnestly pleading voice, invoking the end of the vast conflict, the suicide of civilized Europe...the dark tide of hatred... multiplying ruin and massacre..."

Tom saw pictures in his mind of men killing men with no uniforms or countries identified. He felt anger rise within him. It wasn't until he learned what happened after the Pope's May 5th letter that Tom had become curious. On May 13, 1917, eight days after his letter was sent begging everyone to pray for peace to the Virgin Mary, it was reported that Our Lady appeared at Cova da Ira in Fatima, Portugal, to three young children who

were tending sheep Lucia, Francesco, and Jacinta, Tom wondered if it could be true. All three children said they saw the Lady. And all three were put in jail by the local Mayor, who believed this whole story of apparitions was political. The children of Fatima were challenged to confess they made it all up, but they wouldn't.

Lucia said she saw the Lady open her hands, a ray of light appearing in the direction of the sun. Lucia shouted to the crowds, "Look, look to the sun!". The rain stopped suddenly, and the sun began to turn different colors, illuminating the clouds, the sky, the trees, and even the people. Some people fell to the ground, blessing themselves. Others were skeptical, saying aloud that it was some sort of trick. Still, others realized that all their clothes had completely dried.

Tom had a feisty spirit that often got him in trouble. He'd raise a fist before letting anyone bully him. So, this Fatima story, with its holy attributes, was not an ordinary interest for him, but he knew his mother would believe in this dancing sun. She loved the Virgin Mary, her little shrine by the side door, always holding fresh flowers in the spring and a vigil light in the dark months.

"Boys and girls," Sister Teresita said in a whisper. "Word of this miracle is being written about all over the world. Here's the Lisbon newspaper account:

'On October 17th, O Dia reported the following:

At one o'clock in the afternoon, midday by the sun, the rain stopped. The sky, pearly gray in color, illuminated the vast, arid landscape with a strange light. The sun had a transparent gauzy veil so that eyes could easily be fixed upon it. The gray mother-of-pearl tone turned into a sheet of silver, which broke up as the clouds were torn apart, and the silver sun, enveloped in the same gauzy gray light, was seen to whirl and turn in the circle of broken clouds. A cry went up from every mouth, and people fell to their knees on the muddy ground. The light turned a beautiful blue as if it had come through the stained-glass windows of a cathedral and spread itself over the people who knelt with outstretched hands. The blue faded slowly, and then the light seemed to pass through yellow glass. Yellow stains fell against white handkerchiefs, against the dark skirts of women. They were reported on the trees, on the stones, and on the Serra. People wept and prayed with uncovered heads in the presence of the miracle they had awaited."

Tom listened and wondered. If it was hope that was needed for the world, could this be it?

Chapter 15
Uncle Mike

Fall 1918

Autumn, a crisp day, the air ripe with the smell of apples from bordering trees. Tom sat atop the Waterloo Boy tractor, proud to be doing his chore, plowing the acreage up the road from the farmhouse. Fourteen years old, he was big enough and strong enough to help. His older brother Hugh had been called into the service, joining his peers. There was a war.

On this day, with sunshine and birdsongs filling the air, Tom was feeling particularly tall. He rode up and down the ten acres of land, swinging the tractor neatly at each turn, keeping his rows tight and close. He'd learned well.

He didn't even see Veronica until he was on his last turn. He climbed down to see what the commotion was, for she was waving her arms like a flagman. "Uncle Mike is here. Come quickly. He wants to meet you, the one who has his name," she said breathlessly.

Tom couldn't help himself. He had to finish the rows evenly, as his father had taught him before he'd stop his work. He climbed back up on the running tractor, assuring Veronica he'd come as soon as he could.

He knew only a little about Uncle Mike. It was enough that he knew enough to respect his way of life. His grandfather Thomas, whose name she carried, had been an itinerant migrant worker of sorts, his father had told him. Traveling from town to town, making good wages, and meeting up with grand people. And now he would be face to face with his Uncle Mike, a real hobo. It's not a bum or a tramp. Hobos were different. They worked and worked hard. And kept on the move, looking for an easy mark, the sign with a mark that identified a person or place where one can get food and a place to stay overnight. The sign of the cat, for a kind lady, and the top hat for a gentleman were among the best.

Tom finally shut down the tractor and walked down the road briskly toward the farmhouse, the little green shingled one on the east side of Rochester Road. He saw Josephine standing on the porch, hands on hips like his mother would stand. "What's taking you so long? Mother is already serving dinner. Hurry up, she said."

Tom headed down the driveway to the raised platform with the water pump painted a pristine white, where he splashed fistfuls of water on his face and hands. It wouldn't do to meet this icon of a man with dirt all over him. He pulled his suspenders up on his shoulders, tucked his shirt into his trousers, took his hat off, and pushed open the dining room door.

Maggie, her blue apron wrinkled, red hair dripping from her bun, was placing a plate of mashed potato with a well of gravy in the center with a generous slice of ham in front of Uncle Mike, who looked up when he came in. Tommy saw a wide grin cross Uncle Mike's face, his eyes smiling.

Tommy drank in all he saw. Though he was seated, he was certain Uncle Mike was the same size as his own father. What he hadn't been prepared for was the dark hair and handsome eyes. He thought he was looking at his father's twin.

"Well, young fella," Uncle Mike bellowed as he looked at Tom, "are you the one that wouldn't stop your work 'til the whole row was tilled?"

Tom felt his face flush.

"I am," Tom said shyly, trying to find a way out of the spotlight. He scooted around the end of the table where his father was seated and slipped into a chair alongside Loring, his gaze on Uncle Mike. Jerome was opposite and next to Uncle Mike, his slim torso taller by a head.

Tom sat straight in his chair, listening as the older ones talked with Uncle Mike about the farm, the draft, and the war. Then, the talk turned to Tom.

"He's been a bit of a runt, Uncle Mike," Loring said, nodding towards Tom, his elbows on the table, "but he's diligent and a good worker. Pa says he reminds him of you."

Tom didn't mind the comment. He was eager to know more about Uncle Mike. Had he been in the service yet? Where was he working now? How much money did he make? Where did he sleep? Did he have any girlfriends?

Tom's mother served him a smaller portion of the same potato and ham. He ate hungrily, surprising himself with his appetite. He listened as Uncle Mike told of his latest adventure, where he saw an X inside a circle, a sign that meant this place was good for a handout. He told them that what he didn't see was the other sign on the fence, four prongs inside a rectangle. Before he knew it, he was running from a vicious dog that made hope of a handout impossible.

Those gathered around the table were enthralled as Uncle Mike finished his tale. "As I began to hightail it over the fence, I felt a nip at my boot. Only by the grace of God did I get both feet over and, with a good push, there I was, arse over teakettle on the other side, both feet still on me."

Tom sat staring at Uncle Mike, finding himself holding his breath, thrilled to hear of these adventures. He hoped to have some of his questions answered but was interrupted by his mother, who excused him from the table, reminding him after he brought the tractor back, he had studies to attend to. Tom dragged himself away, wishing he was older and could go on the road with Uncle Mike. He hoped for more stories in the morning. For now, he'd found the perfect subject for the essay he had to write.

Chapter 16
Michael Thomas

Fall 1918

Tommy watched as Uncle Mike walked down the highway, a cloth sack that doubled as a pillowcase slung over his right shoulder, the stripe ticking the same as on Tommy's pillow. In his left hand was a brown paper bag filled with ham sandwiches and molasses cookies that Maggie had packed for him. Uncle Mike turned and waved a final goodbye as he moved alongside the black Model T cars filling Rochester Road.

Tommy read about it in Hugh's letters.

He remembered one that Hugh wrote from Baltimore about his job prospects and returning to Michigan as Superintendent of Sales for the Northern Michigan Ford Branch. And another one in

January 1917 from the Fort Pitt Hotel in Pittsburg:

Dear Mother,

Your communication of a recent date caught sight of its destination this p.m.

Tom admired Hugh's gift for clever phrases. Another letter went on about wages he could earn for farming if he weren't going to war. Ever hopeful, he wrote:

"I believe the next time I make a good killing, I will buy a farm somewhere near home to keep the family busy on it, and so they will have a good landlord."

In a May letter from Bay City, Michigan, he explained,

"I am still kicking and really have no complaint to make. I am inspecting 4-cycle motors to be used in a govt. contract at Nashville, Tenn now and hope to get done here soon."

Finally, by July, he wrote from East Lansing, Michigan,

Dear Mother,

I am writing this on my straw bunk and in a U.S. Uniform. It's a fine place here and plenty to eat, and it looks like a fellow is better off here than in the truck business now - we have been drilling so far this week and start our mechanical work next Monday.

Tommy thought about the world Hugh was in now, his automotive work on hold while he served in the U.S. Army. Tom wondered if he'd like such a life, being told what to do and when to do it.

He looked up the road again to see Uncle Mike, his stride jaunty as if he didn't have a care in the world. His dark cap was tilted forward, his jacket flapping in the warm autumn breeze. As Uncle Mike disappeared up the hill toward Livonia, Tom felt a desire to go with him. Ever so slowly, he turned and came back to the house, the leaves on the two great chestnut trees in front moving rhythmically, filling the air with hope and possibility.

While Tommy's fourteenth birthday had confirmed his rite of passage to operate the tractor, he had yet to fulfill his desire to travel as Hugh and Loring did. This new chore of driving the tractor didn't seem like a chore at all. While he was nothing like his brother Bernard, who was studious and steady, who never allowed anything frivolous to distract him from whatever he set out to do, acting in plays and holding class office, Tom could be steady in his farming skills and help around the farm.

His sisters Gene and Veronica seemed endless in their requests for his help. They wouldn't think of pestering Bernard but were always begging Tom for favors and help. He generally complied.

"Tommie, dearest," Gene would say, batting her hazel eyes and pushing her dark hair back to mimic red-haired Veronica, "won't you help lift down the boxes from the chiffarobe in the upstairs hallway? Pretty please with sugar on top." They teased and carried on enough to make him laugh, something he was glad for amidst some dark days.

As much as school wasn't his favorite place to be, he found much to ponder. The 1915 sinking of the SS. Lusitania, the Fatima story, and the Zimmerman telegram all captured his interest. He listened at dinner as his father railed about the Germans on nights when his mother would allow it, realizing how deep the disdain for Germany was and how inevitable the United States' involvement had been.

With Hugh off to war, Sandy, Lucky, and Vic each off on their own, and Bernard studying to be a teacher, Tommy had been the one left to be the man about the farm. In addition to cleaning out the chicken coop, milking the cows, feeding the horses, and plowing the fields, he had schoolwork to do. He savored his memories of times with his brothers down on the creek, swinging on low branches, jumping in when the water was high enough, playing ball, and even chasing after the kittens, who seemed to come in endless quantities. He loved the wild roses, their fragrance intoxicating. Those days were fast becoming the past, making it inevitable that he had to let go of childhood.

Another letter from Hugh confirmed that notion:

September 8, 1918

Dear Mother,

Just received your letter O.K. and am glad to hear everybody is O.K. You would not worry about a fellow in the army, lots to eat and no chance of getting sick. I never felt better in my life, and the training is hard work, I guess, but it doesn't bother me. I am going to remain here as an Instructor on Tractors - Gas Engines - and Motor Trucks - Ignition, and lighting; the rest of the bunch are leaving next week for somewhere. There were 5 with an expert all-around rating out of 540 men, and I am 4 points ahead of the highest man, so you see, I have 2 good trades down pat...

In any case, I believe the people have to worry more than the soldiers do - which I suppose is quite natural still when you see so many people every day around a camp visiting their relatives and all with the same story. It is a funny world, after all - but when we get a few more of those square-head Germans, I don't think there will be much more trouble. Well, I believe I must get this off tonight, so I will close with love to all.

I am, as ever, your loving son, Hugh.

Tom wondered how soon his own turn at soldiering might come.

Chapter 17
The War

Autumn 1918

John scratched his graying head as he headed to the barn. He slid the big door to the right, glad he had chosen to paint it a bright fire engine red to contrast with the yellow, standing out against the wheat in the height of summer. As five or six - he couldn't keep track anymore - gray and white cats scooted by, John wondered how, in God's name, he would ever get all that needed to be done finished in time. The harvest was upon them: the corn was ready. The neighboring farmer would bring the binder that would be hooked up to the two mares and pulled through each row, sending the sheaves, ears, and all into shocks of eight to ten where, with enough helpers, his children included, the shocks would be loaded onto the hay wagon.

John's hope was that these cool, dry days would stay with them long enough to get everything done in time. While he counted on both Loring and Jerome to rig the wagon up, pull the machine, and run the binder, Jerome was the most reliable one these days. Loring had a wanderlust in him that John couldn't account for, but it was definitely there, maybe like his own desire to come to America. He knew nothing would have stopped him. His father didn't even try. There was nothing to keep him, nothing to keep his brother Michael or sister Annie. His father knew that, and so did his mother. It was what happened to young people who felt they had no future. They left for America.

John remembered the days not too long ago when Loring and Jerome worked up on Doran Road before John owned his own farm. Jerome lived with the Decker family and served as hired help, while Loring lived and helped on Frank and Mary

McDonald's dairy farm further down Doran Road. John knew they could learn better from others what an honest day's work meant, and the pay helped them keep at it. It was good these last days to have their help again, if only for a time.

Thankfully, both boys had gotten a deferment, their status as farm laborers keeping them from war. So many are being uprooted, everything topsy-turvy. While he wasn't actually against the war, it surely didn't do the harvest any favors. The war, the bloody war.

As a young man, John had grown up with talk of war, always hearing the men in the pub speak of winning Ireland's freedom from the British. He knew the fight for freedom was ever alive in his Irish countrymen. Even the recent 1916 battle, the Easter Rising they were calling it, proclaimed Ireland a Republic in an attempt to overthrow the British. Its success was still to be determined. There was no sympathy for the British. Of that, he was certain.

And now, America was at war. He'd given Wilson credit for his neutrality. War never solved anything. But how do you ignore the German bullying? The Lusitania was the first blow. He remembered hearing one man up at the American Hotel say that he was neutral, all right. He didn't care which of the Allies beat the Germans. Enough was enough.

John was pleased that two of his boys were able to serve in the United States military. All four boys had willingly registered as required. John was already fifty-two years old, and though he couldn't serve, his interest and support were keen. His sister Annie's girls, Frankie and Lizzie, had signed on, their nursing skills desperately needed. They had shipped out almost immediately to France. Annie's letters shared her anxiety for the girls, but she would do the same thing, she said, if she were younger and able. Three-quarters of the country were anxious about their children as well.

How John wished it were different. He worried a bit for Hugh, who had been on his way to his own career, a bona-fide car salesman with his own business. John hadn't done much to encourage him, telling him cars were a fad that would never replace horses for travel. How wrong he'd been, though he'd never admit it.

Hugh had been building his own company and had the markings of success. His enthusiasm shone through his letters from Baltimore, Pittsburgh, and Milwaukee, but his last one from Lansing, Michigan, where he'd been stationed, brought assurance to them all that he was adjusting to army life.

It's a fine place here and plenty to eat…a fellow is better off here than in the Truck business now…

John was pleased that Hugh was not too distraught over leaving his newly established **Hugh M. Donegan Motor Company** in Columbus, Ohio. Hugh had included a photograph of himself with his dealer insignia on the back of his car. He also promised to send more details for Loring as a salesman and Josephine as the bookkeeper so they could carry on his business for him during his time in the Army.

Jerome, who at age twenty-five had good common sense and an even disposition, gave John a feeling of calm. He was unlike Hugh, who was maybe too smart and too sensitive for his own good.

As John stepped into the barn, his gaze went to the handsome chestnut beam that supported this massive structure, its hayloft dominating the upper level. Opposite the ladder, three horse stalls held their handsome mares, sixteen-hand horses, each of them in a spacious and well-ventilated area. John was glad for this well-built barn. He had owned this farm for five years already without a single regret. As he climbed the ladder and pushed the remaining hay back on the platform, making room for the new harvest, he supposed it was a prayer he sent off for these boys of his.

The country was learning that war and influenza were not a great combination. These recent days were uncertain ones, good health not a guarantee for anyone, the Spanish influenza ravaging the country. Daily reports of deaths were startling, a global disaster. With the war winding down, the help of American soldiers bringing it closer to an end, this heartrending health pandemic was killing more every day than the guns of war. Of all the U.S. soldiers in the war, half died from influenza, the sudden onset and symptoms often leading to death within a day. John heard a story uptown at the Hotel about four women who were reportedly playing bridge late into the night somewhere in Buffalo. The next morning, one called for the others only to be told they each had died. Other stories were told of people on the way to work being stricken and dying within hours.

Reported cases in neighboring Rochester were up to thirty-thousand. Deaths occurred weekly. Both Buffalo and Rochester shut down schools, theatres, and even churches in an attempt to slow the spread of this relentless virus. Cases reported in Lima so far were limited and contained. A few elderly victims were taken, though those in their twenties and thirties were more prevalent, an unusual event. John could only hope they'd all see their way through these days without becoming victims to this vicious and senseless death.

Even in the throes of war and influenza, there was joy to be found. Young John Victor, still a pup in many ways, had fallen in love. Married last October, just a month before his twenty-first birthday, it was a joy to watch this fourth son beguiled by a handsome young woman who seemed to keep his heart pounding. He noted Vic's gray eyes sparkle like never before.

Margaret Owens was her name. Their wedding had been in nearby Geneseo, where her people were from and where Vic worked for the telephone company. Another new-fangled gadget John thought was just a flash in the pan. Like the motorized car, would it prove to be more trouble than help?

John did remember his own heart beating like Vic's, once upon a time. The diminutive Maggie Buckley had beguiled him with her wit and bits of wisdom when he'd first met her at his sister Annie's home. Annie and Maggie had been pals when they worked as parlor maids on New York's prestigious streets: Park Avenue, Fifth Avenue, and Lexington. Thankfully, John thought, they'd found a way out of that city of fetid air and overcrowding. It was this land that he dreamt of that was overwhelming him now, the land that he loved. Land he'd live and die on. Unlike his father before him, he would stay. He wouldn't pick up and go on to the next farm as an itinerant worker. He would stay as a landowner, and the land would be a gift to his children and grandchildren and their children, too. The land they could till and plant and sow and reap.

John plucked his rake and hoe from the hooks above him and walked out to his twenty-seven acres, glad for the additional ten acres up the road he'd been able to acquire. A feeling of pride overtook the feeling of exhaustion as he moved into his rows of corn.

Chapter 18
The Fire

January 1919

"Tommy, wake up," Bernard whispered as he shook his older brother's shoulder. Tom rolled over and rubbed his eyes. Before he could speak, Bernard hushed him. Then he whispered with urgency.

"Listen to the fire bells. Something big is happening uptown. Can you hear them?"

Tommy turned his head to the small oblong window above their beds. Darkness pervaded. Bernard waited and then said, "Let's go see what's going on. It sounds pretty serious." Tommy nodded and threw his legs out of bed, pulled on his overalls, and found his wool sweater. The cold air inside was not much warmer than the outdoors. He could hear a light rain falling.

Bernard's eyes gleamed in the filtered light of the room as he put on his trousers and jacket. Both boys took their boots in hand and tiptoed down the staircase, through the dining room, and out the door to the stoop. They sat in silence as they put their boots on, listening to the continuous clanging of the fire bells. Whatever was happening was big. Neither of them remembered experiencing anything so potentially dangerous before.

Bernard stood up and waited for Tommy to finish tying his shoes. In a hoarse whisper, he said, "Shall we saddle up Jenny?" The ten-year-old mare had been born when the boys were five and three, an animal they knew well. Tommy nodded in agreement, still not saying a word. He trusted his father wouldn't hear the fire bells; his own snoring as loud. His mother and sisters were apt only to roll over, the sound not one they would do anything about. The boys walked stealthily out to the barn and, as quietly as they could, slid the massive door to the side.

Jenny followed Bernard with a shake of her head but without a sound. Tommy pulled the saddle and harness off the hook and carried them outside. Their eyes smiled as first Tom mounted the horse, and Bernard climbed up behind.

With a kick and a pat, they were off down the road to the south. In a mile, they would be at Route 5 & 20, and from there, surely, they'd find where the fire was.

Tom spoke softly to Jenny. Her cream coloring made her stand out among their other horses, but it was her temperament that made her special- smart, agreeable, and gentle. They trotted along under a black sky, the misty rain thankfully slowing as they traveled. When they reached the four corners, their suspicion of something big occurring was confirmed. Folks staying at the American Hotel stood out on the sidewalk, looking down the road to the east, craning their necks to see. They wore overcoats over bathrobes and shivered in the dampness. The American Hotel, a landmark since the 1830s, stood on the far corner, lights on and bedrooms lit up like a Christmas tree. As the boys turned to the left onto Main Road, they noted porch lanterns casting yellow streaks across the road. They continued down the road. In less than half a mile, they could smell the charred wood. Flames shot up above the tree line.

"Should we keep going, Tommy?" Bernard asked his older brother, his own confidence in this adventure wavering. He wasn't sure he wanted to actually visit the site of this destruction.

Tommy turned his head and talked over his shoulder. "We've come this far, and who knows, we might be of some help."

As they continued another thousand feet, smoke darkened the sky. They knew by now that it was the insulator company, filled with kilns and clay, that had caught fire. Neither boy had ever been inside, but they knew the children of men who worked there. They knew the ovens inside that baked the insulators reached mighty high temperatures.

Both boys had learned about the porcelain insulators high up on the telegraph and telephone poles along the highway when their father pointed them out. The insulators were designed to keep telegraph, telephone, and electric lines separated so the current could be transported without leakage.

Jenny carried them down the road, the dark cloud of smoke covering the building, small licks of flame still visible.

"Maybe it's time to turn back," Bernard said again, coughing as the smoke thickened. His resolve to even think about helping was seriously weakened. He worried about being discovered. "Pa and the others will be getting up soon for the milking. He'll see Jenny missing."

Tommy considered this information. Bernard had a point. "Let's just ride close enough to see what's happening."

Since Bernard had no control of the reins, he acquiesced as Tommy shook Jenny's lead and, with a gentle kick, told her to go into the yard of the company. Bernard was fearful the mare would get spooked. Before they'd gone but a few yards, a man covered in soot and standing not too far from the building called out, "Boys, you'd best get out of here. This is a dangerous place for anyone right now. Go on. Get home before your Pa knows you're gone."

Tommy, not knowing the man or if he knew their father and being ever so inventive, knew how to act innocent. "We came to see if we could offer any help. We hope no one was hurt in the fire. Our school chums have family that work here."

The man approached them. Bernard shivered.

"It's a generous thought, but it won't get you into this area. No one's been hurt, and we'd like to keep it that way. Now get on home before daylight leaves you staring your Pa in the eye. Go on now."

With that, the man slapped Jenny on the rump to get her started out. Tommy knew when he'd been defeated. He pulled on the reins and turned Jenny around. Bernard heaved a sigh of relief as they headed home.

They turned down the road, and Tom steered Jenny onto College Street, which ran at an angle beside 5 and 20. "At least we won't go through the town again," Tommy said to Bernard. "No sense having the other farmers see us riding by."

"You think Pa will be mad at us for going out?" Bernard's innocence surprised Tom.

"You're still a little wet behind the ears if you think he'd not fuss about this adventure. It's getting near to dawn. We're just lucky it's not a school day."

"But you can tell him we came to help, and the man wouldn't let us. He'll believe you. He always does."

The mist that had stopped earlier suddenly started again. The darkness spread out before them like fog. The smoky skyline had cleared a bit, and, in its place, came sweet, gentle raindrops, helping to quell the flames.

"What do you think started that fire, Tommy?" Bernard asked. "I hope it wasn't mischief like some of those boys talked about after school."

Tommy knew what Bernard meant. There were boys who came from up beyond the town to the south. They wore tattered clothes and sometimes smelled. They went to the public school. He'd not had much to do with them, that was for sure.

"I wouldn't know what caused that fire, Bernard, but I would know we shouldn't say anything about it 'til they tell us of it in the morning. That way, we'll be innocent of any talk that goes on. Do you hear me?"

"I do, Tommy," Bernard said.

The next morning came sooner than expected, the rooster announcing the dawn. Bernard and Tom poured out of their single beds to begin their chores, cleaning out the horse stalls and forking hay in. The hired hands had already seen to the milking. Jenny gave no indication of her recent jaunt to town, her rubdown on their return an hour earlier helping to return her to a calm state.

At breakfast, the fire was the topic of conversation.

"I must have been sleeping soundly," Maggie said as she brought the sausage and egg platter to the table. "I never heard the fire bells or any alarm. Your father said he didn't either."

John turned from washing his hands at the little water pump on the sideboard. "Well, it's a mile or so away. It wouldn't have been too loud, I'd say. Mr. Wemett came over this morning. He was there. The wind made it difficult to contain the blaze. He said no one was injured, but the damage was great. It'll probably not reopen for some time, if at all."

"What might have started the fire?" Gene asked as she took eggs onto her plate, her curiosity aroused. John turned to her, glad for her interest.

"I suppose it could have been carelessness by one of the workers. Those kilns get heated up pretty high by the coal. One stray cinder could be the beginning of the end."

"It's funny," Veronica said as she took the platter of eggs and sausage from Gene. "I smelled smoke upstairs when I woke up. It couldn't have come all the way to our house, but it sure was a strong smell."

"With the winds as strong as they were, they certainly fueled those flames. Maybe the smoke traveled," John offered. "They sometimes only have a skeleton crew on overnight. Not enough to check every potential fire threat, I don't suppose."

Tommy and Bernard said not a word. The mention of Mr. Wemett and the smoke gave them pause. As far as they knew, their foray into the night was still their secret. A glance between them said they sure hoped so.

Chapter 19
Vic

January 1919

"You don't mean to tell me they rode out in the night to see that fire, do you?" Vic asked as he stood in the dining room doorway. The dinner dishes were done, and the rest of the family scattered, doing lessons or chores. John was seated at the small kitchen table, a yellow-plaid cloth covering the white porcelain enamel top. He smiled and nodded as he listened to Vic, the *Lima Recorder* spread out in front of him.

Vic was dressed in his chauffeur's uniform, cap in hand, his double-breasted overcoat with buttons parading down either side of his chest, giving him an air of authority. His metal chauffeur badge on his cap with the embossed number and status indicated he'd been certified.

John had just told Vic of Tom and Bernard's escapade during the night. John's own surprise and dismay at sleeping through all the commotion was doubled when he learned the next day at the Hotel that his boys had been there. John's friend, Ted Doran, made mention of it as if John already knew about it. "Your young ones were cautious enough not to get too close," Ted had said to him. "You've trained them well to be wary of fire." Not well enough, John thought, but he said nothing.

John was glad to hear Vic's dismay. It matched his own. Vic continued, "I'd never have done anything that foolhardy when I was their age." To hear this young man, recently discharged from the service and returning home safely to his wife, waxing forth gave John a chuckle with a tinge of pride.

Vic, named John Victor in honor of his father, the youngest of the "four older boys" and the first to marry, just a month shy of his twenty-first birthday. Margaret Owen's agreement to marry proved to be a wise move since "limited service," the status given to married men, meant "not suitable for combat."

The hope that he would be safe encouraged everyone, and Hugh's September 8th letter brought some comfort.

"If Vic is in limited service, he will not have to go across. In any case, I believe the people at home worry more than the soldiers do - which I suppose is quite natural..."

Vic's October 11th wedding had been a simple one. St. Mary's on Avon Road, with its majestic steeple and cross at the apex, lent an air of solemnity to their day. No extra attendants, no procession. Margaret Owen walked down the aisle with her father, organ music, and a vocalist accompanying them, close friends, and family members in attendance. Margaret's sister, Isobel, was her maid of honor. Vic asked Loring to stand up for him, though he wished it could have been Hugh. Vic had fallen hard for this attractive woman. Her glowing complexion, hazel eyes, and delicate lips all drew him in.

Her generous laugh and careful listening made him feel safe, reminding him of an angel. He'd met her on a Sunday morning after Mass at St. Mary's Church. She was from a family almost as big as his, with 9 brothers and sisters. Margaret had been a housekeeper at a home on Route 39, just down from where Vic rented a room. Her fair hair and pleasant demeanor served as a good counterpoint to his brown hair and occasional gruffness.

As Vic's service began, talk of the war's end was already afoot. The Lima Recorder wrote of the Spring Offensive, a successful series of tactics that seriously weakened the German ability to retaliate. It gave them all hope.

On September 3, 1918, Vic reported to Fort Adams in Rhode Island, at the elbow of Newport Harbor. It served as headquarters for the coastal defenses as well as a training facility and depot for units departing for service in France. The United States Army Coast Artillery Corps handled all the US heavy artillery, their expertise singular in using big guns. Four regiments and two brigades from Fort Adams served in France, with troops from Maine, Rhode Island, New York, and other Coast Defense Commands serving as cadre.

Proud to be a part of it all, Vic's assignment servicing engines and motors suited his ability. John had talked himself blue, trying to bring Hugh around to see the importance of farming. It turned out that Vic was as eager as Hugh had been to work with engines. John finally knew enough to say nothing. Vic also discovered during his training that his brothers weren't the only ones who teased. Soon, he was able to stand up for himself and to the challenges he encountered, even forming some good friendships.

He loved looking over Narragansett Bay, his mind wandering to thoughts of Margaret. She was faithful in her letter writing, and while he wouldn't call himself a great correspondent, he sent enough replies to keep her writing back. Soon enough, the time arrived when they would be together again.

The great war had ended. On the 11th day at the 11th hour of the 11th month, across the ocean he so loved, the guns went silent. It was a day and time he would never forget. He remembered Saturday, December 14th, a crisp, sunny morning when his group was finally discharged. He stood at the ocean's edge and saluted a silent goodbye.

As he stood talking with his father about his brothers' escapade, John realized how much he'd grown up. "I hope they'll learn to take precautions in the future. A dose of the service would be good for them." John smiled again, sharing Vic's hope and feeling satisfied that this fourth son had grown into a fine young man.

Chapter 20
Teacher

August 1919

"Well, you've your name in the *Recorder* today, Veronica," Maggie said from her seat at the kitchen table. Veronica glanced over at her mother, her hair piled high in its familiar bun, her house dress showing signs of wear around the hemline. The most recent *Lima Recorder* newspaper was opened in front of her on the table.

"Next thing we know, you'll be running for president. It's you and the Harrington girl who will straighten out these young ones coming forward." Though her mother looked weary, the laughter in her voice was welcome. Veronica never knew her mother to boast about anything or anyone.

Veronica had seen the article earlier and was silently bursting with excitement. She left it for her mother to read with her tea as she often did after dinner while John went out into the fields for a smoke. She continued drying dishes, pleased that her mother spotted the notice and was commenting on her accomplishment. She was thrilled to be recognized in the newspaper but felt a bit intimidated as well.

After all, a teaching job, so soon! It was scary. The fact that she was already slated, along with her classmate Eileen Harrington, to teach in one of the district schools was a thrill she couldn't quite get used to. She trembled to think of it.

Maggie folded the newspaper and picked it up. Veronica knew it would be saved in the special drawer where her mother kept family letters and mementos, eventually maybe even put in the little green valise where she kept such things. Now, her mother ambled off to see the younger two children before bedtime.

As Veronica put the last dishes up in the cupboard and wiped out the sink, she drew in a deep breath and felt satisfaction in the simplicity of this chore. Dishwashing has always been easy. Pumping water and putting it to boil in the kettle had its own danger if she wasn't careful with splashing. She enjoyed how grease slipped off the plates and glasses and into the suds. She folded the dishcloth over the edge of the sink and closed the damper on the white porcelain stove to smother the flame within, grateful for the faithful service it provided.

Thankfully, tonight was not bath night, so her chores would end as soon as she folded the laundry left from this afternoon when she had walked out back into the fields instead of finishing up. She knew she'd have time tonight, but not how many days the rain would hold off for her walk. She took advantage of the sunshine she saw glinting on the remaining corn stalks and the light breeze that accompanied these autumn days. She savored her time alone with no little ones tagging along.

Veronica loved them all right, but she needed to start her own life soon. She was growing weary in her role as next oldest daughter, missing Josephine terribly. She didn't begrudge Josephine her studies and was actually glad for her. Nursing had been Josephine's passion since she was young. Veronica remembered her fixing nearly every scraped knee and bee bite since she was a little girl. Even though she was only two years older, Veronica depended on her sensible guidance in managing the smaller children and doing things the way her mother wanted them done.

"Ma likes the ironing done on wash day, so you'll have to figure that in when you come home after classes on Monday," Josephine had told her as she readied to leave for her schooling in New York City. "If you can't get to it, put it aside. There's sometimes too much to do at once, and Ma knows that."

Maggie was nearing fifty, and her daughters noted her graying hair and expanding girth as she slowed down. Her blue eyes looked a bit paler. They'd both been schooled to help, and they did.

As far as the kids went, Tom and Bernard weren't so much to manage, except when they squabbled over who was right in some tug-of-war game or race that they'd concocted. Rather than having to take care of Gene, it turned out this little sister was actually helpful with the laundry and sometimes the dishes, besides being smart as a whip at school. She was good at assisting the others with homework and was always happy to read a story to Betty and Donnell. She kept her own things picked up and regularly cleared the table after dinner.

Veronica knew things were shifting within her. She found herself impatient with the endless laundry and ironing and tired of the whining of the two littlest ones. She knew they were young, but she wished they'd leave their mother alone.

While doing dishes was one thing, picking up after all of them, especially the older boys who were old enough to do it on their own, annoyed her. Betty wasn't so bad now, at age seven, becoming a bit more responsible. It was actually cute to watch her getting herself and her dolly ready for bed. After she had her own nightie on, she'd put one on dolly Rosie and tuck her in.

Donnell, at age four, was definitely his mother's pet and could do no wrong. In fact, Veronica thought, he did plenty wrong with his messy ways, leaving his soldiers and building blocks underfoot. She was constantly after him to pick up his clothes and wash them thoroughly. Any intervention she performed, like taking the washcloth and scrubbing his face and neck, met with yelps and brought Maggie to his rescue.

"He's still young. Leave him be," Maggie would say as she shooed Donnell off to play with a pat on the head.

Veronica longed for a visit to New York City to see Josephine at her job at Lenox Hill Hospital and to visit Aunt Annie's like her older brothers had. She could talk with her cousin Margaret, who was also a teacher. Josephine had become pals with Hughberta, called "Bertie," who was also already working as a nurse at Lenox Hill, the new name for the German Hospital since the war.

Learning about her New York cousins from their letters and postcards, Veronica had begun to save their correspondence to her, mostly postcards from Josephine. In one from last April, she wrote:

I wish I could join you for Easter.
It would seem more like Easter… Josephine.

She'd received a similar message from her young cousin, Anna Kerrigan. She was glad to learn Vic and Frankie, the older Galena girls, had returned safely from their nursing duties in the war. She couldn't wait for the day she'd finally meet them. Veronica trusted that Gene was most likely doing homework in between giggling with Tom and Bernard. The three of them were sometimes as good as gold and other times as mischievous as thieves, telling stories and making up games into the night.

Someday, she hoped she would be keeping house somewhere else, to whatever place her teaching career took her. Yet the thought of leaving home was both exhilarating and scary. At least the first part of her dream of becoming a teacher was about to come true, and she had so much more to look forward to.

She certainly knew about children. She'd been taking care of little ones since she was a youngster herself. As one of the older girls, she'd been called into service plenty of times to help the younger ones take their baths, dress, and play nicely with each other.

"Tommy, this time let Bernard be the fireman, and you be the farmer," she'd counsel as she saw Bernard's eyes darken when he was being overshadowed.

She also remembered Baby Rose's death and seeing her mother cry. That was the worst part. She would do anything to dry her mother's tears and soothe her heart.

Her mother had assured Veronica that she was a born teacher, the boys generally listening to her voice of authority.

She'd studied her lessons well, graduating with honors from St. Rose's School and going on to be in the first Lima High School class. She developed a love of dramatics and starred in several locally written school plays. A way to escape the drudgery of the ordinary, she thought.

This honor of being selected from among other applicants to teach in a district rural school, Number 3, was one she'd always savored. She'd continue her studies at Geneseo Normal School over the next few summers and looked forward to a job somewhere in a neighboring town. For now, she'd stay on and help as she could.

As she folded the last of the shirts and trousers, putting things that needed ironing into a separate basket, she began to imagine what she'd wear on her first day as a teacher. Josephine would know how to advise her, even though Josephine only got to wear a white uniform. Maybe there'd be an extra dress or two left behind in her closet. With that, she put the baskets away and smiled as she went in search of possibilities.

Chapter 21
Hugh's Visit

Fall 1919

"Ma, you mean Hugh's driving here all the way from Ohio? Will he drive his new car?" Gene asked, her hazel eyes focused on her mother, her brown hair adorned with a white bow. Answering her own question, Gene continued. "It's been a long time since Hugh's been home. He'll be certain to drive his new car so he can show it off. It will be so good to see him. He's so special."

Maggie smiled to hear this twelve-year-old. "Lucky says he'll be here in a week's time. He says Hugh and Vic are going to be looking into auto sales in this part of the country. Maybe we'll see even more of them."

The kitchen table was covered with flour, Maggie's apron splotched all over. Gene was so enamored with her big brother she was beside herself. She would tell Hugh about her nickname and her mother's insistence that there be no "Jenny" since that was their horse's name. She'd had the idea of spelling her nickname with a 'G,' Gene.

Maggie wiped her hands on her purple gingham apron and turned her attention to the rising bread dough on the sideboard. It was good to have this Saturday to bake and spend time with this daughter, who was often overlooked when her older sisters were around.

"Do you remember the postcards he sent me when I was little, Ma?" Gene asked as she sat watching her mother knead the bread.

Maggie did remember the postcards. She'd saved as many as she could. Hugh was prolific in his correspondence, complete with clever witticisms in so many of his cards and letters.

"Ma, do you still have the little case of his cards? Can I get it and go through them?"

"Yes, I still have the box, but I would prefer to go through it with you if that suits you. There are plenty of letters all mixed in there. Maybe you and I can sort it out together."

"Shall we start this afternoon?" Gene asked. Before Maggie could answer, Gene said, "I'll get the box, okay?"

Gene was off like a shot, poking around on the shelves in the front parlor amidst the games and the piano music. She spied the little green suitcase, tucked toward the back of the bottom shelf, next to boxes of pictures. Those would be fun to go through on another day. Today, it was this little case she wanted. It was just the right size for what it contained. Not business papers but memory things.

Gene remembered the joy Hugh's letters brought her mother and how thrilled they all were when they assembled around the table to hear them. The postcards were just as thrilling. Gene loved the chance to organize the letters and the cards with her Ma and read again what Hugh had written her so long ago. She was glad that Betty and Don were out in the yard so she could dare to get into a project with her mother without their interference.

Gene carried the discovered case to the dining room table. Without waiting for her mother, she looked at the little brass button to the right of the keyhole. The key had been misplaced long ago. No need to lock these treasures away, her mother had said. They were treasures for all of them.

Gene pushed the button, and the latch popped up. Her mother called to her, "You'll wait for me, won't you?"

Maggie slid the knife across the top of the brown bread in the form of a cross, something she'd seen her own mother do before it was placed in the oven. She'd said it was to ward off the devil. Maggie learned a more practical reason from the women in the Altar and Rosary Society who talked of the importance of the slashed cross letting the steam escape. Either way, Maggie wouldn't dream of baking the bread without cutting a cross on the top. She slipped the bread into the oven and went out to join Gene.

With Josephine off to New York City to study nursing and Veronica now teaching at a rural school outside of the village, District School Number 3, Gene had become Maggie's biggest helper. Betty had become a good companion for Don, who was already four years old. My, how the time flies, Maggie thought.

Sometimes, she felt guilty about the amount of time she found to be with little Don. It was more than she'd ever spent with any of her other children. Yet she was desperate for it to help soothe the broken place in her heart where Baby Rose's sweet face dwelled. Funny, she thought, her oldest boy, Hugh, and her youngest one, Don, both stole a place in her heart that didn't have words.

Gene was kneeling on the dining room chair, the green box opened, and the letters and cards of all shapes and sizes.

"You did wait for me," Maggie said. "Good for you. Now, which cards are you after?"

"You remember, Ma, the ones Hugh sent when I was just little," Gene said as she gingerly lifted letters and cards out, one stack at a time.

Maggie enjoyed these letters and postcards as much as anyone. Most of them were from Hugh, with a few Easter or Christmas wishes from the New York cousins. Hugh's postcards had come from all over the country: Long Island City; Cleveland, Ohio; Birmingham, Alabama; Washington, D.C.; Bay City, Michigan; Salem, Oregon; and even Windsor, Ontario. As Maggie picked through them, she watched Gene organize them into separate stacks.

"This pile is for ones addressed to you, Ma. And these two piles are addressed to Josephine and Veronica," Gene said as she held up a well-worn letter. "And look at this one. It's from this year, telling Sandy about a car. It's addressed to Mr. J. Donegan. How come Jerome is called Sandy, Ma?"

"Oh, your father and your brothers started calling him that because of his hair color. On his draft registration card, it said, Color of Hair - Sandy. The name just stuck after that," Maggie said as she pulled a pile of cards toward her.

"Now you're looking for postcards, right? Look at these," she said as she handed a few to Gene.

"Oh, Ma, this is the one I remember you always telling me about. You saved it for me." Gene read it aloud.

Lansing, Michigan August 1911.
Miss Genevieve Donegan.

Dear Sister,
You are not a very good correspondent. You should write oftener. Hugh.

"He's so funny, Ma. I was only three years old. How could I write to him? She put the card on the table and continued. "Oh look, here's one from the next day. From Salem, Oregon. He says he expects me to answer this card myself. He signs it, *'Your loving brother Hugh.'* I love that he says that. When I write letters, I will do that too."

Gene's excitement spilled over onto Maggie. She remembered when the postcards arrived addressed to Genevieve. It was seven years ago. How clever Hugh was in remembering his little sister, who was seventeen years younger.

As they looked further and sorted some more, they found one written to Jerome from Salem, Oregon, on August 5th. *"Received your postal will write a letter soon."*

"He had many places to visit, and he kept in touch with as many of you as he could," Maggie said. "Here's one more for you, Genevieve, from October 18, 1913, from Bay City, Michigan. It's signed *"From Hugh."*

"I was lucky to get any at all, don't you think, Ma?" Gene asked. "That one was kind of close to my birthday."

Maggie smiled as she realized how diligent Hugh had been in staying in touch. She found one from Windsor, Ontario dated February 16, 1911 that read. *Rec'd your letter today wrote you yesterday. Hope you get it.*

Maggie was glad for this time of remembering. It helped her look forward more than ever to Hugh's visit. She stood up and patted Genevieve on the shoulder.

"When you've finished sorting, tuck them away again, like the good girl you are."

"Ma, I have them organized by date and person, if that's okay with you?"

"It's just fine," Maggie said as she went back to the kitchen and the bread. She couldn't help but smile to watch this little daughter who reminded her so much of herself. Her own older sisters, Mary and Julia, had never taken an interest as Maggie did in organizing. She could put a room in order while the two older ones just talked about it. And here she was now, watching her own little Genevieve organizing to her heart's content.

Maggie felt her heart fill with gladness, if only for this brief while, letting her other sorrows fade. Soon enough, her oldest boy would be home.

Chapter 22
June

October 1920

"He's here, Ma," Gene called from the dining room door. "And wait 'til you see his automobile."

Maggie came from the bedroom and stood beside Gene. "Hush, now, and don't be yelling when he brings his new wife to the door."

"She won't hear me, Ma. She's still in the car." "Just the same, mind your manners."

As the afternoon sun arched over the big barn, they both watched as Hugh got out of the handsome black Model T Ford. He wore a stylish, long blue-gray overcoat that flapped open to reveal a smart-looking white shirt with one of those new collars and a sky-blue bowtie that matched his eyes. His three-piece suit lent him a sophisticated look as he came around to the passenger side to open the door for his wife. He took her hand as she stepped onto the running board. She stepped down, and he leaned over to whisper in her ear. She blushed and looked at her.

Maggie and Gene watched as the newlyweds walked toward them. She wished John had come in from the fields to see them on arrival and hoped when he did come, he would be kind and not bring up farming again. Maggie noted that Hugh was maybe seven inches taller than June, who was probably five feet five, taller than any of her girls. Well, she's someone who can stand up to him, Maggie thought.

June wore a dark gray mid-calf cape with a large collar over an ankle-length beige pleated skirt and a white blouse with a

matching beige jacket. Gene immediately liked her brown felt hat with the beige bow along the side. Even her purse and gloves were beige.

"She's stylish, isn't she, Ma?" Gene asked.

Before Maggie could reply, Hugh and June joined them at the doorway.

"Mother," Hugh said, "may I present Mrs. Hugh Donegan, the former June Jesse Austen?"

He stepped aside, and June extended her gloved hand. Maggie took June's hand in hers and gently squeezed it. "It's delighted we are you've come to pay us a visit. We're so happy to welcome you to our little village of Lima and our farmhouse, such as it is. I imagine Hugh has told you much about us here."

June looked toward Gene before replying to Maggie and said, "You must be Gene. Hugh told me all about you."

Gene, who had worn her favorite dress with the gray-ribboned waistband, smiled, and Hugh tousled her hair. "You're too big for me to put on my shoulders anymore," he said. "I'm getting too old anyway." Hugh would be thirty next month; Gene had just turned thirteen a week ago.

"Come in and tell us all about your trip," Maggie said as she ushered them into the dining room, where tea had been set with biscuits and cheese. Gene was soon joined by Betty and Don. As if on cue, Don extended his hand and offered to take June's cape. He looked up at Betty to make sure. They all laughed. Hugh slipped it off her shoulders and folded it into Don's arms, who carefully walked toward the parlor with it.

"We've fixed the front bedroom upstairs for the two of you. It'll be the most private for you," Maggie said as she put the teapot in the cozy.

June smiled.

"The girls will see to anything you might need. And you know little Don is at your service. Please make yourself comfortable."

Once tea had finished and Hugh and June had settled in upstairs, Hugh appeared and asked, "Who wants to go for a ride in our new automobile?"

"I do, and so do we all," said Gene, nodding her head as she gestured to Betty and Donnell. "Can we all fit?"

"Certainly. You'll fit like a glove. It's one of Henry Ford's proudest achievements, a family car. Where's Ma? I hope she'll come."

Maggie stepped out of the bedroom. "I wouldn't miss the chance. Do I need to dress the part?"

Hugh smiled and said, "You're fine, just as you are. June says she'll rest while we're gone. The journey was fatiguing."

Hugh ushered them out to his new car. The first thing he commented on was the advertising that had been engraved on the spare tire cover. White letters on a black material around the circumference and in the center stated his business name and information.

H.M. DONEGAN MOTOR CO.
Motor Trucks, Motor Buses and Tractors
277-78 N.20th St. Col.O.

Maggie touched the letters, noting the Columbus, Ohio location, and then looked up to Hugh, "You've achieved a lot for a young man. And now you have a wife. Congratulations!"

Hugh smiled down at her and blushed. He'd worried about her acceptance of June. She wasn't effusive about much, so he took this compliment with relief.

"So, what about this ride?" Gene said. "Where do we sit?" Betty, Donnell and Gene climbed in the back seat and then

Hugh helped Maggie into the front. "For someone almost fifty years old, you're pretty spry," Hugh said. As he pulled out the throttle and started the engine, Hugh asked about Tom and Bernard. He thought they'd have been home by now.

"They had to stay after," Betty explained. "They are in some club for speeches and this is their day to be there."

"The club for speeches," Maggie explained, "is the elocution class taught by Ms. Chapin."

"She's still at it, is she? I remember her from when I took lessons from her. She was a good teacher."

Maggie was often pleased with her children's appreciation of education. The fact that they were good students gave her confidence. A stepping stone for a fine career, whatever they chose.

Hugh moved the clutch into position and, with the smoothness of a professional, moved the car forward. The oohs and aahs from the back seat thrilled him. As he maneuvered the car from the yard onto the main road, Don asked, "Can you make it go faster?"

"But not too fast," Maggie said, holding tight to the inside door handle. She'd been in Veronica's car and in one of Vic's cars, but this one was a bit more lavish. Shiny buttons and gears dazzled the dashboard. And Mr. Ford had been right. The interior was roomy enough for a family, albeit a small one. Betty peeked out the back window, watching the road behind them disappear.

Hugh drove uptown and surprised them all when he tooted the horn at a familiar acquaintance, Don Doran, E.P. and Ann's son.

"Do it again, Hugh, do it again," Don cried.

"We'll get arrested if we make too much noise, Don. When we get home, I'll let you toot it. How's that?" He was certain Don wouldn't let him forget. As they turned into the driveway, they discovered Veronica's Model-T pulled up by the small yellow barn.

"Very impressive," Hugh said. "She made a good choice. I'm glad she took the advice Vic and I gave her. There's lots to know when you're spending good money to buy a car."

"She's saving a lot while she lives at home," Gene offered. "And once she graduates from Geneseo Normal school, she'll need money for an apartment if she gets a new job farther away."

When they stepped inside, they found Veronica and June in the kitchen peeling potatoes. June turned to greet them all and went over to Hugh, who kissed her on the cheek. She asked how the ride was and Don piped up with his story of the horn. "Hey," he said as he finished telling about the loud sound it made, "I'm supposed to toot it here at home so we don't get arrested."

"Right, you are, young man. Come out with me and anyone else who wants to plug their ears." Betty and Gene followed along. Maggie took her apron from the hook near the water heater by the back room and pulled out eggs and the fixings for her popular caramel pudding. It was a special treat for dinner tomorrow. Sandy and Vic planned to join them. Maybe even Vic's wife Margaret and their one-year-old daughter Ruth if it worked out. She was grateful for Veronica, who was overseeing the whole operation. She knew Josephine would also be a great help when she and Loring arrived. Their train, the Empire State Express, was making the trip in less than seven hours. A tip of the hat to modern transportation, Maggie thought.

"How did you two meet?" Veronica asked as she wiped her hands on the towel and placed the last potato into the pot. She and June were finishing up their potato peeling, the pot three-quarters full of Yukon Golds, ready to be sliced tomorrow for the au gratin potatoes.

"It's really quite a story," June replied as she placed the last batch of peels into the bucket for use in the farmyard. "I was the secretary in a local Columbus Automobile company. Hugh came in to see what he could learn about their business. He explained he was in the business himself and wanted to learn more about his competitors. He was amazingly polite and witty." She lifted the pot of peels to the stool by the back door, instinctively knowing how to chip in and help. "He asked if there was anyone he might talk with about their business. I was the only one there and invited him to sit and ask the questions he had. I couldn't keep my eyes off his, blue as the clearest sky ever."

She looked off in memory momentarily. "Anyway," she continued, "he seemed satisfied with the information I was able to share numbers of cars sold, current inventory and number of employees. He was cordial in his thanks and left. I couldn't keep him out of my mind. I even wrote his name on my notepad."

Her cheeks colored a little and she wondered if she was telling this new sister-in-law too much. She decided to go on a bit. "He returned the next afternoon. I was surprised to see him and delighted. I wondered if I hadn't answered his questions adequately. Instead, he asked if I would join him for dinner after work. As soon as my heart stopped pounding, I said I'd be delighted."

Veronica hefted the pot of potatoes over to the sideboard and said, "Well, that's quite a fine 'how do you do.'"

And you've been married now for a little over a month.

Mother is thrilled you're both here for a visit. We all are."

Maggie turned around from her bowl of caramel decadence and added, "Though we wished we could have been at the wedding, we're glad now you're here for our wedding feast tomorrow."

June smiled deeply and said, "So am I, so am I."

Chapter 23
Wedding Celebration

October 20, 1920

Josephine sat back from the table full of her family. She was seated in the prized Windsor chair by the telephone stand, a new arrangement for the telephone. She watched as they sipped tea and listened to Hugh regale them with his latest ventures. She felt affection for each of them.

Here was her older brother, handsome as ever, his hair becoming a darker red, his eyes a more brilliant blue than she remembered. But, of course, they would be. He was in love. And this celebration was for him and his bride, June Jesse Austen.

She was thrilled to be a part of this occasion, savoring every moment.

She remembered how bereft she felt at not being able to attend her brother Vic's October wedding, her nursing hours and wartime schedules making it impossible. She was glad that she'd met his wife, Margaret Owen, when she was home over that Thanksgiving. If it was true that men married their mothers, then Vic's choosing someone with his mother's name was a start. Margaret's light reddish-brown hair and hazel eyes fit in fine. The challenge for her was to keep up with the banter that swirled around them all.

Josephine was also delighted that Margaret brought her precious little Ruth, just a year old, this week. She was a solid child, looking for all she was worth, like her mother with her golden-brown hair and hazel eyes. As the women fussed over her and the men smiled, it was a great entrance for the first grandchild of the family.

It was good, too, to see Gene and Veronica in true form as they cleared the good china dinner plates with the delicate blue trim and set out the matching dessert plates. Her gaze fell on Gene. How good to see her more in the center of things, taking up the space she left by going off to nursing school. She could see Gene's resemblance to her that others had noted, the dark auburn hair and hazel/green eyes so much like her own. It pleased her to think that her little sister, eight years younger, was growing so responsible.

Josephine had seen to the main meal of ham and au gratin potatoes, her specialty. They'd all been glad to be done with Meatless Tuesdays and 'Wheatless' Wednesdays, part of food conservation for the war effort. She remembered hearing it called Hooverizaton after Herbert Hoover, who served as head of the United States Food Administration during Wilson's presidency.

Josephine saw her mother's eyes sparkle as the girls presented the meal. Maggie held court from her chair at the end of the table nearest the kitchen where she always sat. As the family's favorite dessert of caramel custard was served, her delight was evident in her smile. She only made it for special occasions, and this, indeed, was one. She was doubly pleased because she thought this batch had come out better than ever.

Next, Josephine turned her focus to June, the new bride. She and Hugh had been married just a little over six weeks ago, on August 31st. The talk of Hugh's marriage and his 'honeymoon' visit to the farm had filled their letters and postcards. Now they were finally here.

June was medium height with dark, chestnut brown hair and coffee-colored eyes to match. The key feature that Josephine noted was her smile. It was radiant and frequent. Another thing she noticed, as the tea and custard were served, was how June looked at Hugh. It was pure adoration. She wouldn't be surprised if they were holding hands under the table, though she couldn't see from where she sat. It was gratifying to hear June tell of Hugh's enterprises with such pride in his accomplishment of owning his own motor company.

"To see him out there, shaking hands with his customers and congratulating them on their choice, you'd think he was running for office." June looked at him as she spoke, thrilled with his smiling reaction.

"Well, I imagine he received a good enough background after teaching all those classes in the army," John said from his seat opposite Maggie. "I couldn't interest him in farming, but it seems he found his way just the same."

Josephine was relieved to hear her father finally talk reasonably about Hugh.

"It was just last year," John continued, "that Jerome held an auction once he decided to give up farming. You sold darn near everything, didn't you?" he asked, turning toward Jerome, sitting with Loring at the far end of the table.

Jerome sat forward and said, "The article in the Lima Recorder was a great help. They listed the whole shebang: seven horses, the 4 cows, the cultivators, wagons, plows, harnesses, and potato crates. I even sold my Ford car, with that Ames-built body, and got a good price." He beamed. "I was just a kid when I got that car."

"If I'd been staying around here, you could have given all that equipment to me," Loring chimed in, his blue eyes looking like his mother's. "Too bad my timing with my New York City business didn't work out."

"At any rate," John added, "Jerome made a good bundle in spite of the money he had to pay to the auctioneer. Folks around town say that fellow G.H. Pierson is a known crook. But our own "Sandy" made out alright for himself, didn't you?" John asked, then added, "Crook or no crook."

"I'm doing all right in my new business," Jerome said. "There's lots of money to be made in trapping and trading. How's the business for it out in Ohio, Hugh?" he asked.

Josephine's attention drifted. These men could talk for hours about cars, hunting, trapping and trading furs. It was of little or no interest to her. She was off to her own thoughts, thrilled with her choice of nursing and that her degree was only two years away.

She felt fortunate to be mentored by her cousins, both registered nurses, who had served in the war in France. She was eager to hear more of their war stories. Soon enough, she thought, soon enough.

Now Josephine's attention was drawn to her father, who stood with his teacup raised. He looked older to her somehow, his dark hair streaked with silver, his eyes tired. It was hard work he did, and she was in awe of him. He never complained except that he wished his boys were more interested in farming than in automobiles and fur buying. "No car ever fed a family," he'd often say. But tonight, he seemed serene. He waited for their attention and asked that they all raise a cup to welcome their newest relative, June.

Then, nodding to Margaret, he added, "It isn't every family that's blessed with two lovely daughters-in-law. Let's cheer them both."

June and Margaret, who were sitting side by side, blushed. Hugh, never one to miss an opportunity, stood near his father and said, "Let's raise a cup to the lovely Lord and Lady of this home for their hospitality and welcome. Here, Here."

"And let's cheer the horn on the car," Don said to laughter from them all.

Chapter 24
A Letter from June

Summer 1924

Maggie held her teacup in both hands, letting the warmth soothe her. Her green case with the letters was perched on the table, this letter from June open.

She re-read it, hoping to find some clue to what was happening.

Columbus, Ohio December 30, 1922

Dear Mother,

The chickens arrived in fine shape, as Lucky has told you, and we surely appreciated your remembering us. So glad to hear that you all had a nice Xmas, though rather a lonesome one. We had a fine Xmas too. Were invited out to turkey dinner. Pat (Hugh) has not been feeling so well the past few days. Nothing seriously wrong only he has those severe coughing spells more frequently. I think this changeable, damp weather is hard on him. I do hope he will soon be better, but as you say, I guess it will have to take its course. Loring is just fine, and I am surely glad to have him with us. He seems to like Columbus real well. Suppose Veronica is as busy as a bee with her school work. Tell her I will write her soon, but it really keeps me busy with all my correspondence as I'm so far away from my people and have to write to them all every week. Wish she could see my Xmas tree. I think it even prettier than the one I had last year.

With love from us all to you all. I am as ever
Yours
June

She smiled when she saw the name Pat with Hugh in parentheses. While in the service, his Irish heritage landed him the nickname "Paddy" and "Pat' stuck. June knew he would always be High to Maggie. Maggie was grateful the chickens had arrived successfully and pleased that the mail-order chick business started almost five years ago and guaranteed delivery within seventy-two hours. It was a good way to send something from the farm to remind her son of home.

June was right. That year, Christmas had been somewhat lonely. While all her brood had been at home at the October wedding celebration for Hugh and June, before she knew it, the older ones were all gone, back to their lives in other places. Hugh and June to Columbus, Loring there with them; Jerome setting up his meat dealership in readiness for his May 2nd marriage; Vic in Avon, his job as a chauffeur still paying the bills for his bride and baby girl, Ruth. Happily, Josephine had received her Nursing certificate, but her full-time work at Lenox Hill left her with little time to visit. Veronica was indeed as "busy as a bee," her teaching as satisfying as she had dreamt, with new interests and friends. While Maggie was pleased for her, she wished Veronica could spend more time at home, her schedule so full of meetings after the school day and social activities. Veronica even kept in touch with Miss Chapin and her dramatic work.

My six oldest ones, Maggie thought, *settled and on their own.*

And now, this letter that she didn't know what to make of.

Tom walked in as Maggie was putting the letter back in the case. His recent high school graduation had him looking for work in Buffalo, where job offers for good tradesmen were plentiful. He'd been helping his father on the farm, but he wouldn't be here too long if he could avoid it.

Tom slid into the chair opposite as Maggie folded the most recent letter from the Henry Ford Hospital. It wasn't anyone else's business to see this letter, not yet, at any rate. John knew of it and her letter of inquiry. She slipped the typed letter into the case, just next to June's letter.

"More news about Hugh?" Tom asked, reaching for the letter from the hospital. Maggie snapped the case shut.

"Just what June's already written. His cough has been mild but persistent. They don't know how long they'll keep him for observation. I just re-read June's letter about the dampness that is so hard on him. That must be it," she said as she took the case from the table and placed it on the floor at her feet.

The call from June, just after the New Year, had prompted Maggie to write to the hospital. June had been almost incoherent as she spoke about behaviors Hugh displayed that Maggie couldn't believe. It was not like her boy to speak sharply or nastily to anyone, let alone the wife whom he adored. June went on with unbelievable stories of sarcastic remarks, vicious looks, and verbal barrages and tirades. Thankfully, there had been no physical assaults. The reply from Henry Ford Hospital had just arrived last week.

You are undoubtedly aware of Mr. Donegan's recent change of attitude toward Mrs. Donegan, his wife. His condition, in her opinion, warranted hospital observation to determine, if possible, the cause of this change.

Maggie had told John of the reply but no one else. She didn't want to believe June's allegations, but this reply made it difficult not to.

Maggie knew this was not something Tom should know about, not now, at least. From the time he was a little lad, Tom had adored Hugh, coming in from the fields whenever he could to visit with him. Learning news like this would devastate him, but she had an idea that would divert his attention.

She slid her teacup away from her and leaned toward Tom in a conspiratorial tone.

"Would you be able to take Donnell out to the chicken coop and show him how to collect the eggs? He's old enough now, and he looks up to you." The ten-year gap in their ages made this a fine time for Tom to become someone special in his little brother's eyes. Tom nodded in agreement, his eyes taking on a glint that made Maggie hopeful, something she needed right now.

Chapter 25
Veronica

Winter 1923

Veronica slipped out the front door just as dawn was breaking. The winter sky, streaked with orange and yellow, outlined the limbs of the great oak tree that stood next to the barn. A good day despite the cold. She was determined to get the school warmed up before the children arrived. She'd paid several of the older boys to chop the wood after school yesterday, so she'd hear no more complaints from Mrs. Marsdale, who was so vocal in her comments about her son being sent to school for an education, not to chop wood. He could do that at home. The Marsdale boy was not one she included in the paid work.

Her Model-T started on the first try, and Veronica was off. The school, just down Main Street a bit more than a mile, was small, but what thrilled her most was that it was hers to run with only occasional visits from district supervisors. She pulled into the driveway on the left of the small, white clapboard building into the cleared space reserved for her car.

The pile of wood was just under the steps. She'd brought dry kindling from home, a trick she'd learned over her three years at District Number Three. The reprimands about having the children cut wood gave her the idea to offer money. It had been a dream scheme and helped provide enough wood to warm them through the coldest of days.

Despite her black wool coat and gloves, Veronica shivered as she pulled her school bag and the kindling that she'd wrapped in an old black shawl from the back of the car, the rumble seat serving as storage space. She unlocked the school door with the key she'd been given upon securing the job. The door stuck, but with a little effort, she pushed it open to find frost covering the windowpanes. She could see her breath as she sighed.

The room was filled with student desks clustered around the pot-belly stove in the center of the room. Her desk was just beyond the stove. She put her bag down and brought the kindling sticks closer to the stove. Removing her gloves, she lifted the latch on the front of the stove and inserted the kindling. She blew on her hands, went out the door again, and bent below the steps for the first log of what she suspected would be a five-log day.

Once she had more wood inside the stove, she wadded up old newspapers and tucked them strategically under the kindling, then placed the log on top. She struck a match, satisfied to see orange flames lick upwards. As the room warmed, Veronica went about tidying desks and putting *Puns to Ponder* on the blackboard for their morning exercise:

Include Your Children when Baking Cookies
Two Sisters Reunited After 18 Years in Checkout Counter
Local High School Dropouts Cut in Half

She chuckled as she wrote the last one, knowing her brother Tom would especially like it. He'd graduated last spring, though he'd often threatened to quit school and be done once and for all with Sister "Lucifer." "She's got a bit of the 'divil' in her, that one," he'd said of Sister Lucinda.

As the children straggled in, hung their coats on the rack near the stove and got into their desks, Veronica felt the same rush she had since she started this job. She loved the chance to encourage and enlighten young minds. Many of the children came from surrounding farms where education had not been available to their parents. She felt fortunate that her parents had valued reading and writing, though their own schooling years in Ireland had been limited. They also encouraged extracurricular talents of singing, piano playing and acting. Veronica had been singled out for her talent, performing solos in yearly recitals with Miss Chapin and being cast in leading roles in many plays.

The youngsters who sat before her were fresh with possibility, and she was determined to help them make the best of their lives despite the Sister "Lucifers" of the world.

As the children opened their copybooks and began their work, Veronica took attendance. As they answered with the response, "Present," she noted several students who came from West Bloomfield, where her brother Jerome would soon live with his bride-to-be, Rachel Sullivan. She wondered if any of their parents had read about his new business venture advertised in local papers.

Mr. Jerome J. Donegan, Lakeville, NY
Dealer in Livestock and high-class meats and vegetables
Service and Quality is our Motto.

Jerome's marriage planned for the spring had story-book romance to it. Rachel Sullivan was one of six children. Her mother, Mary McNamara and father, Michael A. Sullivan solid citizens of West Bloomfield. "He's chosen well," Maggie had said to Veronica, "and so has Rachel. Jerome is an enterprising young man with lots to offer any woman."

Veronica had only been nine years old, but she remembered Jerome complaining at Sunday dinners about the terrible hours he had to work, up at dawn and too tired to go off at day's end to have some fun. Their father had no sympathy. "Fun wasn't part of the Lord's plan," he'd counter. "Hard work and good food, that's what's fun."

By age twenty-seven, Jerome got the gumption to get out from under the plow. Auctioning off everything he owned, he threw his hat into the meat dealing business. No more milking at early dawn for him. He'd had enough of separating wheat from straw. He had a mind for business and he intended to use it.

The plight of farmers wasn't getting any better these days. Since World War I, they had overproduced to feed the European market and now prices were plummeting. A crisis was looming. Attempts to increase corn harvesting with Husking Derbies and improve methods of egg production and marketing strategies were discussed at "egg circle" sessions. But these efforts didn't have enough appeal to the many returning soldiers who had survived the hell of war.

At one point, Jerome boasted to Veronica that he could buy and sell and make a handsome profit without ever getting up before the sun. She thought of her own dark winter mornings during these first years of teaching. When she finished her studies next year at Geneseo Normal School, she would receive a permanent teaching certificate and new jobs in more established school districts with school rooms warmed in time for her arrival at respectable morning hours.

With the January passage of the eighteenth amendment that put prohibition in full swing, things changed for Veronica and her brothers and sisters. Decent events for socializing were scarce. The popular dance halls were not approved of by the Church, the priests speaking out from the pulpit about the near occasion of sin they represented. The speakeasy at the American Hotel didn't offer much in the way of a good time, mostly filled with older folks. Pool halls were out of the question, the work of the devil. As they discovered, Prohibition hadn't eliminated drinking. Rather, it just went underground.

The fact that women all around the nation had finally secured the vote underscored the fact that the times were changing and, in Veronica's opinion, for the better.

All in all, Veronica thought, as the children lined up at her desk to have their work checked over, her brother Jerome was one of the lucky ones in these times. He'd found the girl of his dreams right in West Bloomfield at a church-sponsored Saturday dance. Despite some downturns, Veronica hoped things were looking up for the Donegan family all the way around.

Chapter 26
Tom

September 21, 1925

Tom was up before dawn and slipped out to the barn alone. Soon enough, his father and brother Bernard would join him, but for now, he craved this time alone. He didn't tend to any chores just yet. Instead, he grabbed hold of a rung on the ladder and climbed to the hayloft. This haven away from the others brought him a sigh of relief.

Tom's eyes searched the rafters. No birds about, though he could hear an owl from the large opening in the back through which the hay was loaded. Its sound comforted him. He breathed easily here where no one could see him, not even Jenny, the faithful horse whose stall below him was on the opposite side of the barn. He pushed a mound of hay aside and found a corner to sit against.

Today was his 21st birthday. A man by any standards. Yet the last thing he felt today was manly. He'd watched his older brothers go out and make their mark. Hugh, married now to June, had his own motor company. Jerome, his recent marriage to Rachel, now had his own meat dealership. Loring was living in Columbus, Ohio, helping Hugh with his business. Vic was making a great success as a chauffeur, his little girl Ruth beguiling them all, Tom included, as his family expanded with the recent birth of his son Harold.

They're all getting settled in a trade, Tom thought.

And what good am I? Even Bernard's gone on to take classes at Genesee Wesleyan Seminary to better himself. And he's younger than me. Bernard had told him that at one time, he'd thought of going off to the real seminary, the one that shared his name, St. Bernard's, in Rochester, where young men his age studied for the priesthood. For now, he was keeping at his studies in the hope that one day he could move on.

Loring's stay in Columbus was longer than any of them expected, Hugh's illness extending beyond the initial symptom of the cough to something that appeared to be far more serious. Even Hugh's business seemed to be suffering and the business Tom had hoped one day to join.

Tom pushed the hay with his foot into a circle around him, trying to collect his thoughts. He overheard Josephine, who had been doing Hugh's books, telling their mother that Hugh's company was in trouble.

"Ma, I've paid all the bills that he had. He's all caught up. He hasn't taken a bit of money for himself in over six months. The rent is paid, and he doesn't owe his creditors any outstanding amounts, but when all's said and done, he's nearly broke. Lucky isn't taking any salary, though he was supposed to be paid. It's not good, Ma. I'm telling you, it's not good at all."

It all was adding up to trouble. Tom begged to help, but his father wouldn't hear of it! "You'll stay right here where you can fix anything that goes wrong. That's the fixing you'll do. Your brother Loring is doing what needs to be done in Ohio! For now, I need you and Bernard right here to keep our farm afloat."

Tom knew he was stuck for the time being. He'd been told since a small boy that he was smart and clever. His father told him as much when Tom was only eleven and was called upon to fix the fencing around the pasture, something Bernard had no aptitude for.

A few years ago, when it came time to replace the chicken coop with a more substantial arrangement, Bernard took over the milking so Tom could do the measuring and designing for it. He'd worked at the kitchen table with his father into the night, drawing sketches of a structure big enough so they could double their profits by doubling the space. He knew how to handle the two-by-fours and had the know-how to frame the little building to include windows, far beyond what his father expected.

"Why, you're building a real Taj Mahal for these creatures," his father had said. "They'll be laying golden eggs before long!"

Tom rolled over on his side in the hayloft. He put his hand up to support his head and smiled as he recalled the work that hen house had been.

He had measured the right size for the dozen hens they had, fixing the nesting boxes with a place for the eggs to drop safely and be easily collected without disturbing the hens.

He'd managed to match the details of the hen house architecture with the big barn and the smaller storage barn, using the same trim and angles for the roof. He even coordinated the colors of yellow and red with the other buildings. He positioned the hen house to the left of the other outbuildings and away from the farm tractors. He'd thought it through thoroughly, and it came together perfectly. All this while he was finishing high school. It was work he was good at. Work he loved!

Tom sat up feeling a simple satisfaction. He heard his mother's words again, "You've a fine head on your shoulders. Your father couldn't get along without you."

Tom sighed as he looked around the hayloft. For the time being, he'd be saddled with staying at home. But not forever. He had dreams and they weren't in Lima. He'd talked with the fellows at the Hotel uptown and learned of other opportunities, some as far away as Buffalo.

He straightened and looked up at the rafters. He found himself thinking about a way to strengthen the master beams in this big barn. As he studied them, he considered a way to shore up the main chestnut beam that ran lengthwise across the rafters. He was fairly certain he could make it hold for years to come.

The sound of the barn door sliding open jarred Tom from what had been his birthday reverie. As he climbed down to begin the day's work, he was greeted by Bernard, who said, "Pa says he'll be right along. He wants us to work in the south pasture today before the rainfall. I'll saddle up Jenny."

Tom smiles despite himself. His birthday was not mentioned, but the day was young. He knew his mother would remember. She always does.

Chapter 27
The Music

With yet another string broken, the old square piano left by the Lays family finally sang its last note. Made by Henry F. Miller Company and dressed in Brazilian Rosewood, it had been a beauty in its day. It was popular for a long time throughout the country but didn't satisfy the need any longer. Its bulky presence and Victorian ornamentation had gone out of style as sleeker models were manufactured.

Maggie's love of music, starting with her own button accordion that she had carried on the ship to America, had been a constant in her life. She was vehement that her four daughters would have the opportunity for piano lessons.

Without much difficulty, Maggie won out over any financial objections John posed, knowing he loved their times around the piano as much as she did.

The day the new upright console with its dark mahogany satin finish arrived, Maggie felt unexpected joy. The Chickering and Sons piano fit neatly on the inside wall of the parlor just outside the south bedroom. It gave the parlor a more spacious look, the old square piano gone from the far wall where it seemed to dominate the room, even covering part of the window. Maggie had already arranged for more chairs in the room so more of the family could easily gather about.

Josephine was home for a visit, adding to a festive atmosphere. Thirteen-year-old Betty sat now at the new keyboard playing her lesson piece, Percy Grainger's *Country Gardens*. She was

Miss Chapin's newest student. Her sisters, who had spent long practice hours on the old square monstrosity, were pleased to hear this new sound.

Betty finished to applause and next, Gene played her favorite *Humoresque*, which she had memorized as a younger student. Then Josephine accompanied Veronica as she sang a melody from one of her past performances at high school events. Then Betty returned and they all joined in singing *Danny Boy*. With Miss Chapin's help, Betty was perfecting her own rendition of it with a few extra trills.

Maggie couldn't have been more pleased as the singing continued.

"It's a Long Way to Tipperary" was one of John's favorites. Made popular by the famed Irish tenor John McCormick, the song's comical lyrics brought a laugh from them all.

Paddy wrote a letter to his Irish Molly O,
Saying, "Should you not receive it,
Write and let me know!

On occasion, Maggie would dance a jig for them, tapping it out to the same phrase she had learned, with *a heel and a toe and a heel and a toe*. Her ability to perform from childhood memory awed them all.

The other thing they teased Maggie to do was play her accordion. Maggie had an ear for music that was fine-tuned, and she was glad her children had inherited it.

She remembered the night before she left for America when her Ma had given her the accordion to take with her on her ship, the S.S. Etruria. She had protested, saying, "Ma, I can't take yer accordion. What'll ye play? Where will the music come from when I'm gone?"

She remembered her mother's reply. "That's the question I've been asking meself since I knew ye were going off to America. Where will the music come from?" Maggie could still hear her ma's promise. "I don't know the answer, but I guarantee I'll find it."

And find it she did. Her mother had been well cared for by Julia, Maggie's older sister, and kept the farm in Ahadallane, County Cork, where she lived among her friends for as long as she was able to. Julia had written that she took their mother for her last days to Mrs. Crean's, where she died as she'd lived, simply and peacefully. The parish priest had given her last rites, and Julia had written that there'd been music playing in the courtyard at her last, her promise to find the music fulfilled.

Remembering home brought such bittersweet memories. The heartache and leaving mingled with the joy of America. She'd not forget home nor the people who made America home.

The air tonight was clear, the front door open, and Maggie suspected stars were shining. She sat back in her rocker and watched as the girls gathered 'round, their father in his chair by the side window, tapping his toes as *Finnegan's Wake* was played. Then Veronica sang the love ballad by Thomas Moore, Believe *Me, If All Those Endearing Young Charms*, a bittersweet melody that Maggie understood only too well.

Their song fest lasted into the night, the wonder of it all filling Maggie with a delight she hadn't felt in so long. She lost herself in the melodies, the lyrics and the love. There was nowhere else she wanted to be.

Chapter 28
Genevieve

October 2, 1926

Gene folded her letter of acceptance, its bold RBI insignia displayed prominently across the top. She placed it carefully in her dressing table drawer for safekeeping, tightening the brass knob after she opened it. This drawer, she thought, would be like her mother's green valise that held mostly Hugh's letters. This is where she will keep her acceptance letter, the beginning of the path to her dream.

She sat on the stool and looked in the mirror connected to the pine dressing table. Her chestnut brown hair was bobbed in the style of the day, close to her cheeks with no curl. Her hazel eyes gleamed back at her. This day, her nineteenth birthday, felt like a special one. Everything seemed to be falling into place, her acceptance to RBI top on her list.

Rochester Business Institute was a venerable school founded in 1863 and located on Clinton Avenue in Rochester. Josephine's choice of nursing and Veronica's as a teacher led Gene to the next alternative, becoming a secretary. She'd been good at writing and language skills since a child, helping her mother with letters to the New York relatives and to Ireland, where her mother's sister still lived. Gene was happy to serve as her backup secretary when needed, as Josephine and Veronica had done before her, helping to dot i's and cross t's.

She pulled a small pile of *Lima Recorder* clippings from her drawer and smiled to see her name in print along with others of her classmates and chums. Like Veronica, whose name had been in the paper often during her senior year with her various vocal achievements and plays, Gene now found her way as

Senior Class President. The June 17th edition listed Genevieve Donegan as delivering the Class Prophecy. She'd been careful not to offend anyone. Her best pal, Claire Doran, who was Salutatorian, laughed when she heard Gene's draft.

"I love that you call him Father Joe. He's been more like a brother to us. Well, maybe a little bit more."

Both girls giggled as they spoke of "Father Joe," their good friend Joe O'Connell, who was headed for St. Andrew's Seminary despite their efforts to dissuade him. "You'll have to wear a dress and get up early every day," they taunted him.

In the class prophecy, Gene wrote that they'd see Claire Doran leading children around the world, her dream of travel finally realized. That seemed to please Claire, for she was full of fun and adventure, one of the reasons Gene liked her so much.

She was pleased to see her older brother Bernard mentioned for having completed his course in the teacher training class at Canandaigua Academy. His career choice was unique, only two out of ten men choosing education these days, farming often taking precedence. He would make a fine teacher, Gene thought. He was patient and smart, a good combination.

The May issue had mentioned Gene as part of the High School Prize speakers. Her friends Claire Doran and Joe O'Connell were prize winners, too. Her essay was "A Second Trait." Joe's story of "The New South" and Claire's "Joint Owners in Spain", a one-act play, the other listings.

Gene wished she could keep copies of all their works, for who would remember or even care in years to come? Maybe one day she'd have a daughter who would write about her. For now, she was glad to be mentioned in the September 23 issue under the title *Away At School*. She and Elizabeth Sheehan, who had written and read the Class Poem at Graduation, would be at RBI, Claire off to Buffalo Normal for teaching and Joe to St. Andrews to be a priest, of course. Other classmates were attending a variety of schools: University of Rochester, Rochester Normal, Buffalo University, Sacred Heart School, Notre Dame University, Alfred University, Canisius College in Buffalo, Colgate, Mt. Holyoke, Keuka and Geneseo Normal.

Gene was glad to be going 'away,' even if it wasn't as far away as Josephine in New York City. Her plan was to get an apartment once she found a roommate to share expenses. In the meantime, she was pleased to be a part of the family hustle and bustle, each of them coming and going, their lives leading them off into the world, but their hearts at home.

Next month, Hugh and June would be coming to visit. It was to be his birthday celebration. His last two letters indicated his health hadn't been improving.

"…They tell me I nearly cashed in my chips. But I am on the gain again and hope to be out of the hospital in a few days but will have to be careful for about two months. No need for anyone to come and will not need any help unless I go broke on Doctors and hospitals. Tell the kids to write me a line and awaiting your reply.

I am as ever Your loving son, Hugh

The next letter followed two weeks later.

Dear Mother,

Lying in bed for these three weeks and liable to be for three more weeks. I am gaining rapidly in weight although l lost quite a bit while I was the worst off. Why don't the kids write me some letters? I live to watch the mailman and read letters. The doctor says I will be better than ever when I get up this time. I hope so as it was three years last August since I was first taken sick. Well, my nurse says I must stop now so I will close with love to all.

I am as ever Your Loving son, Hugh

Gene wondered how much sorrow her mother could bear. Uncle Jeremiah, her mother's brother, had died just two years ago. Maggie had learned from Aunt Molly that, like their brother Tims, alcohol was the problem.

Gene still remembered his address, 756 2nd Street, and often wondered what it was like to live in New York City. She knew Aunt Molly lived on 82nd Street, not too far from the Metropolitan Museum of Art, another place she longed to visit.

She knew very little about her uncle Jeremiah except that he was a twin and had been named after his father. His twin sister Lizzie and he had come to America in 1889, a year after Maggie had come. He had been in the Manhattan State Hospital, and Gene had overheard her mother telling her father that it had been the same for Tims. Nothing to be done.

Now Gene wondered about Hugh. She hoped upon hope there was something that could be done, this oldest brother a joy to her since she was a small child, often carrying her about with him on his visits around the fields of the farm. He was seventeen years older and seemed magical in his energy and spirit, his visits always memorable.

Jerome married just three years ago and now had the dearest little red-haired girl, Cecilia. When they visited, Gene would carry Cecilia around and show her the farm, as Hugh had done for her. She felt so grown now. Whenever she thought of her four oldest brothers, she felt a certain pride. Hugh, Jerome, Loring and Victor. And she'd not forget Tom and Bernard nor even little Donnell. All seven brothers made her smile.

Now, as she tucked her treasures securely into the drawer, she smiled, certain her mother would make this a special birthday. Like Tommy, she knew her mother always did.

Chapter 29
The Chestnut Beam

November 19, 1926

Hugh slid open the barn door wide enough to slip in. He glanced at the full moon overhead, bathing the fields in light. He'd loved these fields, his childhood memories of walking to the creek flooding him now. He carefully pulled the door back along the track to shut it, creating the privacy he had craved all evening.

He gazed around the interior, his eyes drinking in all that he saw: the collars for the workhorses hung on the wall by the loft ladder; the ropes and lassos and saddles; the hay bin filled to the brim with this season's harvest; the pitchfork randomly placed by the last one to pitch hay. It was just as he imagined and remembered it. He'd never forget. He looked up at the chestnut beam Tom had been so proud to have reinforced. Two new oak beams shored it up. It was perfect, Tom's skills unsurpassed.

Hugh looked over at the middle stall where the family's favorite mare stood watching him, curious, he supposed, whether he had brought her something. The two empty stalls would be filled as money became available for a new mare that Loring knew about. Money. How Hugh wished he could help. How he wished so many things.

He reached into his pocket and pulled out the few sugar cubes he'd taken from the table to give Jenny. "You'll spoil her,

Hugh," his mother had warned each time she saw him gather some treat for her. He could hear her voice clear as a bell. Today, it was his intention to spoil her. He stroked her mane, her golden Palomino coat shining, her brown eyes almost smiling as she ate the sugar cubes from his opened palm. Dear Jenny, who'd been around almost as long as he had. He felt the warmth of her as he brushed her down, recalling their rides off into the fields when she took him to the open places where his mind could wander, where he could daydream and imagine all he would become. Days that were long gone.

Everything seemed jumbled up now. He was so tired. All he wanted to do was sleep.

Tonight had been overwhelming. Seeing them all celebrating him felt wrong. He was nothing to celebrate. He was a failure. Ask his father. Ask June. He'd said such horrible things to her he didn't even want to recall them. Now, here they all were saying nice things to him. "Hugh, you are such a good storyteller."

"You're my favorite big brother," Betty had said. "You are the smartest of us all." He knew better. He knew he was nothing. That was certain.

As he stroked Jenny, the songs, the good food, the stories, and Maggie's dancing came to him. Saying his good-bye to them all tonight had been worse than he thought. Seeing Jerome and Rachel and their two little girls so happy made his chest ache. Having children of his own was something he'd never know. June would have loved them, but during their six years of marriage, it wasn't to be. He believed it to be his fault, this damned illness taking so much from him. He was confident enough in June's love for him, yet he desperately wanted so much more for her.

The company he had built from scratch was under collapse. Whatever this cursed thing he suffered from was, it took him off the road and put him in bed. No way for a man to live. Days of doctor appointments and hospitalizations had given them no hope for a cure, no one certain what this ailment was. It was no way for June to live, taking care of an invalid who could only sleep the day away. He wouldn't allow it.

As he shook hands with his brother Loring earlier, he put his left hand on Loring's shoulder and looked into his gray eyes.

"Take good care, Lucky," he said, using the family nickname. He hated to see sorrow in Lucky's eyes, the recent loss of his first little girl weighing on him. Lucky had been a real pal to him, staying by his side through the worst of his illness. It didn't seem fair that a man so giving would have the gift of a child taken from him. Yet he knew they'd have more children, his wife Peggy a real survivor, her sweet round face and her infectious laugh making her a great, welcoming spirit. June had liked her instantly.

And then there was his pal, Vic, who loved cars as much as he did. His two children were growing up so fast. Pity about their little Harold's death last year from that damned pneumonia. Yet, they'd have others, too, he predicted. Vic's wife Margaret, though grieving now, would go on, her spirit strong.

He intended to head to the barn after these goodbyes. He had no idea how they'd tear him up. When he turned back into the dining room to find dear Josephine, his dark-haired beauty of a sister, bookkeeper and nurse all rolled into one, his heart stopped. She was gorgeous. He'd never really seen her 'til now. Her face was radiant and open. Another stab to his chest. June would always have a friend in her. And red-haired Veronica shone through like none other, keeping everyone happy, not counting the cost to herself. They were lucky children she was teaching.

When he found Bernard, whose eyes were twinkling, he quickly said his good-bye. You could see he was bound for something grand, that was for certain. He'd already got a good start at becoming a teacher with his graduation from Canandaigua Academy. A good student and a gentleman, with malice toward none. Success would be his.

When he stepped away, Hugh found Tom standing by him, his buddy, twenty-two years old and strong. He had trailed about with him when he was home on holidays as if Hugh was a hero. He even found Hugh's army cap that had been stored away wore it in his honor. Over the years, Hugh had encouraged

Tom in his carpentry skills, making sure to compliment him as he knew his father wouldn't. He'd known his father's harshness, remembering his devastating words when Hugh told him he didn't want to be a farmer.

"No son of mine," his father had said, "is going to go off willy-nilly to follow a fad. Your 'tin-lizzie' isn't going to feed you, that's for sure." Yet this son of his did go off and made a good go of it without his permission or encouragement. Hugh had been angry with him for a time, but as success came, he let go of his resentment. His mother was there and believed in him. That made all the difference.

Then he turned to find Gene, her hazel eyes and chestnut hair so like Josephine. Her winsome ways won his heart. He often took her under his wing, her presence making his visits more special. She'd go off to the barn with him, where he'd hoist her up on the top of the stall gate so she could stroke Jenny. "Folks call girls with the name Genevieve, Jenny, just like this horse of ours," he'd told her.

"Ma says she'd not given me the beautiful Saint's name Genevieve to have it become a horse's name," Gene said punctiliously. She was far too grown up now for him to lift her, a young woman of nineteen, so he gave a special wink. She beamed broadly. He moved on to his last goodbyes, tousling Don's brown head of hair and patting Betty on the shoulder. Earlier, she had presented him with a card she'd made for him. "It's got a picture of Our Lady. She'll always watch out for you.' He'd tucked the card into his pocket. As he headed out the door, his exit to the barn all he wanted now, he walked right into his father, who was on the way in.

"You in a hurry, son?" his father asked. Hugh paused, so desperately wanting relief, yet he waited for what his father had to say. "If you can come with me to the parlor, there's something I want to show you." Hugh followed, not knowing what to expect. His father, three inches shorter and quite a bit stouter, moved through the dining room with Hugh. Rarely had his father asked to be with him. Thankfully, he had taken a liking to June, gentle as a lamb with her. For that, Hugh was eternally grateful. Now, his father went over to the bookcase on the far wall and lifted out the small green valise of letters.

"I don't know if you've seen this before, but as many letters as she could collect are in here. The letters that you sent your sisters and brothers and your mother." He placed the valise on the piano bench and snapped it open. Hugh looked inside and recognized his scrawl. He saw the address of the latest batch, his handwriting looking like some old man's. It was a painful reminder of what had once been one of his greatest sources of pride. After his schooling had ended and he'd gotten his eighth-grade certificate from Genesee Wesleyan Seminary, he promised himself he would practice his skills. And he did, sending a vast amount of communication, keeping everyone in his sights.

Hugh looked down at the letters, his heart heavy, his shoulders slumped. He felt his father watching him, his eyes narrowing. "With you living so far away, this has been a source of comfort to your mother. I thought you'd like to know."

Hugh nodded slowly. John clicked the case shut and put it back on the shelf. Hugh knew this act was meant to be a tender one by his father, but just remembering it all: his early successes, his dreams, his company, and finally, his illness made Hugh want to scream. He felt like he would explode. As he made his way to the barn, he saw his mother watching him. He kept going. He couldn't face her. He wouldn't face her.

He'd been over it a thousand times in his mind. His own June is so brave and so lonely, his lack of stamina leaving her lost. Maybe soon now, she'll find relief. He couldn't think straight for all that needed to be done, for all that had been done for him. He was broke and couldn't, wouldn't ask for another dime. He'd already spent his life insurance policy, his mother getting it cashed once he'd signed it over to her. There was nothing left. The business would bring something for June, he hoped. It was all he could do. All he could do.

He'd thought all the details through on his summertime visit. With determination, he went around the stalls and found what he'd stowed there. He threw the rope up over the chestnut beam, secured it tight, and held on to the other end. He climbed the ladder to the loft.

As his feet swung free, only Jenny was left to hear his cry.

Chapter 30
As Ever, Your Loving Son Hugh

Saturday Morning, November 20, 1926.

Maggie was up before dawn, watching the red ribbon of light unveil itself upon the horizon. She'd slept fitfully, thoughts of last night's celebration lingering. Out on the porch with her robe wrapped around her, she reviewed it all again.

The full moon had illuminated the fields with a glow that looked like daylight. She smiled as she remembered the entire family gathered to celebrate Hugh. June, as much a treasure as ever, drove Hugh nearly four hundred miles from Columbus to make this birthday visit possible.

Betty sang her favorite selections, *Danny Boy*, the one they all requested, and Red Sails in the Sunset, another favorite. Veronica and Gene lit the mood with their antics and stories from some of the shows they'd done for their high school programs and recitals. Maggie, not to be outdone by her children, played the accordion for them and then proceeded to perform a jig, full of spirit and high kicks. They'd seen her do the ordinary steps she'd taught them, but this one had Maggie lifting her skirt high and kicking even higher steps.

"Watch yourself there, Lass," John had called out. "We don't want ye kicking the bucket." They all laughed as Maggie ended her performance, with applause from all and whistles from the boys. The little ones were quite awed. And Maggie, quite spent.

Hugh smiled ruefully, his connection to his mother a strong one.

"Ma," he said, "ye couldn't have given me a better gift than that. I'll remember it always."

With that, all assembled applauded, including the littlest ones.

Hugh didn't look much better than he had in August. He was gaunt, the little weight that he'd gained not significant enough to make a difference. His eyes were ringed with circles, and his hand had a tremble. Even his red hair was dull, the blue of his gorgeous eyes pale and watery. Maggie knew the trip couldn't have worn him out that much. He looked older than his thirty- six years.

Might it be the medication he was taking, she wondered. There'd never been a definitive diagnosis, though sleeping sickness had been mentioned. Maggie had learned from Doc Kober about some of the signs of it: sore throat and fever accompanied by a headache; double-vision and severe weakness; tremors and jerky bodily movements, muscle pain and mental slowness which could increase in severity. The symptoms that worried her the most were the behavioral changes that could include psychosis and hallucinations followed by steadily increasing drowsiness and lethargy. She often remembered the letter from Henry Ford Hospital that had mentioned Hugh's change of attitude toward his wife.

Two years had passed since his hospitalization, and Maggie prayed daily for things to improve. She was glad to have Hugh home on the farm, his love of it so present. Yesterday, Maggie had watched from the back porch as Hugh and June took a long walk out beyond the barn, strolling hand in hand - an encouraging sign.

Whatever it was that was troubling him, he seemed to have found some peace, though no cure. Lucky had been of assistance during his illness, helping Hugh run his Motor Car business from his bed.

As she looked toward the barn, Maggie hoped Hugh hadn't stayed out too late. His frequent napping often disrupted his normal sleeping hours. She'd watched him walk out to the barn, his love for animals never sated. He was probably going to tuck them in for the night. Maggie thought when she'd seen him go out just as she was ready to tuck herself in.

Now, as the morning light illuminated the tree line over the creek, she saw John headed out to the barn. She prayed as she felt the familiar pain near her heart. She'd known it wasn't a bad heart but rather a broken heart that mothers acquire each time one of their children suffers.

How, she wondered, would this energetic, creative, intelligent young man whom they had celebrated in grand style cope with his continuing reduced circumstances? She was so very aware of her love for him. Something she never doubted, no matter what.

It was time to check on food for the kittens. With a full heart, Maggie walked out to the barn.

Chapter 31
Grant Him Eternal Rest

The sound of her mother's sobbing awakened Josephine Saturday morning. She pulled on her robe and tiptoed down the stairs before any of the others awoke. It was just after dawn.

Maggie was sitting alone in her dining room chair, her pale blue dressing gown and robe around her, her faded red hair unpinned and falling to her shoulders. She was holding her valise of letters, hugging the small green case to her breast. Josephine didn't know what had happened, but she saw the wild look in her mother's eyes. It gave her a chill. It was the same look she'd seen when she was fifteen years old, watching her mother's grief when Baby Rose had died.

Josephine approached gingerly, uncertain of what to say or do. Just then, her father came through the door, her brother Bernard trailing behind, too early for an ordinary day. Josephine immediately knew it was Hugh, Maggie's first-born boy, who meant the world to her, who brought her the world with every trip he took, with every letter and card he wrote.

Her father shook his head as Josephine sat in the chair next to her mother. Bernard stood back; his eyes cast downward.

"Ma, what's happened?" she asked.

Josephine watched her mother try to put words together. Maggie drew a breath while rocking her body back and forth and said, "It's our boy, Hugh. He's gone from us."

All the fear and heartache that had accompanied these last years of Hugh's illness came crashing down. Josephine watched as her mother's face crumpled, her lips quivering, her eyes puffy, and her mouth pulled tight. Josephine felt the sorrow for both of them. She reached over and wrapped her arms around her mother and held her, drawing comfort from her.

During her days at Lenox Hill Hospital, Josephine had tried to learn more about Hugh's condition, describing what she knew of his erratic behavior to colleagues. She'd hoped they'd hear something more from Henry Ford Hospital, the only real information contained in the letter Maggie had received about his uncharacteristic behavior toward his wife. June had been open about their hard times, the harsh words, the erratic emotions that Hugh had displayed. They'd all hoped things had settled down since that hospital stay, a hope not realized.

Josephine looked up as Loring came in. Bernard had called him. Josephine and Loring had been able helpers, traveling to Ohio to help with Hugh's business, providing what support they could, neither of them understanding what Hugh's malady was. What they did know was that he'd gone downhill, nothing relieving it. The constant sleeping and lack of energy might have indicated sleeping sickness, but all the symptoms didn't match. Now, it didn't matter. Hugh found his own solution.

Josephine unwrapped her arms from around her mother and went out and put the water to boil. The others would be awakening soon. Her father joined her in the kitchen.

"I've called Father Farrell. He'll come with the coroner," he said softly. "They'll be here soon." Then he stepped toward the little window by the pump and stared out.

"It was your mother that found Hugh. She went out with just her shawl over her night clothes to feed the darn barn cats. I was on my way out when I heard her scream. I couldn't figure out what it could be. By the time I got to her, she was hysterical, telling me that it was all my fault. I brought her back to the house and woke Bernard to come help me."

Josephine put the kettle to boil and looked over at her father, his eyes bloodshot, his hair grayer than she'd noticed before. He looked broken.

"She blames me for this, you know," he said as he continued looking out the little window. "She's blamed me since he went off on his own for his automobiles. I was too harsh, she always said. You didn't understand him. He was sensitive. He might have stayed in town if it hadn't been for you."

Josephine listened, a story she'd heard before. She had also heard Hugh's hunger for his father's approval. "He's been kinder to Vic than to me. It's Vic's gorgeous children that softened him," Hugh had once said, his own lack of children coloring his thoughts.

Now she listened to her father, regret pouring from him. His voice broke as he blurted out, "I didn't know. I didn't know how to do any better." He went out the door, inconsolable.

Josephine wrapped her arms around her waist and held herself. Two heartbroken parents. What's to be done?

When Josephine saw her two sisters come into the kitchen, she felt her eyes well up with tears. How could she tell them?

"Where's Ma?" Veronica asked. "What's going on around here?"

"Is June awake?" Josephine asked.

"She said she wanted to stay in a bit," Gene answered. "She's pretty sure Hugh slept in the barn with his beloved Jenny."

Josephine paused and closed her eyes. "Oh, dear God, oh dear God." Not sure what to do, she asked about Tom. Where was Tom? Tom, whose hero was gone.

Loring came in from the outdoors. The priest would be there soon, he told her, and Tom was nowhere to be found. The coroner would be right along as well.

"Veronica and Genevieve," Josephine began, "there's no other way than to tell you. Our beloved Hugh has died." She breathed deeply, feeling tears run down her cheeks. "Ma found him in the barn this morning."

Josephine couldn't say another word. She waited for the news to sink in. She watched the eyes of her younger sisters, knowing the weight of this loss. Hopefully, they would see to the youngest ones. She would go to June herself later.

As she sat in the front parlor with her father, J.C. Preston, the coroner from Avon, gently asked difficult questions. Josephine took her father's hand, holding back sobs as the details were completed.

Name of the deceased: Hugh Michael Donegan,
Sex: Male
Color or Race: White
Single, married, widowed, or divorced: Married
If married, widowed wife: June Jesse Austen
Occupation: Invalid

How she hated that answer. Yet it was true. He hadn't been able to work these past two years, his stamina lacking. Dr. Preston handed the document to Josephine for her signature. As Josephine scanned it, she read the coroner's statement - Cause of death: Suicide by hanging while mentally unbalanced; of unsound mind for two years and four months. She clutched her heart. Seeing the words in print made it all the more real.

Josephine had been aware of Hugh's troubles since he'd returned from the army. She'd seen him cry sometimes at the drop of a hat, saying he didn't deserve to live. He'd confessed to his mother after she'd learned from a letter sent by the hospital about his "period of hostility" toward his wife. "I wasn't in my right mind," he'd said in his own defense. He'd continued to write letters, but his penmanship, of which he was so proud, was barely legible. He'd pine for letters asking if the 'kids' could write to him, his younger brothers' and sisters' letters something that comforted him.

And yet, on this last trip, it seemed he'd been touched by a magic wand, acting as clever and smart as his old self, telling stories of his adventures around the country. His postcards, collected like relics, were proof of his strength, intelligence, and savvy.

Josephine signed the Death Certificate and dated it.

11/19/26.

The funeral will be tomorrow. Oh, the pity of it, Josephine thought.

Maggie watched from the porch as the wagon driven by Jimmy O'Connell, the undertaker, drove out. Her boy was gone. She blessed herself and awaited Father Farrell. When he arrived, Maggie was ready for him. With her rosary wrapped around her hand, Maggie nodded as the priest said his sorries. He was a good man, and she was about to test his goodness. Josephine served them tea, watching her mother closely.

"Yes," Maggie proclaimed, "there will be a Mass of Christian burial. The poor boy wasn't in his right mind. That's all there is to it. Yes, he will be buried in consecrated soil at St. Rose Cemetery. Isn't he entitled as a child of God? Didn't his own baptism at the Church of the Holy Innocents in Manhattan when he was five days old welcome him into the communion of saints? Didn't Reverend M.J. Doherty perform the baptism and his own uncle, my very brother-in-law Hugh Galena, and our dear friend Agnes McCormick act as his sponsors?"

She drew a breath, tears threatening to break the steel with which she'd spoken. She sighed and said, "Can we not grant him eternal rest?"

Father Farrell knew the Catholic church's stance on the refusal of a Mass and Christian burial for any who died by their own hand. No sacred soil should hold them, he'd learned. He knew it and had long ago used his own discretion in enforcing it. He looked at Maggie, heartbroken, her spirit nearly shattered. He paused and said, "Even if I have to go to Rome to get permission, you'll have a full and right Mass and burial. You need not worry at all." Father Farrell had known Hugh since his youth. This last act of desperation was not to be held against him. It didn't come close to tipping the scale of his pluck polish and perseverance. He was a baptized member of the Church, a Great War veteran, a business owner, a husband and the finest son and brother anyone was ever blessed with. "Indeed, we will grant him eternal rest."

Chapter 32
The Cousins

November 1926

"She's the best of them, isn't she?" Gene asked her older sisters Josephine and Veronica as they waved goodbye to Cousin Margaret Galena. Margaret's smart gray wool coat and matching hat gave her a sophisticated look that Gene, at age 19, admired. Margaret had come up from Long Island City to Hugh's funeral on her own, representing the New York relatives. The cost of her travel expenses was never mentioned, and the affection between the two families solid.

Gene was gaining an appreciation for the importance of family. Hugh's sudden death had stunned them all. Margaret had taken the early Sunday morning train, the Empire State Express, which made the trip more possible and easier than in the past. She arrived in time for the evening wake and stayed over with Maggie for the Monday morning funeral. She brought greetings and well wishes from all, sharing how much her mother, Annie, wished she could make the trip. It was a blessing, Margaret had said, that her father, Hugh, hadn't lived to hear of this news, so proud of his namesake, this death a heartbreak.

The front parlor had been re-arranged with Hugh's coffin placed on the far wall under the window. Gene watched from behind the usually open glass doors that were now closed to separate the dining room from the two parlors. Cousin Margaret, close to Hugh's age, stood next to her, taking her hand. Jerome, Loring, Vic, and Tom served as pallbearers and maneuvered the casket through the front door, each man holding tight as they lifted it onto their shoulders so all could bear the weight.

Each of them did bear Hugh's weight, larger than life, Gene thought. She turned to Margaret and said, "He was the standard by which Ma measured all the boys," her eyes filling with tears. It was a standard they'd mostly succeeded in meeting, though Gene guessed that Tom's absence following the day of Hugh's death was his inability to deal with the loss of this man who had been his hero as long as Gene could remember. Tom had so often shadowed Hugh, going to the barn with him or out through the fields. As he got older and Hugh left home to start his own business, Tom still mentioned him often.

"Hugh will like that when he comes on his next visit," Tom had said to his mother after he'd seen the hen house to completion. Hugh's approval meant so much to him. Hugh was Gene's hero, too, if only for the special postcards he'd sent to her when she was four years old. Their last outing together was no exception. He'd taken her with him to visit Jenny earlier that night. Little did she know it would be his last night.

Gene didn't share her tears with Margaret; she winced as she thought of the pain, they all felt. The tears she did weep were for her mother, who so adored this oldest son. Maybe it was because he was her first, or simply because he was so bright and enterprising. Maggie was just Gene's age now, nineteen, when Hugh was born. He'd been her New York City baby; someone she could hold onto during her days of early love and great change.

"My mother says she'll never forget how good your parents were to her, never," Gene told her cousin. Margaret nodded knowingly and smiled. They'd all heard some of the same stories.

Margaret told them of her sister Loretta's regret at not being able to come, her two children, Anna Marie and James, born in the last few years. "You'll love it when you meet them. They are both Donegans in their looks, with hazel eyes and fair complexion." Margaret proclaimed.

Hugh had made strong connections with the Galena girls and the Kerrigan cousins, too. Margaret, though she had no children of her own, had a motherly and solicitous manner full of comfort as she absorbed the sorrow around her.

As they watched her out the door, Loring driving her to the train station, the three sisters held hands, feeling the gift of cousins. "The best for sure," Josephine said.

Chapter 33
After Hugh

February 13, 1927

Tom climbed the small muddy slope above the creek and started back toward home, the green shingled house set close to the street beneath two horse chestnut trees. He'd been glad for the time alone, the others at church. A favorite place, this stream of running water where he felt his worries slip away, was his own kind of church. He'd grown impatient with words from the churchmen who preached sermons about sin, hell, and damnation. For Tom's money, that wasn't how he saw God. Besides, his faith didn't need a go-between person. He'd deal with God directly. He had plenty of time to tell God what he thought of these most difficult days, days that had no end and no answer.

The sun was melting the last of the snow, and the fields glistened, almost seeming to warm him. He walked back deliberately, veering over by the henhouse, avoiding the barn, still so angry as he thought about what had transpired there. He couldn't reconcile any of it. Loring had tried to talk to him, but there was nothing Loring could say that would help. Tom knew Hugh better than any of them. Hugh had told Tom that he was his special pal. He just couldn't believe he hadn't been able to help him. His Ma had blamed his father and maybe she should have. His father never encouraged Hugh. Anyone could see that. Tom knew how keen Hugh was on cars. "Wave of the future," he'd said. Hugh was smart. Tom knew that.

Tom's anger was ripe. Hugh had been the kindest, smartest, most eloquent man in all of Lima. Even Father Farrell said so. He'd seen Hugh when he made his visits home and always came away with the same compliment. "He's a true gentleman, that one."

After Hugh's death, it galled Tom even more than before to work on the farm with his father, who couldn't see any further than his own fields. Luckily, Tom took the opportunity offered by a neighboring farmer to go with him to Johnson City, near Binghamton, the summer before last for a first job on his own, building silos.

It was the wooden stave silo that was popular these days and Tom was good at constructing them. They were like a large barrel with adjustable steel hoops holding together grooved, vertical staves. Tom had helped out a few farmers in Lima, his carpentry skills, along with his hen house, catching the attention of local farmers. While his father never complimented him, Tom didn't need him to. He'd had Hugh. It was one of their last times together that Hugh had told Tom he could easily find work because he was so skilled. They'd been out on the back forty acres, Hugh reminiscing about the farm.

"Even though I'm not cut out for the farming life," Hugh had said, "it may sound corny, but there's a place in me that is nostalgic for the sounds of the horses snorting and smells of the new-mown hay, the oats when they ripen, the dirt when it's cultivated. I'm even glad for the barn cats."

Tom had listened attentively as they walked toward the creek, a favorite destination. "This is a rough time for someone with your talents, Tom, but I'll tell you now, and you listen well. You're destined for better. "You've got a talent for building. Don't you forget it." Tom's chest ached as he clung to the memory of Hugh's words.

As he came closer to the little green farmhouse, Tom remembered his idea to one day build a porch on the south side of the house. It would give them all a place to sit on a warm evening, away from the noise of the road traffic out front. A garden of peonies could be the scenery. He could see it in his mind's eye. Maybe this spring, he would begin.

Tom had surprised himself since Hugh's death, his ambition completely lacking, and he had little or no interest in anything. Now, finally, he found himself looking ahead. Remembering Hugh's words helped. It also helped that Loring and Peggy had a little girl, Margaret Mary, born just a few weeks ago. The cycle of life?

He laughed as he remembered with fondness the letters his sisters wrote to him while he was away those few months. He hadn't known until he left home that these sisters of his, especially Gene and Veronica, were so fond of him. They looked forward to his return so he could accompany them to the lake. Such gay times they all had at the dance hall on Conesus Lake. Tom met some of his sister's friends, several helping to make the evening's most interesting.

Tom sighed heavily. It all seemed so long ago. He arrived at the house as weary as if he'd worked the whole day. It was barely noon.

Today, because it was Sunday, was the birthday celebration for Veronica. Born on Valentine's Day, her mother had often told Veronica that she had been blessed with a sweetheart. At twenty-six years old, Veronica had already achieved success as a schoolteacher in Pavilion, a town directly west of Lima. She'd been written up in the Perry Herald for her solo, *In the Garden of Tomorrow*, a recently released song composed by George Graff and Jesse L. Deppen. She also directed the Glee Club for the 1926 graduation exercises for the Pavilion Union School District.

While she'd loved her first job in Lima, here in Pavilion, she felt so much more professional. She had a bona fide budget that allotted money for supplies and paid a living wage. The community cared about the staff and school and that made such a difference. Clarence Brooks, the principal, provided professional experiences, conferences and interaction with teachers from other districts and counties. She was eager to learn and happy to be there.

One thing she'd learned early on was to keep proper decorum in this small town; scandal and gossip were too easily propagated. In this time of Prohibition, speakeasies, even the American Hotel in Lima, began serving bootleg liquor on the sly. Spotty enforcement of the law, coded 'word of mouth' details were given for where and how one could procure a drink. Veronica listened and learned, fascinated that bootleg liquor got its name from flasks that had been stowed in the leg of boots.

Women, it seemed, were navigating the times with more and more freedom. Once fashion designer Coco Chanel initiated wearing pants, the way was opened for more fashion flair. The fact that President Coolidge had been re-elected a few years ago during scandals in his administration was a disappointment but not one Veronica allowed to trouble her. She'd watched too many people let politics lead them into the doldrums, unable to change a thing. She was not about to let that be her fate.

As Veronica began her drive home and pulled onto Route 20, her Model-T Ford took the roads easily. She turned out to the right, into the hills of Linwood, mile after mile of rolling terrain covered with melting snow, looking like frosting. It was a thirty- mile ride that she had taken many a time. Today, she felt the heartache of her family begin to creep once again into her soul. It was her birthday and a reason to celebrate, yet sorrow-filled so many of them. With Hugh's death, Tom and Gene, her closest pals, were struggling, as Veronica was, to keep her spirits up. Hopefully, they would all find ways to provide each other some levity, as they had in the past.

She shook her head, her red curls brushing her cheek as if she could shake it all away. She held back the tears, for they no longer helped. Instead, she forced herself to let the words of her recent solo fill her head.

She sang out loud, hoping for relief and inspiration.

In the garden of tomorrow
Will the roses be more fair?
Will we find relief from sorrow,
Will there be more sunshine there?
Ah! For each love flow'r that will blossom,
Some will die and fade away;
Oh! I'd so much rather
All my love flowers gather
From the garden of today.

Maybe she would sing it at the dinner. She'd pretend she was the great opera singer Florence Easton. That might do the trick. She'd also take time to visit Loring and Peggy's new baby girl, whose arrival had been announced in the *Lima Recorder* just this week. Margaret Mary. Such a burst of hope from the garden of today.

Chapter 34
Town Hall Fire

March 1927

The flames licked out the second-story windows, the roof burning now. The crowd stood back as firemen from Honeoye Falls and then Avon were brought in to quell the flames. Avon's pumper was a key to getting the fire under control, the pungent odor hanging in the air.

John stepped forward and quickly back again, away from the intense heat. The whole building, from roof to basement, was engulfed in flames. The fire bell had drawn a sizable crowd from whatever they'd been doing. John had just finished getting a haircut from Ray Bawden, the town barber. Some were lunching at the American Hotel, and several members of the Altar and Rosary Society had been meeting at St. Rose of Lima Church, stopping their work to come watch. It was noon time on March 3rd, a mild, gray day. There is no snow on the frozen ground and none in the forecast.

Last June 6th, a bolt of lightning struck the Presbyterian Church spire and turned the white pine timbers into charred remnants. And now Lima's Town Hall was burning.

John watched the Honeoye Falls firemen arrive, hoses unreeling, eyes alert. They had rendered invaluable aid last June, preventing the spread of the flames to the main building, the spire the only loss. Nine years had already passed since the building that held the Leary Brothers laundry on the floor above the Lima Recorder office was saved by nearby fire departments as well. The neighborliness and resilience were so like that in his memories of his childhood home in Kenagh, Ireland.

He remembered the smell of smoke from the Presbyterian Church fire that seemed to hang in the air ten days later, during the Lima High School commencement. He'd been proud to listen as his own Genevieve, class president, read the class prophecy. She never mentioned the fire, but she captivated the audience with her eloquence. She'd grown into a beauty, that one. Within a few months, she was gone, off to Rochester Business Institute and from there, who could say?

As today's flames were brought under control with verification that no one was harmed, John let out a sigh of relief, grateful for his own good fortunes. While Hugh's death ate away at him frequently in the dark of the night, daylight often found him reveling in the blessing of Jerome, whose quick mind and physical strength made light of so much of the work. He'd begun to realize how much he had underestimated this second son. Even with all he had to do with his young family, Jerome had seen to it that he, Tom and Bernard would handle the major work of haying, turning it into the sport of the day. Cutting and drying were the most boring part, but pitching the dried hay up into the hay loft became its own fun. They competed with laughter and great abandon to see who tossed the biggest amount, Tom frequently the winner.

Never in a million years did John suppose that he would have his own farm or that he would have such a large family. He was proud of them all and, since Hugh's death, had begun to let them know. He'd been rough on poor Hugh. At least Maggie had said so, and he was determined to do better. He was pleased that Jerome thought to include young Donnell when the work wasn't too taxing, and pitching hay became one of his favorite times with his older brothers.

Fur buying also seemed to be quite an interest for his sons. Loring had been back and forth to New York City on fur-buying trips where he'd met his bride, Peg, the mother of darling Margaret Mary. The times were ripe for such a venture, the demand for fur coats increasing with the advent of the motor car. Raccoon coats had become the rage worn by both men and women. John occasionally fancied himself in such a coat, dark brown with a shawl collar and hefty leather buttons but didn't dare go too far in showing favor to any of those fashion "fads," especially related to cars.

Actually, he wouldn't mind wearing one of those coats right now. As the flames were successfully doused, the chill in the air seeped into his bones. At sixty-two years old, he found himself less and less able to take in the cold air, his vigor waning in many respects. Doc Hinman had been straightforward with John about his condition. "You're not the young man you think you are, John. And your heart will get the better of you if you don't slow down."

John had listened and the following Sunday, without letting on there was anything wrong, he announced at dinner his new plan. "To give you young men a chance to get experience for your own farms. If you think farming is for you, I will step down, only giving guidance as required." The boys glanced at each other, suspecting something was afoot. Even thirteen-year-old Don looks around quizzically. No one said a word.

Don had been born a 'runt,' John had told Margaret as he watched this surviving twin develop. He seemed to struggle with even the simplest farm chores. "He can't be left on his own, Maggie, or he'll cause a disaster. Just sawing a board in two for the fence posts seems too much. He knows he's not up to it. He's a sensitive boy. I feared he might cry if I pushed too much."

Maggie had seen the telltale signs of Don's slowness herself, but she would not hear any talk of it. "He'll be just fine. Just you wait and see," she would counter when there was any mention of his inabilities. She continued to spoil him, the older ones often said, but Maggie had no mind to change one bit. She carried his sister in her heart, and she wouldn't ever forsake this little one, not ever.

Betty, nearing sixteen, understood Don. She'd helped with his lessons, rarely showing exasperation as she repeated and repeated her many attempts to teach him his times tables or spelling words.

"You're doing just fine, Donnie. Sister Hermine even said so," Betty would say. She deliberately used tactics of praise, hoping to encourage him. As Maggie watched Betty working with Don, she saw the budding teacher in her and perhaps something more. Only time would tell.

Today, once he had warmed himself upon his return from the fire and had drunk a cup of tea, John asked Don to go with him to check out the hen house. Don scrambled to get his coat; hazel eyes gleaming. As he put on his wool cap, covering his red hair, it was evident that he was eager for this moment with his father. John would tell him about the fire, knowing Don would be enchanted, listening to every detail and imagining it for himself. And that would be just right

Chapter 35
Thanksgiving 1927

Maggie looked up as the outside door to the dining room opened. "Well, hello!" she exclaimed as her heart jumped. The wispy red-haired Margaret Mary, holding on to her mother's hand, toddled her way right over to Maggie and said, "Uppie, uppie." Maggie felt her eyes moisten as she pulled this little one onto her lap. "There you are now with your pretty blue and white dress with your white shoes and socks. A real fashion plate, aren't ye?"

"She's just up from her nap," Peggy said, her kind blue eyes smiling, "and we thought we'd bring her early to see you before she gets ornery."

"Well, it's a fine thing you've done," Maggie said as she kissed the top of her granddaughter's head. She looked down at the tiny girl and continued talking right to her. "Isn't that right now, little lady? You've come to see your grandma and glad she is of it," she said as she hugged the child to her.

Maggie's heart was bursting with joy. This one, with her red hair and blue eyes, just ten months old, brought to mind Maggie's own little sister, Lizzie. Fifty years melted away as she held the little girl, her hair as fair, her eyes as blue.

Occasionally, Maggie pined for her childhood days in Ireland; then along came this child, bringing some of the joy of the old days right back to her.

"She's a bright one, isn't she?" Maggie said to Peggy, who happily replied.

"She's been toddling all over the front room, holding on to the sofa and even petting the kitty. She doesn't seem afraid of anything."

That could be good, and that could be bad, Maggie thought, but she merely nodded and smiled. After raising eleven children, Maggie had a few notions about things, but she kept her thoughts to herself unless asked. Let the young ones find their own way. That's what they want to do anyway, just like babies, all of them exploring and learning. She had always loved the young "I do it" stage, independence blasting forth.

Soon, the house would be full as the families arrived for the Thanksgiving feast. Maggie clucked her tongue as she recalled she had six grandchildren already, and not one of her girls was yet married. There's room for more, she thought.

She knew Loretta, the only one of the Galena girls to have children so far, was thrilled with her two grandchildren, Anna Marie and James. Her husband, John Fennelly, was the manager of the local Country Club and a jewel of a man, they all said. They'd made their home in Harrison, New York, on Coakley Avenue and were as welcoming as could be to her children when they visited the City.

Annie was getting on in years, her health becoming a challenge. Bryan was seeing to her as were her children, skilled seven daughters and a son always available for her care. She knew Annie felt as blessed as Maggie herself did.

It was Maggie's older boys who had started her off with grandbabies: Vic's little girl Ruth, the first and very precious granddaughter, was already eight and her brother Jack, a handsome six-year-old. Harold Francis's death at age 2 from pneumonia was a sorrow they all danced around. The loss of a child never heals completely. Maggie knew that. And that little one had such a light smile that drew you in.

Jerome's two little girls, Cecilia and Marjorie, 3 and 1, were already shining stars and now were joined by Loring's little princess. New life proved to be nature's balm for losses. Thanks be to God.

Maggie shifted little Margaret Mary to her other knee, offsetting the stiffness. It's funny, she thought. After all these children of mine, I can't get enough of their little ones. And always, Baby Rose came to mind. Always.

Maggie set the little one down and stood to hold her hand as she toddled into the front room where the dollies, books and toys were stored. Maggie held out a little stuffed doggie and Margaret Mary reached up for it. The magic of the moment. Peggy was right behind. "She's easily contented," she said, "sometimes."

Maggie smiled, patting Peggy's arm as a way of saying, 'Excuse me,' and made her way out to the kitchen just in time to see Veronica and Gene putting the turkey into the oven. These girls, each with their own lives, starting Veronica in Pavilion and Gene in Rochester, had been lifesavers for her during this past year.

Maggie watched as they patted the bird and ceremoniously closed the oven door. It was a fine bird, one that Jerome had secured for them. He'd been ever-present in his solicitations and help since Hugh's death. He and Rachel and their two little girls managed to visit most Sundays, Jerome often bringing a sumptuous piece of beef or lamb and, this time, a plump Tom turkey.

It would be several hours now before dinner, and the girls seemed to have much of the preparation under control. "Well, you ladies have done a fine job, I'd say," Maggie said as she noted the relish trays with the olives and small pickles all ready to go." Nothing seems to escape your view."

"You taught us well, Mother," Veronica said as she set to peeling the potatoes. Gene had lined up the silverware and plates on the kitchen table and was folding napkins.

"A feast indeed," Maggie said, aware that the girls had been here just last Saturday, coming to town for the anniversary Mass of Hugh's death. At the consecration of the Mass, Maggie wanted to shout out loud to God her anger and sorrow. But she merely wept silently. She had a position to hold, and it wouldn't do to let others see her weeping and wailing. She remembered the keening stories and sounds of her own mother at her losses in Ireland, especially of her first baby, Julia, stillborn. The tale, as she remembered it, was of the haunting sound of the banshee who foreshadowed the child's death.

But this was America. There were no banshees and no keening. One didn't wear one's heart on one's sleeve. She knew her grief. That was the point. It was her grief. She had her living children and grandchildren to think of. That's what Father Farrell had said, and she'd agreed. Her living children were worthy of the best of her.

At fifty-six years old, Maggie felt she had lived a long life. Sorrow was a part of any life and hers was no exception. The beauty of all she had, even with the loss of Hugh, would be her guide. This was her Thanksgiving resolution.

Bernard peeked into the dining room door and then stepped in, bringing with him a basket full of bright red apples, picked and polished to add to the bounty of this day. He hoped a few pies might become a result of this gift since Genevieve was a specialist with crust. He put the basket up on the sideboard, careful not to muss the doily that covered it. He'd been around these women long enough to know that appearances and orders some days were extremely important. He surmised that Thanksgiving Day might just be one of those days.

Bernard was glad for the little ones, who brought so much joy and much-needed relief from the sorrow that lingered. It wasn't right what happened to Hugh, and there were no two ways about it.

Bernard had talked afterward with Jerome, who was so philosophical about it all, his calm demeanor serving as a lifeline. "Only God knows what plagued poor Hugh. It's not ours to understand. We just know how much he loved us, and we loved him," Jerome had said.

Bernard was in awe of this brother, fourteen years older, who was tall and handsome, his sandy blonde/brown hair earning him his nickname. He resembled Hugh yet had a more peaceful demeanor. He was dignified; that was the word Bernard would use.

At age twenty-one, Bernard thought his own life had been going along well, his love of books holding him steady throughout his studies. The completion of his teaching certificate from the Canandaigua Teacher Training Class was a great satisfaction to him.

Glad that Loring had his little Margaret Mary now, Bernard was hopeful he'd be around more often. With thanks to their father John, who started the family on fur trading, Loring and now Jerome were becoming quite the pros.

The fur trade was booming for rural farmers. Not only did they clear fields of pesky intruders on their crops, they developed a side business that was quite successful. Sears and Roebuck, just a few years ago, had begun a mail order service for trappers to send their prepared muskrat, mink, otter, raccoon, fox, badger, beaver, skunk, and opossum pelts to a Sears depot. Sears would grade the pelts and send a check or give credit toward purchases in their catalog.

With so much to learn and his father and older brother to teach him, Bernard had found his own Thanksgiving blessings.

Chapter 36
Jerome

January 31, 1928

As he hoisted his youngest daughter up in the air, Jerome watched her red curls sparkle in the sunshine. Her giggle filled his heart with joy. If only he could freeze these moments. Marjorie would be two this coming March and her sister Cecilia would be four in July. Where did the time go?

Was it almost five years ago he stood with Rachel Sullivan on that early sunlit day in May, the priest blessing their marriage? Rachel, her delicate pink skin, bobbed auburn hair, and no-nonsense ways, had captured him. She was one of nine children, he one of twelve. They understood families and farming. Her mother, an O'Connor and his, a Buckley, Irish ways filling both homes with music and laughter.

They'd married in West Bloomfield, just eleven miles from Lima, where they made their home. He loved the fact that the town was within the historic homeland of the Seneca Nation, and his discovery of arrowheads as he plowed was not uncommon. He felt a tinge of pride that Jesuits were among the first Europeans to visit the area in the seventeenth century, a nod to his Catholic roots.

Lima was settled in 1788, around the same time as West Bloomfield, which was in Ontario County, closer to the City of Canandaigua. It was the town where he'd been born, his parents arriving from New York City that summer. The New York Central Railroad was noted for bringing almost a century of prosperity to the area. The land in West Bloomfield was high and rolling, and he'd heard the town described as "peculiarly pleasant," the soil fertile and well-adapted to raising wheat. Farmers prospered there.

Jerome's first paid work in farming occurred as a hired hand when he was just eighteen, on the Decker Farm on Doran Road. Mrs. Decker, almost eighty, and her son Frank, age fifty-nine, needed additional help. Jane Decker's younger sister Mary lived on the farm, too, and helped with the meals and housework. He'd made good friends with Frank, whom he respected for his know-how. He was learning enough to be a good help to his father as the time neared.

Jerome was just shy of twenty-five when he registered for the draft, glad he never had to go over, his farming trade keeping him stateside. Still, a part of him might have liked the adventure of the travel. Hugh had been crazy for it, talking in his letters about shooting those German square heads. But then Hugh had been crazy for lots of things. Jerome had seen him studying words late into the night, always bettering himself. With a lot of hard work, Hugh finally took on the world with his car dealership. At least he had that before he died. And June would always know he had the soul of a gentleman.

The loss of Hugh was still with Jerome. He couldn't believe that a man as young and strong as Hugh could be brought down so quickly. But today wasn't for those thoughts. Today, Jerome was off with Will Wilson for a new adventure.

Will was a great advocate for fur buying and trading. Since Jerome had sold his farm equipment and become a dealer for high-class meats and vegetables, he continued to raise what he could on his small piece of land, buying from other farmers and making friends throughout the region. It was through such commerce he'd met Will, a fellow just a few years older than he, burly in stature, clean-shaven, fair-haired, with blue-gray eyes.

Will introduced Jerome to the same business Jerome's father had become enamored with and that his brother Loring was getting interested in, especially since travel to New York City was sometimes part of fur trading.

Jerome wasn't interested in that much adventure. His wife and little girls are far more important at this time in his life. He was thirty-six and looking forward to the joy of watching his girls grow into young women. He hoped to give Rachel the status she deserved as a successful man's wife.

Will had talked of spending an afternoon in western Monroe County, where farmers were eager to sell their furs. He assured Jerome that the end of the month when money was sometimes short, was a fine time to make a deal. Many were eager for cash and sold their goods at a great discount. Jerome hadn't traveled much, his work keeping him close to the farms he worked on in Ontario and Livingston counties. Will's talk of the towns of Chili, Gates and Greece had an element of adventure that Jerome hadn't realized he longed for.

Will told Jerome that his light black and gray touring car had been a sound investment. It had brought him safely from West Virginia with his wife Ruth and daughter Mildred to West Main Street in Lima, where they lived. Jerome also knew that Will was a well-respected member of the grange, a solid recommendation of his worth.

Jerome agreed to drive to the American Hotel in Lima to meet Will. He parked his car in the back, joined Will, and they set out on a crisp, though overcast, Monday afternoon, no snow expected. Jerome was glad for his new overcoat with the fur collar. He noted Will had a heavy coat, too, these wintry temperatures testing them both.

The sky was enthralling this afternoon, clouds streaking past like silver-white threads, wisps of blue occasionally peeking through the gray. Jerome was glad he'd accepted Will's invitation and Rachel had been supportive. So many seemed to be profiting these days, trading pelts of all kinds. Jerome had heard Rachel drool over mink stoles, their softness and color causing her to ooh and aah. If he had his way and this new business worked out, he'd see to it that she had one of her very own.

"This winter weather is certainly colder than what I was used to in West Virginia," Will said once they were on their way. "In the daytime, we wouldn't get much colder than thirty-five to forty degrees. Like today. I'm glad we've got some cloud cover to keep us a bit warmer."

Jerome hadn't thought much about the weather these days. There wasn't much you could do about it anyway. But he was glad Will was eager to share his stories.

"My wife Ruth came from the Bacon family. You could guess what we ate for every breakfast. My daughter Millie doesn't even like bacon."

Jerome laughed, enjoying the simple pleasure of companionship.

"My little Marjorie," Jerome said, "thinks I'm a horse. Each time she can, she says, 'Horsey, Daddy, horsey,' and I'm compelled to carry her on my back as I prance around. It's her giggle that keeps me going." He could feel her little hands around his neck as he told the story and basked in Will's laughter.

Their first appointment in Chili found them a quick and decent purchase. Jerome learned that the key to good pelts was the process the trapper used to prepare them for sale. Turning the fur side out for coyotes, fox and bobcats was essential. "They must be turned before becoming too dry and brittle," Will told him. "The flesh gets a glazed appearance and that's key. Then, it's dried at room temperature for four to six hours to make it flexible and soft. Something to watch for."

The men fingered the pelts that were carefully laid on tables. Beaver pelts are the ones Will was after. Jerome watched as Will examined the goods, his expertise reflected in his stance and demeanor, giving Jerome the sense that Will knew what he was doing.

As they arrived at the second appointment, the light of the day was waning. "This one won't take long at all," Will said as he stepped out of the coupe. "This guy's an old customer and decent man. Then one more stop and we'll head home."

"You can tell if they're good by how careful they are," Will said as they headed to the barn. "This guy knows how to skin, flesh and stretch like nobody else. His furs are among the best of any I buy."

The process of skinning, fleshing, stretching, and drying each pelt was common for trappers preparing them for sale. After they purchased three fox pelts, Will and Jerome carefully stored them with the others in the boot of the car with a blanket covering them. Jerome thought he might like the blanket to cover himself, the biting air colder since the sun was down.

"This is the season for these animals. They grow extra fur for warmth, and we get the best of them. Spring furs aren't as plush," Will explained.

Jerome thought of the barn cats he'd grown up with, their fur thicker in the winter. He sure was glad there was no attempt to skin them. His little girls loved the kittens he and Rachel had kept for their small farm. Because the mother cat was most protective of her babies, the little girls knew to be cautious about petting them. "They won't bite you, but you must be gentle," he and Rachel repeated. It was a special time for the kittens and the children.

With one more stop to make, Will and Jerome headed south toward the Statt Road railroad crossing. The idea of home was appealing to Jerome. He'd learned a lot and thought this might be a new venture. He was eager to tell Rachel about it. He thought of his little girls, and a smile crossed his lips.

It was then the locomotive hit them.

Chapter 37
The Day After

February 1, 1928

The paper was delivered early the next day, Wednesday, February 1. The headline read:

Fast train hits Motor Car: Two Men Seriously Injured That was the day Jerome died. And so did Will Wilson.

The paper went to press before their deaths and quoted physicians at the hospital who expressed little hope for Jerome, who had a fractured skull and fractures of both legs. Will was in critical condition as well, with internal injuries and a possible fractured skull. Deputies had been unable to determine which of the men had been driving.

According to witnesses, who were some distance from the scene, the car drove onto the tracks directly in the path of the onrushing freight train.

John folded the paper shut and shivered. He'd gotten to the newspaper before anyone else could read it, fearful of the worst. He could still hear Rachel's sobs on the phone, the young children crying in the background. Her call, telling of the accident, had come in the late evening, Veronica and Gene driving over to be with her. Maggie lit candles and began a rosary, Betty and Don joining in. Tom and Bernard drove to the hospital in Rochester. Nothing John said could stop them.

As the sun came up over the back acreage, a sheen of frost covered the fields. John shook his head and put his hand over his heart. He wasn't sure he could do this. Lose Jerome? His second son and a sometime confidant, as much as he allowed any of his sons to be. Jerome had become the strong one he'd leaned on during rough times. Losing Hugh had been hard enough. He couldn't lose Jerome.

Veronica and Gene had come downstairs from their brief slumber. Last night, they'd both joined in a decade of the Rosary when they came home from Rachel's, reporting that Rachel's mother and sisters had come to stay and the little girls had finally settled down to sleep, but not until Aunt Veronica worked her magic by singing her Sandman song. They hadn't much hope that Rachel would get any sleep.

Bernard and Tom hadn't returned yet, their trip to General Hospital nearly an hour away. No one knew what to do. Maggie was staring straight ahead, her beads moving through her fingers as she rocked in her chair.

"Shall we call Josephine?" Gene asked of no one in particular. "We won't be bothering her 'til we have some news," her mother answered. "She has her own worries as it is."

Josephine was working on the surgical floor now with full responsibility for the staff. She'd risen quickly in the six years since she received her nursing degree, her poise and competence making her an easy choice for promotion.

Loring and Victor hadn't been called either, their young families not needing to be disturbed yet.

As the morning wore on, Veronica and Gene made a simple breakfast, knowing that appetites wouldn't be big, yet some sustenance was needed. Scrambled eggs, sausage and toast were what they settled on, working in unison without much conversation.

It was well after nine when the family heard the tires roll onto the gravel driveway. There was a stillness as they each waited.

John was at the head of the table, Maggie on the other end, and Gene and Veronica on either side. Maggie bowed her head as the two boys entered, afraid for all her life of what they would say. John stood to greet them, then backed away. Bernard's tear-stained cheeks were all he needed to see. Tom nodded towards Maggie and went upstairs.

"They did all they could," Bernard said as he stood in the doorway, his voice cracking with emotion. "The doctors told us it was touch and go for quite a while. If he'd survived, Jerome wouldn't have been able to do much at all. Same for Will. The Police said they never knew what hit them." Then he sank into the chair nearest his mother and bowed his head.

The two youngest, Betty and Don, had to be told. They'd slept late due to the commotion the night before. Gene went to them while Veronica set the table for breakfast. Maggie moved to the front parlor, her beads in her lap, her eyes distant, filled with grief. Soon, they would call Josephine.

Father Farrell knocked gently on the door and peeked in. The family were all gathered at the table, the toast and eggs gone, a few patties of sausage left. Betty opened the door and said, "Do come in, Father. We were hoping you'd be able to come by." Another pot of coffee was put out on the sideboard, a cup ready for the priest.

"I can't imagine it, Maggie. I can't imagine your grief at all," Father Farrell said as he pulled up a chair next to Maggie. John remained at the other end, the others sitting around them. "You wouldn't believe the Lord could do such a cruel thing, and you just wouldn't."

Maggie looked at him, her eyes on fire. "You wouldn't believe it yourself, nor would I," she spat. "He has two small children and a wife whose world revolves around him. No, you wouldn't believe it at all." There was a silence that lay heavy all over the room, no one knowing what to say next.

Finally, Maggie spoke. "And what do we know about Will Wilson's family? He had a wife and a daughter, didn't he? May God be good to them."

Chapter 38
Stardust

February 2, 1928

The funerals for both Jerome and Will were held on the Saturday following the accident. Jerome's service began at nine o'clock from the house and nine-thirty from the church, Father Farrell officiating the burial at St. Rose Cemetery. Will's service was at two in the afternoon, with Reverend G. Palmer of the Presbyterian church officiating, burial at Oak Ridge.

Though she didn't know she had the strength, Maggie, accompanied by her girls, stopped briefly at Will's home before his service. There, she found grief as palpable as her own. In a strange way, it was comforting. Will's wife and daughter, just like her and her girls, were dressed in black and were as inconsolable as Jerome's Rachel and her two little ones.

"I'll say one thing," Maggie proclaimed as they left Will's small house uptown. "These two knew they were loved. That's a certain blessing."

It wasn't usual for Catholics to go to services of other denominations, but then Maggie wasn't usual. For this loss, a sympathy card wouldn't do. She'd come through enough strife over religious differences from her homeland to know that her God was bigger than steeples and altars. She didn't need to speak of it, yet anyone who knew her well was aware of her sentiments.

That evening, the sound of Betty's piano playing filled the small house with strains of Hoagy Carmichael's popular tune Stardust wafting through the early evening hour, the lyrics haunting:

You wander down the lane and far away
Leaving me a song that will not die
Love is now the stardust
Of yesterday
The music of the years
Gone by.

With the meal finished and dishes done, the calm might have been mistaken for peace.

As Betty's playing continued, Veronica began to sing, evoking memories for all of them. Jerome and Rachel's love had been contagious to all surrounded by it, Jerome's joy radiating from him. His little girls were all he spoke about of late. "When there's music on the radio, you should see my little strawberry blonde Cecilia dancing about. I'd say she has real talent." He'd often speak of Rachel as an angel straight from heaven, his arm around her shoulder as he said it. He found his little Marjorie yet another jewel in the fullness of his life. His lavish language of praise was so like that of his brother Hugh.

All too soon, Rachel, draped in black, shivering in the February cold, stood at her young husband's gravesite, her days to be saddled with the grief of loss. All too soon, all too young.

Sometimes I wonder why I spend,
The lonely nights dreaming of a song,
The melody haunts my reverie,
And I am once again with you.
When our love was new,
And each kiss is an inspiration,
But that was long ago,
Now my consolation,
Is the stardust of a song.

Beside a garden wall.
When stars are bright,
You are in my arms.
The nightingale tells his fairy tale,
A paradise where roses bloom,
Though I dream in vain.
In my heart it will remain,
My stardust melody,.
The memory of love's refrain.

Maggie, brought up with music as a constant, jigs, reels and singing a part of every weekend, was consoled to have her own children making music so often. The healing quality of the melody and lyrics proved to be a balm for these difficult days.

The editorial in the evening Rochester Times-Union the day following the deaths quelled any of those who may have thought the men at fault for careless driving:

A Dangerous Crossing
The killing of two more persons at the Statt Road crossing of the Falls branch of the New York Central Railroad, in Gates raises sharply a question as to whether this crossing is sufficiently protected by existing signs and signals. Other fatal accidents have occurred at this point. The fact that it is upgrade on both sides to the crossing adds to the danger, as cars proceeding slowly might stall. Town and county authorities should look into this matter and also call it to the attention of the Public Service Commission.

Lawyers would be involved, that was certain. Both families were young, and this loss could bring destitution if there was no restitution. Loring and Peggy, with their little Margaret Mary, continued to visit, hoping to ease the way as much as they could, advising when asked and listening with compassion. It was what they could do. It was all they could do.

Chapter 39
Christine Grace

March 1928

"She's due any day now. Do you think Ma knows?" Gene asked. "When he told me, I was so stunned, I never thought to ask him. Did you?"

Gene sat at the foot of Veronica's bed in their tiny bedroom. Veronica sat, knees up, her book, Death Comes for the Archbishop, propped open, the powder blue hurricane lamp's upper bulb illuminating the pages.

"How did he ever even tell you?" Veronica asked. Incredulously. "I was sworn to secrecy. I sincerely doubt Mother knows a thing about this."

Gene had just come from a class meeting at Rochester Business Institute, where she served as secretary. As they settled in for a longer chat, the sisters could hear Betty practicing.

"About Tom," Gene asked again. "What do you think? Ma will be devastated. Let's hope she never finds out," Gene said.

Veronica put her book down and looked straight at Gene. "We, dear younger sister, are in a small town. Living in the little burg of Pavillion, where my every move is scrutinized, has taught me that people notice everything. I've learned that even though Lima is bigger, don't trust that Ma won't hear something. We might be better to tell her than let her hear it from some gossip uptown."

Just then, Betty's playing stopped.

Dear Lord, Gene prayed, why did this have to be happening now, on top of everything else? Poor Mother.

Hands thrust deep into his pockets. His collar turned up against the wind, Tom made his way up the highway towards home, his heart full like nothing he'd ever known before. Such tiny fingers and big round eyes, his infant daughter. He wasn't prepared for the feelings collecting inside him, his own self-loathing clouding every step, yet those miniature features, like a baby doll's, chasing away negative thoughts. Her perfection overwhelmed him.

As the wind picked up, so did his pace and anxiety as he neared home. His sisters would want to know. And his mother, too. How could he describe her? The miracle she was.

His thoughts drifted to Lill, whom he'd lost before he ever had her. Lill, whose kindness and compassion had drawn him in. Lill, whose youth and attractiveness had seduced him.

He went back in his mind one hundred times, remembering her loveliness, unlike so many others who only knew him as a clever fellow. She was different. She had listened. She'd heard his confusion, his feelings of loss, as he talked of his hero Hugh, gone now almost six months for no good reason. Tom's loneliness and desperation had overpowered him, his depression holding him in chains.

He couldn't resist her. It was in the depths of his unshakable sorrow that he found comfort with Lill. There in the hayloft behind the dance hall. And it was there, her fair skin and light hair falling around her face, that he hoped he'd brought her joy, for certainly, she had given him more than he'd ever known.

It all seemed so distant now.

He dug his fists deeper into his pockets as he trekked along the highway, cars zooming past. He'd often hitched a ride in cold weather like this, but not today. He had too much to sort out.

Only nine months had passed. His heart needed to harden, the pain of it all too great. He'd married Lill in December but couldn't have her. Her family hadn't wanted that. A young girl, not even eighteen, hitching up with a twenty-three-year-old farmer who lived at home? For what purpose? He didn't know much about love, but he thought of Lill constantly. He could see Lill wasn't in love with him, that sorrow as deep as his other losses. And now they had a daughter.

His little baby girl looked like a Donegan. He couldn't say exactly how he knew. In his memory, he saw his little sister, Baby Rose, who lived only a few days. He remembered her. He was ten years old, and he remembered. That's why this baby, pink and fair and pudgy, was such a gift.

He'd been very willing to marry Lillian, knowing that giving the child his name was important. Never should she be subjected to derision. She'd always known who her father was. He'd dressed in the same suit that he'd worn to Hugh's funeral. He would step up and be the man he'd always intended to be now he was to be a father.

He'd met Lillian's father, John Ward, and his common law wife, Pearl Washburn, who'd lived with him since Lill's mother, Grace Conlin Ward had died, the Spanish flu nearly killing them all. Lillian, her older sister Madeline, and two younger brothers, John and Gordon, left motherless, were all now grateful for Pearl.

Lill's father told Tom that Lillian was not to be tied to him in any way except by the marriage certificate. Tom felt defeated and ashamed. He was longing for this girl, not yet eighteen, and it wasn't to be.

They were in the vestibule of the small white church on Route 5 and 20 in Bloomfield, where he waited with Lillian while Reverend Ralph Shurgur, minister of the Gospel in Holcomb, spoke privately to John Ward and Pearl Washburn, who were witnesses to their marriage.

It was then that Lillian spoke to Tom quickly and quietly. "My father doesn't blame you for anything," she said, her small face close to his, her blue eyes staring up at him. "He's actually thrilled about the baby but doesn't want me to end up as a farmer's wife." She paused and looked away. Tom stood spellbound.

"You know I don't blame you either," Lill added. "I told my father our baby would carry your name and he didn't object. She'll always know who she is and that her father loved her."

He wanted to reach out and hold her, but he didn't. Guilt, shame, and remorse were all he could feel.

As the days awaiting the infant's birth staggered past, with only a month until he would meet his child, his life tumbled upside down. His second brother was struck down.

Jerome's death crashed down on them all. To Tom, it was another senseless loss. He felt anger he didn't know he had. He longed to see Lillian, to tell her, to feel her compassion. He couldn't get to her. Pearl, smiling sympathetically, said no to his request when she answered the door. Her family had made that clear.

In the weeks following Jerome's death, Tom accompanied Bernard on visits to Rachel, taking turns tending to farm chores, milking and feeding the animals. He watched as she hugged her little girls to her, tears pooling in her eyes as Jerome's car sat empty in the yard, something she didn't even know how to drive. The strength of women staggered Tom, who couldn't fathom how they carried on. Rachel, June, and his mother, all carrying loss as deftly as a precious stone, the weight somehow holding them steady.

As the wind whipped up a bit, he was glad to be cresting the small knoll of the road that put him within view of his house, the home he'd lived in since he was seven. Its small front door was painted white, handsome against the forest green shingles. He knew when he arrived, he would find his family around the dinner table. He sighed as he anticipated the inquisition about the baby. His mother had already handled telling his father about Tom's child, that there had been a marriage to assure the child a name. "No shame will be visited upon the child," she had told Tom.

Tom sighed deeply, seeing again his daughter's perfection. He was certain about one thing he was proud to tell them. His daughter was Christine Grace Donegan, the Grace after Lill's mother.

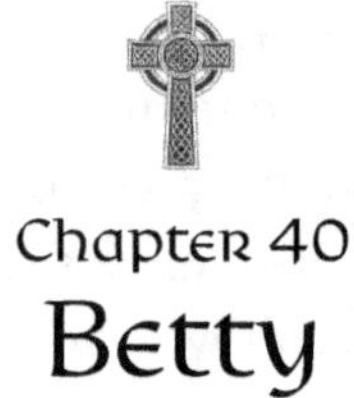

Chapter 40
Betty

August 1929

Betty carefully lifted the statue of the Virgin Mary out of the little wooden shrine in the dining room. The blue interior hadn't faded a bit, protected as it was by the three-pointed arch that covered the structure. She stood the fourteen-inch statue on the dining room table and took a damp cloth to wipe down the statue. She giggled at her devilish thought of painting the Lady's toenails in the fashion of the day. She noted the bare feet of the Lady standing on a globe of the world, a serpent being crushed beneath. Her fourth-grade teacher, Sister Hermine, called this statue of the Blessed Mother, Our Lady of Grace, reading the verse from Genesis:

"And I will put enmity between you and the woman and between your offspring and hers; he will crush your head, and you will strike his heel."

It didn't make total sense to her, but Sister Hermine explained that it was the crushing heel on the serpent that signified the end of sin. That was enough for Betty. She knew that the Madonna's sorrow was great, enduring the loss of her only son. Was there a lesson to learn from the statue?

Betty knew her family's losses and prayed regularly for them all. She'd been just three when Baby Rose had died. Betty remained the youngest girl, a place of importance she was often reminded of by her three older sisters. They taunted her about being spoiled, but Betty knew differently.

The loss of both Hugh and Jerome, who had become heroes to them all, followed so soon by the death of two-year-old Marjorie, had been too much. The newspaper article told the tragic story.

Three weeks ago, after she choked on a peanut and forced it into her lung as she gasped for breath, the 2-year-old daughter of Mrs. Rachael Donegan, of West Bloomfield died yesterday morning in Strong Memorial Hospital of pneumonia. According to the family physician, the baby accidentally found some peanuts Easter Sunday. The mother smartly slapped the infant on the back, after the child choked, and recovered several pieces of peanut and believed none was left in the girl's respiratory system. A number of days later the child appeared ill and a physician was summoned.

The mother did not at once recall the peanut incident, and it was not until last Tuesday that the accident was mentioned to the physician. He took the child to the hospital here immediately for an X-ray of her lungs.

It was discovered, according to the physician, the particle of peanut had reached the child's lung and caused an abscess. It later resulted in pneumonia of which the child died.

The funeral service with the tiny coffin was so painful, so reminiscent.

A year later, Vic and Margaret's seven-year-old boy, Jack, became violently ill with a sore throat and a fever so intense he was sometimes delirious. Splitting headaches, frequent vomiting and a red rash on his face with a 'strawberry' tongue were all symptoms that he was one of the victims of the horrible Scarlet Fever, with no known cure. Frustration mixed with sorrow filled them. His two-year-old brother, Harold, had died four years earlier of pneumonia and with Jack's loss, consolation was difficult to find.

While at her high school graduation, Betty received a floral bouquet from the mother of her favorite flower, wild roses. She loved the song, *My Wild Irish Rose*, as it seemed so fitting to her memory of her little sister, Rose. "My wild Irish Rose, the dearest flower that grows..."

As the years passed, Betty had learned not to speak of Baby Rose, recalling how Gene or Veronica would hush her if she mentioned the baby. "Don't upset Mother," they directed.

When it came time to get her Lima High School class ring, Betty switched her own middle initial, "A," which stood for Adona, and used the letter "R" for Baby Rose. "E R D," it read. Though she couldn't speak of her, she'd not ever forget her.

Betty tucked the Lady back into the Shrine, her reverie for the moment completed. She stepped into the yard, gazing at the fields behind the house. The golden grain of August could be seen for miles, the smell of the sweet grass perfuming the freshly mown hay. It seemed just a short time since crocuses and primroses had pushed through the recently frozen dirt. She sighed, rejoicing in how wondrous new life felt, her own just beginning.

In April, at the end of their class trip to Washington, she and her classmate, Loretta O'Connell, had been granted permission to slip away for a side trip to New York City to be with her sister, Josephine, a thrill indeed. They stayed for several days and were able to see Shakespeare's The Merchant of Venice at the Broadhurst Theatre on 44th Street.

In May, Betty sang a solo in the Lima High School concert and had a part in the class play, a comedy titled The Bride Breezes In. Their class picnic in early June was followed by another solo she sang for the 7th District American Legion at the Town Hall. As if all this weren't enough, at her high school graduation, besides singing the solo, she was the Class Valedictorian.

The August 22nd *Lima Recorder* summed it all up for her:

Elizabeth Donegan, secretary of the Class of 1929 of Lima High School, will attend Nazareth College in Rochester this coming year.

She could hardly wait. As she cut out the article to add to other clippings, she laughed out loud when she came across the August 8th clipping already in place.

The PINCO (Porcelain Insulator Company) picnic, well enjoyed by so many, announced the winners of the boys' pie-eating contest. The second prize went to Donnell Donegan.

Good for him, Betty thought. At age fifteen, her youngest brother was being recognized for something that brought a smile.

Chapter 41
Donnell

June 1930

Fifteen-year-old Donnell hitched Jenny up to the hay wagon and drove down to the lower part of their twenty-seven-acre field. He hoped to scoop up some of the haystacks before the skies opened. He'd noticed the clouds mounting in the sky and the couplet his father had taught him came to mind: When clouds appear like rocks and towers, the Earth's refreshed by frequent showers.

As he and Jenny neared the stream, Donnell's shoulders relaxed. He ran his hand through his auburn hair and let his green eyes soften as he listened to the sound of the running water gurgling over the rocks. His memories of summers past, swinging on the rope across Honeoye Creek with his brothers Bernard and Tom filled him with joy. Their kindness touched him. They included him when they could with gentleness, encouraging him to hang on tight. Bernard was already twenty-four and Tom almost twenty-six, yet occasionally, they still took time to play out on the creek with him as they had in their younger days. Donnell treasured the memory of a special time when Bernard gave him a ride, swinging him over the center of the rushing water below. It had felt good to have Bernard's arms helping him hold on.

John wasn't up to such 'tom foolery' these days. Their father had slowed down, the boys had said. "He's not up to much, that's for sure," he'd heard Bernard say to Tom. "He's usually spent by the afternoon." His father's naps in the front bedroom in the late afternoon were a telling sign.

Donnell knew his father missed Jerome, though he never heard him speak of him out loud. As he worked side by side with him in the fields, loading the hay wagon or pitching hay into the loft, he could somehow feel his father's sorrow. He watched him as he moved heavily, speaking less and staring off into the distance more often.

Donnell missed Jerome, too, more than he missed Hugh. He was so young when Hugh struck out on his own, only five when Hugh went off to war. But Jerome had stayed home and had been a pal, seeking Donnell out when he drove the hay wagon, teaching him how to pitch hay so it ended up where you intended. He showed him how to handle the pitchfork so he wouldn't hurt himself or anyone else.

Being the surviving twin, Donnell had heard about Rose and who she might have become. He sometimes felt overlooked and even a little guilty for surviving. Thankfully, his mother's extra time and attention helped him to feel more confident. He was slower in his school lessons than his older sister Betty, that was for sure, and he wasn't as quick as he suspected little Rose might have been, judging from all the promises she represented, but he was certain he wasn't dumb.

When the right time came this past week, and Donnell showed his father what he could do with the radios that he had been collecting, he felt a glimmer of real pride. His father's interest felt genuine as he listened, his eyes widening as Don explained the circuitry he'd created and demonstrated the wide range of stations he was able to tune in.

"Well, our youngest may yet be our best," John had announced one night around the dinner table where Bernard, Tom, Veronica, Gene, and Betty were gathered. "Wait until you see the elaborate systems Don has concocted out in the barn. It's a real haven of wires and bulbs, with stations all the way from Canada."

Donnell felt his face flush as he listened to his father tell of his accomplishments. Unlike the others, he'd never had any accolades about his schoolwork discussed at the dinner table. If it were up to him, he wouldn't bother with school at all. Reading was hard and nothing else he was taught seemed very interesting. If there'd been a machine shop, that's where he would shine.

In one of his prouder moments, Donnell followed up on an advertisement he'd heard about on an important new show. With his direction, the family had gathered around their new Philco burled wood console radio that had been a family Christmas gift from Josephine and Veronica, the two money-makers in the family. He was pleased to invite them all to listen to the first episode of The Shadow, the Detective Story Hour, that started with the ominous voice saying, "Who knows what evil lurks in the hearts of men. The Shadow knows!" They loved it.

With his new-found acclaim, Donnell felt that his time spent in the barn was finally seen as a legitimate activity. Now he could listen, mostly undisturbed, to music of the era without feeling guilty that he wasn't spending all his free time with books. Paul Whiteman and Fletcher Henderson had become his two favorite band leaders.

The American Hotel in town featured some of this same music, yet Donnell knew he was still too young to go up to the speakeasy there. He was delighted when Veronica and Gene occasionally visited him in the barn to hear some of the music that was popular and being played in Canada. They would practice jazz dancing around the barn, laughing and causing Donnell to laugh out loud, too. He wasn't surprised when Betty didn't join them, her sights set on something a bit more devotional than jazz.

One of his favorite songs was one he'd learned by heart. It conveyed so much of what he felt about his own mother, his chum.

That Old Irish Mother of Mine.
In her eyes there's the blue of Killarney
On her cheeks the rose of Kildare
On her lips just a bit of blarney
and the rose of Kildare in her hair
She was cradled and born
on St. Patrick's morn
with a smile on her face so sublime
She's as sweet as the day
She stole Dad's heart away
That old Irish Mother of mine

His mother had been there when no one else understood, kind and thoughtful, treating him so gently, never once asking him to do more than he wanted. When Betty had pushed him to do his lessons, he could be sure she would defend him. "He's had a rough day today. Let him rest now," she'd say ever so gently. "There's time enough tomorrow." His mother was his protector and champion. He had no ambition for any other life.

Don struggled in his own way with the loss of Rose, his mother telling him of her beauty and her rose complexion, "as sweet as any flower you've ever seen." He knew the others had struggled with her loss, too, yet he knew Rose had been closest to him. And that was the truth. It was his truth.

Chapter 42
Faith, Love, and Loss

Autumn 1930

Maggie settled into her rocking chair in the front parlor, her hot cup of tea just off the boil on the nearby small mahogany table, a biscuit tucked on the saucer. The cup and saucer were a gift from Josephine, their green shamrock pattern on the delicate porcelain with their identifying black marks of Fermanagh and Belleek.

She picked up the first of the pile of newspapers she intended to catch up with, the Canandaigua Daily Messenger. She was particularly happy when she came across items about Jerome's Cecilia, a promising young one. She was all of six years now and was just last week mentioned for her role in a school play. She was a grand girl for performing Maggie thought.

At one time, Maggie was certain she would never recover from Baby Rose's death. Now, she was recovering from additional sorrows she never thought possible. Yet, as she sipped her tea, she felt a peace come from deep within. She couldn't say how it was, yet she was able to go on. Sitting with a cup of tea on a lovely autumn day had its joys and never did she take them for granted.

As she perused the paper, she was glad to see a familiar name: young Joseph O'Connell, who was off to St. Bernard's Seminary, a favorite among so many of the young people. Betty's name appeared as one who would be returning as a student at

Nazareth College. She and Joe were thick as thieves. She often wondered about their friendship and if there was anything more to it. Time will tell.

As she turned to the business page, she thought about Genevieve, who was certainly handling her life admirably. Once she'd finished her schooling at Rochester Business Institute, it didn't take her much time at all to find a job and an apartment. Following the trends of the day, she found work as a secretary in the Lewis General Tire family business on East Avenue. With her classmate and friend, Dorothy Dunn, she rented ideal housing in the sophisticated Third Ward located on the banks of the Genesee River, an area sometimes called 'the ruffled shirt district.' Within just a year, they had scraped together enough money to buy a used Model-T. That carried Genevieve to work after she dropped Dorothy at her job.

Maggie enjoyed seeing Genevieve so proud as she came to Sunday dinner with Dorothy and the new car. This past August, Genevieve had been a bridesmaid at Dorothy's wedding, her peach-colored taffeta dress with hat and shoes to match, a stunning look. She and the other bridesmaid also carried peach-colored gladiolas and thankfully, Father Farrell didn't quell her excitement despite church prohibition of Catholics participating in Protestant weddings. These two friends didn't intend to convert to each other's religion. They were simply celebrating love together. Maggie was glad Father Farrell understood that.

Religious rules that prevented love were something that Maggie could never comprehend. She was devout; there was no doubt about that, but she was level-headed about it. John didn't interfere much in her raising the children to believe. He'd been raised in the Church, but like so many men, he didn't darken the doorway very often. Weddings, funerals and high holy days were the extent of his presence, along with his adherence to the sacraments and his celebrations of Baptisms, First Communions and Confirmations. Maggie wouldn't ask much more of him.

As a child in Ireland, Maggie's faith was nurtured by priests who talked of love. She'd learned to say her Rosary there, which, to this day, brought comfort. And she cherished her memory of the one-time visit they had with Father John J. Riordan, the cousin who was the head of the Mission of Our Lady of the Rosary for the Protection of Irish Immigrant Girls in New York City. The fact that there was a Mission with a relative in charge was one of the reasons Maggie's father consented to her emigration. He'd been dead set against losing another daughter to America, Mary having broken his heart three years before Maggie proposed to go. It was Father Riordan's visit to Ireland and reassurance of the protection provided to Irish Immigrant girls that softened him. Charlotte Grace O'Brien, the daughter of William Smith O'Brien, one of Maggie's father's heroes, was the guiding force responsible for the 1848 rebellion that helped move toward an independent Ireland. With passion, Father John Riordan, a cousin on her mother's side, spoke of the Mission's goals to give information and counseling to the young immigrants, an immigrants' chapel and a temporary boarding house where immigrants could be safely sheltered while in transit or while waiting for work.

Maggie had dreamt of the day when she would arrive and be sheltered so safely. And she remembered her tears when word came that Father Riordan had died before she even got to emigrate.

This disappointment, while not her first, had stayed with her. Her eventual arrival and the welcoming arms of her older sister, Mary, became her new memory.

When Father Farrell had asked her about her emigration experience, she had shared the story of Father Riordan, his good work and his untimely death. He'd known of him, and this familiarity brought Maggie a degree of comfort and confidence in him. Gratefully, it was Father Farrell who settled the question when it arose about whether Hugh's burial could be in Catholic consecrated ground due to the manner of death. Father Farrell hadn't hesitated, defaulting to love, not rules.

Friendships with priests, while keeping reverence intact, was something Maggie had grown up with. Visits for heartrending deaths were coupled with celebrations of birth and marriage. The comfort of it all was beyond words for Maggie and for John as well.

John had suffered these last few years more than she could have imagined. Other losses he'd never spoken of surfaced as he struggled to deal with the loss of his two oldest boys. His gruff edges were gone and replaced by a quietness that might have bordered on depression. Loring's growing family brought some consolation; two-year-old Bobby and the spring birth of baby Jack kept Sunday dinners full of antics, the two red-haired boys adding much to the mix. That they lived just down the street made it easier for everyone. Peggy made frequent stops to visit when she could with a sweet treat or an extra handful of fresh vegetables. John seemed appreciative.

John's stamina was becoming of concern to them all. Maggie knew that talking to him about it would be of no help. Her chats with Doc Kober gave little solace. Each time Maggie found an opening, whether after church or on a visit to him with one of the children, he said little.

"His color isn't as good as it might be, would you say?" she'd said gingerly enough. But Doc Kober just brushed off the concern, saying, "There's no need for alarm. He's just slowing down. And he deserves now to rest a bit." Maggie knew John and sensed there was something more. Grief can't kill you, but sometimes you might wish it would.

John's sister Annie told stories of their early years in Ireland. One always stayed with her. Their brother Mike was too young to remember, but it had stayed with Annie, and she was certain with John.

Their mother, Bridget, had been out in the field digging potatoes for a farmer in Kenagh, where they had a small cottage with a main keeping room and one sleeping room. The newest babies, twins, were snuggled in a cradle by the hearth. Annie and John had been put in charge of watching over them. It was never clear what actually happened, but when their mother came back, the twins were gone. Gone to heaven. In their sleep. Annie remembered the horror as if it were yesterday. John never spoke of it.

John never spoke of any of their losses either, Maggie knowing there was no consoling him. Rather, she continued to lie by his side in their bed, holding him when she could, grateful for all the world she'd found such a good man those many years ago, on the streets of New York.

Chapter 43
John's Birthday

Autumn 1930

"A surprise party?" Maggie asked. "We'll be the ones surprised if his heart doesn't take the shock of it," Betty's plans for John's upcoming birthday cause a stir.

"Well, we could tell him we're having a birthday dinner for him, just not tell him that everyone is coming. How would that be?" Betty asked, not quite knowing how to carry out the ideas she'd been asked to implement by Josephine, Veronica, and Gene. Easy for them, she thought, to have all these highfalutin' ideas and be off in New York City, Pavilion and Rochester, leaving me to do all the arranging and convincing.

As she folded the dish towel and headed for her chair to put her feet up, Maggie saw the consternation on Betty's face.

Dinner was over, the dishes were done, and the light of the day was already fading. "Don't trouble yourself. When the time comes closer, it'll all work out. It always does," Maggie said.

Betty didn't take much solace from her mother's counsel. She wasn't the one listening to her older sisters talk up the idea of a special birthday party for their father, who would turn sixty-five, the bona fide retirement age suggested by Social Security, though John was vehement that he had no intention of retiring. The fact that he'd been slowing down for several months, however, did lend a sense of urgency to celebrating him, his heart trouble an unspoken worry.

"He's not one for a party," Betty had said to Josephine when she was home visiting, but Josephine dismissed her worry.

"He'll be glad of it once it happens," she had said.

It had been a rough time at home. The loss of her brothers over these past years took its toll on all of them. Betty's studies were her saving grace. She traveled daily to Augustine Street in Rochester for her college classes, thoroughly enjoying them and wishing she could spend more time learning all there was to learn at Nazareth College. She was glad to be lifted from the weight of sorrow, entering a new world of wonder and wisdom and even some wit. She'd met classmates from other parts of the country who shared stories of travel. Mary Grace Wilson's father, who was a Navy Captain, had moved his family to Rochester to be a part of Kodak's program to provide supplies of cellulose acetate for coating airplane wings and producing unbreakable lenses for gas masks.

Mary Grace provided Betty with a much-needed diversion, talking continuously about boys and encouraging Betty to join in the school dances. Betty drove the old Model-T that Hugh had driven home on what turned out to be his last trip. Ironically, his wife June couldn't use the car since she didn't drive. Vic fixed the car up and before Bernard got his own car, it became the family car. Betty was pleased to be able to get back and forth to Rochester on her own, take her mother shopping and go to church when she could.

Betty knew that troubles had beset farmers in the wake of what was now called the Great Depression. She also knew that while the mortgage on the farm had been paid, there was little extra money for anything else. Bernard was helping out on the farm and Loring, Veronica, Gene and even Josephine occasionally helped with some bill paying whenever Bernard alerted them to the need. Luckily, food and shelter were more than adequate.

Thanks to Bernard and Donnell's help, the harvest this year had been successful and, while it was smaller than they hoped, there was enough grain, oats, and corn to keep them going.

Eggs, while selling for half what they did the year before, were continuing in plenty. Betty and Donnell shared the task of checking the hen house in the morning and early evening. They knew to slip the eggs out and keep out of the way of the mother hen who might peck at them, the little ramp Tom had designed making it safer and easier.

Bernard became key to their stability, keeping the farm going, his dream of teaching slipping away. Being at home to help had become a priority, Donnell the only other help available. Tom was off in Buffalo with a prosperous carpentry job and Veronica's new teaching position in Niagara Falls kept her away for weeks at a time. Gene had found a new job in Rochester, secretary to Miss Ailers, the head of nursing at Strong Memorial Hospital. Her new apartment on Fairview Avenue, close to the hospital, was an almost new 1924 two-family house, a fine place to host friends, her social life burgeoning.

John's birthday was on Friday, October 10th and it was coming quickly. Betty had alerted Vic and Loring about the planned celebration, providing enough time to get their children's schedules set. Veronica notified Tom in Buffalo, and Gene was in touch with Josephine. John was none the wiser about this family dinner in his honor. Maggie had been right. Things did fall into place nicely.

Betty, Bernard, and Donnell had joined John and Maggie for an ordinary Friday night meal, with no hint of anything special on Saturday. Since Josephine had the farthest to come, they planned an early dinner on Saturday. All afternoon, those from away arrived. Vic, Margaret and their two children; Loring, Peggy and their three children, their youngest only seven months old; Tom, Veronica, Gene and Josephine all joined Bernard, Betty and Don at the family home. Throughout it all, John's heart was fine.

"Well, a fella has to get pretty old to have all this fuss made about him," John said as they sat at the table. He seemed pleased with the gathering. However, saying little, his peaceful smile satisfied them all.

The meal was one of his favorites: roast lamb, mashed potato and peas. Maggie took charge of the potatoes. John had often said that no one could make them like she did. The gravy was seasoned perfectly, butter making a well in the middle of the potatoes. John felt the joy of home, a meal attended by them all.

As the meal ended and the table was cleared as if on cue, there was a knock at the door. There stood Rachel, Jerome's widow, and their surviving child, six-year-old Cecilia, ready to add to the festivities that were about to begin. Josephine invited everyone to join in by the piano for a special treat. In no time, Betty and Veronica, accompanied by Josephine, were singing the treasured favorite, Danny Boy, easily reaching the broad range of haunting notes. The song, whose words were written by Fred Weatherly, an Englishman, had become Ireland's unofficial national anthem.

Then, as if on cue, Vic's eleven-year-old Ruth, along with Tom, gathered up the children, and they all danced a jig while Tom whistled the accompaniment and the three littlest ones jumped up and down for all they were worth to the joy and laughter of everyone present. With a glance at John, Maggie stood and nodded to Josephine, who played The Irish Washerwoman jig. Maggie sang out to the little ones as she danced, "And a heel and a toe, and a heel and a toe." Laughter, joy, and applause filled the room for the second time.

Soon, Veronica and Gene carried in the cake. Candles ablaze. Piano notes led them as they all joined in singing Happy Birthday. Squeals of delight reached around them like a hug and John, misty-eyed, blew out the candles.

The cake was ceremoniously carried back to the dinner table, plates and forks ready. As they ate the chocolate-frosted yellow cake, John's favorite, a lightness of spirit filled the room, a spirit that had been missing for a time. Children's voices rang out with abandon.

Soon enough, the little ones were being bundled up to go out into the crisp October evening, blowing kisses and saying their goodbyes. Finally, John excused himself and headed out to the barn, first stopping by the hen house, Tom's fine little building.

He remembered helping him with the dimensions and being so impressed with his son's skills. Tom could eyeball a board and know within a fraction of an inch where to make the cut. John taught him the adage, "measure twice and cut once," though Tom didn't appear to need such advice, precise since he was a young lad.

How he wished Tom hadn't gotten himself into such a predicament with that young girl, Lillian. A baby, too precious to let go of, a family not willing to let Tom get too close. He'd given the only advice he knew to give, to always support the child as best he could. The new job Tom landed in Buffalo would help for certain, but he missed Tom's help at home. Thank Heavens for Bernard, who remained vexed as could be at Tom for his irresponsible ways. "He should have known better," was all he would say as he added Tom's chores to his own. He never made further comments.

Bernard's skills were broader than Tom's. Book learning is one of his specialties. He read voraciously, his academic work at Canandaigua Academy something to be proud of. He was almost as popular as his outgoing sisters, who were always putting on a gathering of some sort, like the one they set up for John this afternoon, every single one of them showing up. It was really something. His whole crowd, the brood, as Maggie called them, all together to celebrate him. He wasn't one to be too emotional, but when he looked around and saw them all as they sang Happy Birthday, the littlest ones clapping, he choked up.

John clucked at the hens a bit, satisfied they were settled for the night. He moved on to the garage, where all kinds of gadgets and gear for the tractor and car were stored. He still preferred the pony and trap he'd grown up with to those horseless carriages that were cluttering up the roads. Hugh had become so enamored with them, with Vic making a living as a chauffeur. Imagine.

The cluster of radio wires and setup that Don had configured made him smile. That youngest boy had some talents, just not schoolhouse ones. He thought of his own schooling, not quite as available in Ireland then as it was here in the States. He and his brother Mike had finished up to sixth grade, quite a feat at the time. He pushed past the tractor and looked up the staircase at the end of the building. He could only imagine what had accumulated up there over the years. They'd bought this farm in 1913, seventeen years of labor, advances and antiques all stored somewhere. As he left to go to the barn, he moved past the Model T Ford that Betty was using to go into Rochester each day. He worried about her, especially in the winter months, but there was no stopping young people when they had a mind to do something. And there was no shortage of more young people coming along.

Just this past March 19th, Loring and Peggy's newest baby boy, John Joseph Donegan, joined the family, his name a tribute to his grandfather and St. Joseph, on whose feast day he was born. Their other red-haired baby boy, Robert Francis, had been born the July after Jerome's death, new life refreshing them all. The birth of Vic and Margaret's newest son, William Alfred, that same November also helped soothe their losses. Folks don't get over those kinds of losses, John thought, but they do go on.

What is there, John wondered, as he slid open the barn door, that helps folks heal after loss, if they heal at all? He gazed up at the chestnut beam from which Hugh had hanged himself and reached in his pocket for the words of Abraham Lincoln that Josephine had brought home to them on a card from Lenox Hill Hospital, where staff members were so often called upon to give solace to families:

You cannot now believe that you will ever feel better. But this is not true. You are sure to be happy again. Knowing this, truly believing it, will make you less miserable now. I have had enough experience to make this statement.

John was grateful for the sentiment, Lincoln's loss of two young sons giving him credibility to make the statement. John felt the loss of his own two sons keenly. Young men full of promise and potential were still with him.

He wasn't sure he'd ever recover from Hugh's death. Any glimmer of joy was dashed when Jerome was killed in the train car crash less than two years later. Amazingly, strength came from somewhere as bundles of new life joined the family. The birth of Tom's little girl a few years ago, Christine Grace, might have brought more joy, except for the shame that kept the families apart. Still, Tom's marriage to Lillian counted for something that was certain.

John slid the barn door closed and headed back to the house. He could hear the music and laughter spilling out.

Was it only six months after Jerome's death that his dear sister Annie had died? His Annie, who'd brought such love into the world, her family a part of his. Annie, who had meant the world to him. Yes, indeed, the years had passed and as he recalled the joy of this 65th birthday gathering, John knew that Lincoln was right.

Chapter 44
Farewells

May 1931

Within two months of John's October birthday party, in early December of 1930, the family all assembled again, this time to bury their father. John's death came after a month of bed rest for congestive heart failure. They'd been prepared but not ready. When Betty sang her solo of *Danny Boy*, her voice faltered ever so slightly. She'd performed in high school and at Nazareth, yet always felt nervous, only consoled when Veronica told her she often had similar emotions when she performed.

The collective grief of John's children, like immovable boulders, found them all searching for new ways to be with one another, the silent oarsman who steered them now gone. He'd often said his blessings far outweighed his sorrows, which had been plenty, a fact they held onto.

The funeral Mass, said by Father Farrell, whose friendship and guidance had been valued throughout these many years at St. Rose of Lima, was simple. Flowers filled the altar, and friends and family sent their love and blessings. Roses accompanied by winter greens were sent by the Ted and Ann Doran family, special friends for so many years, who sat front and center across the aisle. Other friends gathered for rows and rows, overwhelming the whole family with the presence of love.

Her girls surrounded Maggie with solicitous love and support, guiding her to her seat in the front row on the right side of the church, where she sat with tear-stained cheeks, memories of John flooding her, from that handsome man in Manhattan to the gentle father of their children, to the quiet man who listened. She would miss every facet of him.

As the casket was carried down the main aisle, Ted Doran, in the lead, was accompanied by John Flanagan, Matt Dalton, John Byrnes, and Marty Cummings. The wake had been the night before in their front parlor, as it was for Baby Rose and both of their sons. In the tradition of their homeland, songs were sung, stories told, and spirits shared. The most memorable moment of the evening was given over to Father Farrell, who spoke of John's quiet humor and captured the traits that his sons were demonstrating now.

"He wasn't what you'd call a church-going man now, but he had a faith as deep as any of us," Father had said. "I was new to the parish, testing the waters a bit, and of a Sunday, I said to him, 'John, I haven't seen you at Mass lately.' He looked at me with that look you all know so well and said, without a pause, 'Funny, Father, I haven't seen you either.'

The next day, in his funeral homily, Father Farrell added, "He was a man of few words. Everyone he spoke counted."

That was John Donegan. Not saying much, just enough. *The Lima Recorder* called him a "well-known nature lover and trapper." It acknowledged his well-established business in raw furs, which was now operated by his sons. "He worked in New York City for several years and was married there in 1890 to Margaret Buckley."

John's death created a space in their world that wasn't to be filled easily. As the coldness of the season settled upon them, the family looked for warmth and comfort from each other. Though the winter roads didn't easily allow travel, phone calls and letters were exchanged that were tender and timely. The Christmas holiday found them reaching out to one another and watching out for Maggie. Each took turns visiting, bringing news of the day along with a sweet treat, one of Maggie's favorites - a Hershey's 5th Avenue candy bar of chocolate-covered peanuts, which reminded her of New York City.

Carrying on without John was what they had to do and what they did. Bernard saw to the farm, taking over his father's role of coordinating things. He was grateful for Loring's help and advice. Their business of fur buying was growing, their farms providing food for the family and access to beaver, raccoon, muskrat, and sometimes even fox pelts. Clearing the land of these animals, who were often destructive to the crops, also provided needed additional income. Loring's young family was his focus, his wife now pregnant with their fourth child.

Donnell, for the most part, remained a faithful worker, which pleased Bernard greatly. He'd always admired the youngest of the family, the surviving twin saddled with a slighter and smaller physique than his older brothers. While Bernard watched Donnell, now sixteen, pull his weight, hefting bales of hay heavy enough for two men, he feared for his thinking himself a man as he began to snitch the drink. He hid it well enough for now.

Meanwhile, Betty startled Maggie with a decision she'd made. As they sat doing their tatting work, a skill brought from Ireland, Betty followed along the intricate knotwork as her mother had taught her. The Presentation Sisters in coastal Youghal, just east of Cork, taught the refined skill to those in need to help them support themselves in the aftermath of the famine. Maggie found the new craft addicting, her new skill producing attractive and delicate pieces to sell at the weekly market. As they sat with their shuttles and fine thread, Maggie raised her voice.

"You've applied and have been accepted? To become a Sister of St. Joseph? Is that what I'm to understand? And you have decided this is what you want?" Maggie stood up and went to the window.

She turned, hoping to modulate her tone when what she wanted to do was shout and holler. This was one thing too many. Jesus, Mary and Joseph, she said under her breath, not as much a prayer as an exasperated sigh. She knew it was an honor to give over a child to God, so many families were proud to have one of their children serve the church. Yet not this child, not now.

It had only been six months since John's death. Thank God he wasn't here for this next chapter of loss. Their baby girl was going to the convent. Glory be to God.

Betty moved the threads over and under and followed the intricate work as her mother had shown her. Maggie watched and remembered so much. Betty had an intense nature and a devotion to prayer. After all, she'd been at Maggie's side, a three-year-old, when Baby Rose died. She'd knelt with her mother and followed along on the Rosary beads Maggie had given to her. She'd held her dolly and taught it how to pray along.

"You say the words and then say Amen," Maggie heard her instruct, Betty holding the dolly in her arms. Before Maggie knew it, Betty had graduated as high school valedictorian, was chosen to sing a solo, and enjoyed dozens of friends and parties. Then, there was more achievement at Nazareth College, where she was elected to Our Lady's Committee this past spring and served as the Glee Club secretary. She'd even been chosen to sing a solo performance on the radio.

The world was hers. Whatever was she thinking? She even had a friendship with Don Driscoll, who could certainly become someone special. Glory be to God. How could it be that she would give up her life and talents to live in a convent? A calling, Betty had said. Hmmm.

Maggie wondered about the influence these very Sisters of St. Joseph who ran Nazareth College had on Betty. Her earlier signs of devotion, the seasonal decorating of the dining room shrine, her pious behavior at church, never looking left nor right but straight up to the altar while her sisters were whispering gossip to each other, never seemed anything but a childhood fancy. Yet, here she was, choosing to make a life of such devotion. And just now, when Maggie was most in need of her at home. John was gone and soon Betty would be too.

Maggie drew a deep breath, turned to face Betty, calm returning, "Well, all I can say is that you'll make a fine Sister. There's no doubt of that. Those nuns are lucky to have you. If it's the Lord's calling, as you say, things will work out for us here. Especially because we know you'll be praying for us."

A late August visit from Maggie's niece, Margaret Galena, the schoolteacher, was a welcome one. She brought Loretta's daughter, her niece, nine-year-old Anna Marie Fennelly, as sweet a child as ever. It was a perfect treat for Betty, who filled the days before her Convent departure, spending time fussing over Anna Marie as if she were a doll.

Margaret, Annie's third daughter, often reached out to keep the connections going. She'd come to Hugh's funeral and, while she wasn't able to come to John's, she sent letters and postcards with regularity on holidays and birthdays, bringing a strength and sense of family that brought peace to Maggie. She hoped her own children would savor these relationships, a part of the soul of a family.

This summer visit was just what Maggie needed and it was an extra treat to meet Loretta's daughter, Anna Marie. Yes, a well- timed visit, Maggie thought as she prepared herself for Betty's departure.

Chapter 45
Pittsford

Tuesday, September 8, 1931

The feast of the Holy Name of Mary was the designated day for Betty to arrive at the Motherhouse on East Avenue in Pittsford. It was a grand enough structure, the building was just barely four years old. As they drove up, Bernard pulled the car into the big circular drive-in front to help unload Betty's small trunk. They were greeted at the door by a Sister who identified herself as the Mistress of Novices, the title, Maggie noted, holding its old-world meaning. Betty stayed with Bernard and her few belongings, awaiting direction, while Maggie was led up the front steps and into the chapel with its remarkable stained- glass windows. "Each one of the windows depicts a female saint," the plump middle-aged sister explained. "Except for our patron, St. Joseph." She pointed to the window located above the altar with St. Joseph holding the Christ Child.

Such elegance was not something Maggie had been accustomed to, nor were her children. St. Rose's church was stately, but this was beyond that. She sighed and was reminded of the young people in Ireland who often left their poverty- ridden homes for religious life. Though Maggie knew her children weren't exactly poor, Betty would definitely be experiencing something grander.

The Novice Mistress continued to give explanations of the artwork within, explaining that the raised reliefs were the Stations of the Cross created by the Meyer Studio of Munich, Germany. Maggie was grateful when Bernard and Betty appeared at the doorway before any further descriptions could be given. Maggie's interest today was on Betty, not building details.

"We can take you now to see Betty's cell," the Mistress of Novices said. They were led down a polished main hallway to an elevator, where Bernard seemed relieved to slide the small trunk against the wall.

Betty exited the elevator first and turned to the left toward a large 'dorm' room, consisting of a series of sparse, curtained-off spaces, each containing a bed, a nightstand and a chair, not much smaller than her bedroom at home. A wall of wooden cupboards provided a place to hang clothing. Lavatories were down the hallway, with marble trim no less. Opulence was the word that came to mind. Betty's eyes were aglow. Maggie didn't say a word.

As they returned on the elevator to the main hallway and front door, Maggie nodded to the Mistress and then turned to Betty and opened her arms. With tears pooling in her eyes, she held this youngest daughter, trusting in a God who'd certainly given her enough to bear already. Similar tears in Betty's eyes told Maggie that the child might indeed have a calling. Why else would she inflict this grief on them both? Maggie let Betty go with the word Sláinte, the Irish word for health. It was enough. They turned and with a wave and a bow, mother and daughter parted.

Maggie and Bernard walked slowly to the car, which Bernard had parked a few yards away from the front cement stairway. The surrounding grounds were groomed and luscious, with tall poplar and fir trees creating a world of quiet. The sound of birds chirping and the breeze playing through the branches soothed Maggie. If this was God's will, so be it.

As Bernard turned the car toward the driveway, Maggie looked back at the enormous building. A huge statue of St. Joseph stood above the main entrance amidst the pillars and ornate carvings.

Her daughter's new home. They headed out the gracious tree-lined driveway to East Avenue and turned to the right. They'd be home in time for lunch and Maggie would take a rest, something that had become quite important these days. She didn't have a thought for dinner but would rustle up something. Don would be looming about; his school days had not quite ended, but he was. His attendance had dwindled and his chance to graduate almost evaporated. Bernard had tried to encourage him, but there was no use. He was hooked on his gadgets; his radio signals a main preoccupation. He helped Bernard with the daily chores, but his heart wasn't in it. Maggie dreaded the possibility, but she feared Donnell was becoming like her own brother Tims, the curse of the drink taking him over. She could see it in his eyes and in his soul. She knew there was little she could do about it. Just sixteen years old, he'd several times come home mumbling and stumbling, his repentance and tears more than she could bear some days. She took a deep breath in preparation. She'd grown up with this heartache and here it was again.

As if reading her mind, Bernard turned to her and asked, "Shall we have a bite to eat at Tyler's?" It was an old and favorite location in the village of Pittsford since the building of the Erie Canal almost one hundred years earlier. Known for many years as the Phoenix Hotel and a variety of other names, it was a place Bernard had been familiar with due to his travels for fur buying. A classic old building in the Federal style of the day, it served the community well, not unlike their own American Hotel in Lima. They had both dressed up for the occasion of taking Betty to the Motherhouse. With that mission accomplished, they could enjoy a bit of socialization and a bite to eat. Perhaps some Shepherd's Pie with a tall glass of ale. Just the ticket! There was time enough to go home to the new emptiness of their little house on Rochester Road.

Chapter 46
Bernard

Autumn 1931

Rows of tasseled corn stretched out under a deep blue sky that only autumn could host. He would remember this sky, Bernard thought. His father had told him many truths about nature that he'd brought with him from Ireland. The singular beauty of an autumn sky was true, his father had said, in both countries. The moist earth brought the deeper blue. He spoke with authority.

His father's ability to read the sky to predict the weather rivaled forecasts found in the Farmer's Almanac. Gazing up at a crescent moon, its points turned upward so it could hold water, he'd predict a clear day with no rain at all, and he was usually right.

As Bernard walked through the fields, the late afternoon sun illuminated everything it touched. He surveyed the hay that was still to be harvested and then felt a jolt. He was surprised to find himself missing his father, who'd been gone less than a year. He always knew John's gruffness was a cover for softness, yet he found it annoying to have to dig down to get a share of kindness. John had driven Tom away with his sharp tongue; Donnell didn't seem to pay much attention to 'the old man' as he called him. It was Bernard who'd borne the brunt of him, Bernard who'd been stuck on the farm helping him, letting his teacher certificate lapse, and staying close to home. And now what?

Bernard worked his way back toward the creek, the crisp air and clear blue sky seeping into him, soothing him. Bitterness wouldn't become him, he thought. Yet heartache held his hand as he walked.

His mind went back, as it often did, to that November morning almost five years ago, when he'd cut the noose down from the chestnut beam, handing off his brother Hugh's body to his father, who laid him in the hay. Bernard hated the memory of it, the drooping head, the bulging eyes. He hated watching his father's guilt and sorrow go underground. There is no logical way to deal with it. His own anger festered. This brother, who was sixteen years older, was a hero to so many, leaving them all with the burden of his death. None of this loss made sense.

On the bank of the creek, wildlife scampered as he approached. A great blue heron lifted off, and two otters swam up past him. Bernard settled down on the log that stretched along the western bank, watching the cardinals and robins flutter from tree to tree. Bernard spotted a beaver swimming downstream, its shiny coat catching the sun's rays. He'd learned much about these creatures from his father and Loring, who'd been his guide since Jerome's death.

Bernard first began to learn in earnest about pelts and furs during his three years of teaching in rural schools in Ontario County. Besides what his father and Loring taught him, the fathers of the children he taught shared other tricks of the trade regarding trapping and tanning. He'd become so involved that he ultimately was invited to become a member of the Raw Fur Dealers Association as its youngest member, an honor he was most proud of. Men who had known his father and his brothers Jerome and Loring spoke of their regard for them as fur buyers. He was glad now to be among those who knew the trade so well.

The association's objectives included the conservation of wildlife and fur-bearing animals in New York State. He'd heard others talk of hunting as a sport without any regard or thought of conservation. Yet it was in the late 1800s, Bernard learned, that real hunters, as well as anglers and recreational shooters, became the driving force behind principles that set forth the radical idea that wildlife belongs to everyone, not just the rich and privileged. Through his membership in the Raw Fur Dealers Association, Bernard learned that preserving the land for wildlife was crucial to their continued existence.

Proud that the twenty-seven acres of their land on the east side of Rochester Road served as home to a great number of small animals, among them foxes, gophers and beavers, Bernard was glad it was a kind of sanctuary for their propagation. And he was proud to be keeping his mother safe from the well- intentioned salesmen who could also be potential predators, trying to convince her to sell her land. She was not about to, the land as important to an Irish immigrant as it was to their descendants. He included himself as one who saw the power and possibility of owning land and living from the fruits of it.

Bernard stood up from his contemplation log, a light breeze pushing through the branches of the oak tree above him. He felt as refreshed as if he'd had a swim, his love for this land deep within him. No, there'd be no sale while he was around. This would be his mother's home for as long as she lived.

As he wandered back toward the barn, he eyed the lane to the north of his homestead. The hen house stood within view, prim and painted, the steady sound of clucking coming from inside. It would take several years to do it, but he would plant a row of trees to mark the property line nearby and assure that the grandeur of swaying branches would bring breezes for generations to come.

Somehow, despite so much that had gone astray, it felt good to be alive.

As he approached the barn and eyed their mare, Jenny, grazing just beyond, he thought it high time he took her out for a jaunt. A trip to pick up ice cream for tonight's dessert would be just the right distance and the right treat. His mother would be pleased.

Chapter 47
Barn Fire

Loring Francis, Sr

December 8, 1931

The quiet of the early morning before the boys got up was a time Maggie savored. She could sit with her cup of tea and let the day unfold. The winds blew cold, and she was happy to be inside for a bit longer before it was time for Mass. She looked out the north window as snowflakes covered her spent roses. She'd carefully nurtured this particular bush, which she had planted in the side yard, not far from the hen house. The roses will be back in spring, she thought. Wild Irish roses, she'd called them, remembering similar ones from home in Ireland. She also recalled her childhood window in Ahadallane, where she got lost in thought, often dreaming of America. Her mother recalled Maggie speaking of seeing angels, her childlike innocence allowing her that spiritual gift. How Maggie longed now for some of that innocence that so often gets lost with age.

It was just over a year since John's death. As she thought of him and their times together, their marriage, their twelve children, a fine home and so much more, she felt overwhelming gratitude. She picked up her prayer book to contemplate the December 8th feast day before Mass time, a Holy Day of Obligation. Bernard had been such a gift, taking her to her devotions while keeping up with the chores. She'd remember him, especially at Mass today, the feast celebrating the innocence of the Virgin Mary. She was deep in thought when Bernard burst in. He shook the snow from his jacket and said, "The fire's finally out."

Maggie turned in her chair, stunned. "Where was there a fire?" she asked incredulously, her eyes wide, her heart pounding.

Bernard stomped off his boots and hung his damp coat by the warmth of the heatilator, then continued. "It was quite a blaze and little Margaret Mary was awake most of the night. Peggy and Loring have just now settled back to bed. It's still smoldering."

"Whatever are you saying? Was there a fire at Loring's? What happened? Is everyone alright? Holy Mother of God," Maggie exclaimed.

Bernard took a deep breath, realizing his mother had no notion of the events of the evening. He thought she'd have heard the fire bell as he had. But she was sleeping more soundly these days than she used to, her household down to two residents beside herself, both grown, with Donnell seventeen and himself twenty-five.

"Yes, it was Loring's barn and garage. It's a mighty mess," Bernard said, rushing to add, "but no one was hurt."

"I never heard the fire bell. How'd you know about it?" she asked, looking quite stricken, her blue eyes pale and laced with concern.

Bernard sat beside her and took her hand. "I'd say it's good you didn't hear it. I came in quietly enough sometime after eleven o'clock last night. Our fur-buying trip was successful, though the roads weren't the best. We'd taken our time and when Loring dropped me home, you were sound asleep. I didn't want to wake you. Don had already gone up to bed. It was the fire bell that woke me sometime after one in the morning. I slipped out the door, not knowing if you'd hear it or not."

Bernard paused. "Evidently, Peggy discovered the blaze around one o'clock. Lucky sure has the right nickname. The fire trucks saved the house and the chicken coop that had a flock of fowls. It's the garage and barn that are completely gone."

"A good thing that little one has such an appetite," Maggie said. "They might have lost a lot more."

Bernard reached over and poured more tea. "Loring says he pulled the car into the garage and left our lot of furs inside. It was almost $100 worth. He was as tired as I was when we got back and went off to bed before putting them away."

Maggie thought about how tired Loring might be. He was well on his way to forty, with four young children, the youngest just two weeks old.

"However, did it start?" Maggie asked as she sat forward in her chair, her agitation now turning to curiosity.

"They still aren't certain how it started. One thought is a spark from the car since we'd just come home."

Bernard eagerly told the next part of the story.

"Mother, you would have loved little four-year-old Margaret Mary. She was sitting on her mother's lap, looking out the window at all the firemen working diligently to control the blaze. When Loring came in, she jumped down and ran to him. Quite sincerely, she asked, 'Daddy, why did the firemen put our barn on fire?'"

After Bernard assured Maggie that the family was safe, he continued. "While the firemen finally did get the blaze under control, over five hundred dollars' worth of raw furs stored in the upstairs of the barn were lost, with no insurance to cover them and the sedan was also damaged. Luckily, the buildings were insured.

Once Maggie was satisfied that everyone was safe, she encouraged Bernard to get out of his smoky clothes. "Get yourself some sleep," she said. "We'll go to the 10:00 Mass this morning. Maybe Don will go with us. This afternoon will be time enough to visit up at Loring's." She'd make some biscuits, she thought, to take up to the children. They always loved her biscuits.

Bernard nodded and went upstairs. She listened for the quiet to return as she fingered her rosary. It never ceased to amaze her what life brings. She thought back to her Irish window from childhood where she could see the angels. They were still with her, she believed, as she watched the snow slow and a stream of sun peek through.

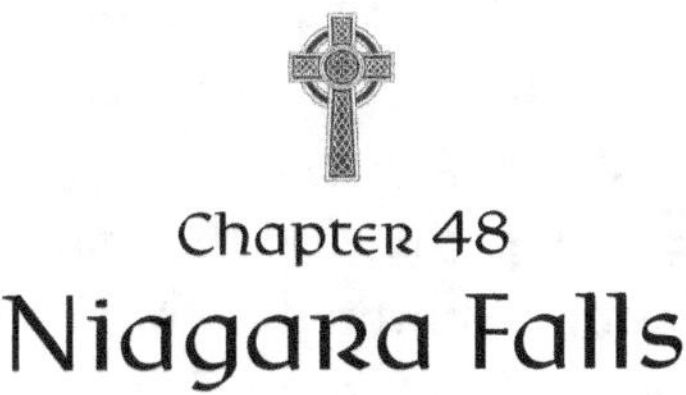

Chapter 48
Niagara Falls

October 2, 1932

"Hugh was right all along," Gene said to Veronica as they made their way from Veronica's apartment to the majestic Falls just a few blocks away. "Automobiles are not only here to stay. They are the way." She pulled the collar of her camel hair coat closer and nodded to the traffic that rushed past. They both smiled. Hugh was often in their thoughts.

Veronica, her red hair pinned up high, her short navy cape covering her tailored gray suit was pleased to have Gene visiting from Buffalo and looking forward to showing off her easy access to this natural wonder.

As they crossed Jefferson Avenue to 3rd Street, the Falls roared, a sound Veronica vowed she'd never tire of. The deep resonance filled her with awe at the power rushing past them. She'd moved from her beloved Pavilion, where she'd had great success during her early years as a teacher, school play director and performer. She reluctantly left the beauty of the rural countryside in response to a job offer in this much larger school district, where she found adventure at every turn. A pal from Lima, Mary Tubbs, another teacher, became her roommate, which made it possible to live in the posh Jefferson apartments, built just five years ago and a short walk to the Falls.

Ever the teacher, Veronica, said to Gene as they neared the Falls, "That 12,000-year-old glacier sure ripped a good one for all of us."

As the roar of the Falls swallowed the sound of Gene's laughter, Veronica continued. "At 176 feet high, the American Falls is the pride of this city."

Standing at the railing, viewing the majestic spillway of the Bridal Veil Falls, Veronica ventured, "That's what your wedding veil will look like when you get married."

Not one to miss a retort, Gene held her hand to her very straight, coiffed brown hair and said, "At least I won't have to bother curling my hair."

The two sisters, six years apart, had become fast friends through their share of family losses. They'd learned how to cook, serve meals for dozens, and clean up after dessert, coffee and tea with ease and conviviality. Gene was a master at mashed potatoes and Veronica cooked delectable moist chicken, always a hit. They'd had their squabbles, but none that mattered much. They knew deep in the recesses of their being that their friendship made life much sweeter.

Neither of them had a serious beau just now, though that might be changing. This afternoon, they'd be meeting their brother Tom at The Como, a stylish restaurant up on Pine Street. He was bringing his boss, Freddie Hendler, to a celebration for Gene's twenty-fifth birthday and a 'welcome' dinner as well.

Gene's recent arrival in Buffalo had been the result of a job promotion to secretary to the president of B.F. Goodrich. She had loved being secretary to the head of the recently opened School of Nursing at Strong Memorial Hospital in Rochester, Miss Leona Ivers. Unfortunately, with the depression, funding for it ended.

Luckily, she landed a job at BF Goodrich on Main Street in Rochester, which led to her Buffalo promotion. Automobile tires are in constant demand, business is booming, and BF Goodrich is an up-and-coming company. Not bad, she thought, for a country girl.

Her move to 245 North Street in Buffalo, a recently completed apartment building, proved far more enticing than her Knights of Columbus high rise in Rochester with its iconic sign: If you lived here, you'd be home by now.

As part of her initial training at BF Goodrich, Gene learned about the founder, Benjamin Franklin Goodrich. She was fascinated to learn he was once a surgeon and helped the Union Troops during the Civil War. The latest source of company pride was that the airplane, the Spirit of St. Louis, was fitted with BF Goodrich tires as it made the first non-stop transatlantic flight.

Her new boss put her in mind of Hugh, gentile, bright and polite. She'd known plenty of women who were treated more like servants than competent employees. Here at BF Goodrich, Gene felt genuine admiration and appreciation. She remained one of 'the girls' at lunchtime when she was able to join the others while enjoying some definite perks due to her senior status. Among them were complimentary Silvertown tires that were the rage for Ford. Her purchase of a used 1929 Model A with its iconic blue oval logo was a perfect means of transportation for her, though she was frequently reminded of the risky business cars were, her father cursing automobiles after Jerome's horrific death.

The Como restaurant, opened just five years earlier by the Antonacci and Colucci families, was one of the more popular Speakeasies. While prohibition, known as the noble experiment, never really limited alcohol consumption, it did provide creative ways to serve it without being arrested. Private rooms, separate entrances, and walls that opened into back rooms and bars became the norm. Secret words and intrigue accompanied many places. Italian restaurants with possible Mafia connections were always suspect. Tonight, as they stepped through the front door, the openness and warmth of the welcome struck them. A well-groomed middle-aged man in a pin-stripe suit with dark hair and mustache greeted them.

"Welcome, Miss Donegan," he said as he nodded to Gene. "Your party is in the other room, and we'll seat you as soon as you'd like." He led Veronica and Gene through a private parlor with flocked red wallpaper, floral paintings, and scenes of Italy. Though dimly lit, they saw Tom and Freddie get to their feet to greet them. Instantly, Gene liked what she saw. Freddie was a well-built, fair-haired man in his forties with polished shoes, creased trousers, a pressed shirt, and a well-knotted tie topped by a tweed blazer. Gene watched for Veronica's reaction, wondering if she was attracted to him. She followed her sister to the small corner booth.

As Tom introduced them, Gene saw a side of Tom she'd always known despite his supposed distaste for formality. He wore a dark jacket with a red-striped tie, his dark hair parted and combed, his mustache well-trimmed. "Fred, I'd like to introduce my sisters, Veronica and Genevieve, whom we all call Gene," Tom said. "Gene just moved to Buffalo recently and today we're celebrating her birthday."

Fred nodded and took his seat across from Gene and Veronica, who had seated themselves on the inside of the booth. Tom sat next to Fred and nodded to the waiter, who brought two whiskey and water drinks to his sisters. They were up for a good time, Gene suspected, as she watched Fred settle in, his debonair manner lending a good feeling to the group.

As the evening wore on, they adjourned to the dining room for their meal and learned the story of Freddie Hendler, who had started his own business specializing in experimental and production patterns for airplanes, motor cars, steam, and diesel motors. He was unassuming and enthusiastic about his company, Aero Pattern Works.

Tom had been his employee for a time, Freddie complimenting him most highly. "Your brother Tom has an ability, unlike any I've known, to measure accurately with just a visual check."

Both women listened attentively, glancing at each other as they continued to size up Freddie. They knew Tom had been acknowledged for his good carpentry skills, but there was a more technical entrepreneur speaking. Very impressive.

As the conversation continued, they learned that Freddie not only founded the Aero Pattern Works but also belonged to the Society of Automotive Engineers, the Buffalo Athletic Club and was currently the Commodore of the Buffalo Launch Club.

"I'd be delighted to host you all for Sunday dinner at the Launch Club some afternoon, followed by a boat ride on Lake Erie. It would be my pleasure," Freddie offered, looking at each of them for acceptance.

"You'll find no argument from me," Veronica offered. "I'd love a boat ride and a bit of excitement. How about you, Gene?"

"I couldn't think of a finer invitation to receive on my birthday. Is it too late in the season to plan a time now?"

Freddie smiled and said to Tom, "You were right when you told me about your sisters. They do get right to the point."

As they walked back to the front rooms, only vaguely aware of being in a clandestine venue, Gene watched how polished Freddie was as he tipped the waiter. Far more mature than others they'd palled around with, he might just be the ticket for Veronica, Gene thought. Dinner and a boat ride would certainly help determine the next steps. Gene stepped outside first, and breathed in the evening air and thought, as she looked up at the stars, what a lovely birthday party it had been. What else might be in store? She wondered.

Chapter 49
Beulah

Early March 1934

She was gorgeous. A real looker, Tom thought. Soft, auburn hair framed her freckled cheeks and green eyes that seemed to smile. No one had captured him like this since Lillian. Beulah FitzGerald Maloney had a soft spot for almost everything. "Look at those little puppies," she'd swoon as they walked along the banks of Honeoye Creek, spotting a yard full of the tiny creatures playing. She'd chattered on about this and that like a magpie when they first met, her love of her hometown, Rush, where she'd lived all her life, her love of her husband, Ray Maloney, who died a little over two years ago, whom she missed terribly. He was a World War I veteran. She'd proudly told Tom and a member of the Smith-Warren post of the American Legion of Scottsville.

Tom had quickly grown quite fond of Beulah's company throughout the winter months, going on sleigh rides and meeting up at dances. They even met with his mother and Bernard at the Christmas tree lighting uptown.

He'd first met Beulah at the Creekside restaurant in Rush, the neighboring town to the northwest, where she was a waitress. Tom had taken a mind to stay out of Lima for his socialization as often as he could, getting away from the American Hotel where everybody knew his business. In a rush, he could be his own person. Also, Beulah helped him feel like somebody, listening to stories about his work and his success as a silo builder and carpenter.

As he told of his recent work with Freddie Hendler in Buffalo and the good income it brought, he mentioned the extra credits he'd earned for introducing Freddie to his sisters. Veronica and Freddie appeared to get along, often going for boat rides on the Niagara River with Freddie's twelve-year-old daughter, Mary Jane.

Mary Jane, Tom told Beulah, had lost her mother when she was only a year old. With her schoolteacher's wisdom and natural way with children, Veronica became a good friend, and she and Mary Jane became fast pals. Shopping together was one of their favorite pastimes, and Freddie was relieved to have someone help his teenage daughter come of age. Tom was given credit for the budding relationship.

Dating Beulah kept Tom in Lima for a time. He knew Bernard resented being 'stuck' at home, Don not much of a companion or significant help. Don's preoccupation with gadgetry and radios, coupled with his thirst for beer, made him less than dependable. While Tom was willing to help temporarily, he didn't take a fancy to fur buying and selling like Loring and Bernard did. However, he did have a knack for trapping muskrats and beavers, a contribution Bernard valued.

With the late afternoon sun sending sparkles over the creek, Tom and Beulah strolled along Honeoye Creek, hand in hand. They'd been an item for several months now and contentment was filling their time together.

"Tom," Beulah asked quietly, "do you have a sister Genevieve?"

Tom was surprised by the inquiry. Before he could reply, she pulled a folded piece of newspaper from her pocket and handed it to him. He knew what the paper said. He'd seen it just yesterday at home, his brother Loring bringing it with his report of the events after his visit to St. Jerome's, the Batavia hospital.

Batavia, March 4, 1934

Three of five persons injured in a head-on automobile collision two miles west of Batavia on the Buffalo highway late last night are still in St. Jerome's Hospital here today. Most seriously injured was Miss Genevieve Donegan, 26, of Lima, who received a broken collarbone, a cut over the right eye and a possible spinal injury. She was riding with Mr. and Mrs. Gerald Busch of Buffalo, both of whom also were hospitalized with cuts and bruises. Anthony Matrone, 25, driver of the other car, was treated at the hospital for cuts on the face and hands, and his sister Rose, 21, riding with him, was also treated.

"Did you know the fellow who was driving?" Beulah asked. Tom did know Gerry Busch, a family friend, for years.

Originally from West Bloomfield, Gerry taught for a time and got his PhD from Notre Dame before joining Socony Mobil Oil in 1931. He was a fellow on the rise, an industrial relations manager. They'd all laughed when Rose O'Connell married Gerry and became Rose Busch.

Loring had visited Gene yesterday. Today, his mother and Bernard were planning to go. When Tom told Beulah of his intention to visit, she was eager to go along. Gene would love Beulah and it might be a tonic for her to know he'd fallen in love for real this time.

Their hospital visit was appropriately brief. The Buschs had already been discharged. It was evident Genevieve had taken the brunt of the impact. The driver had been treated and released that same night, as had his passenger, another woman named Rose. Funny, Tom thought, two wilted Roses.

When they arrived at Gene's room, they found her propped up in her bed, looking quite uncomfortable. A bandage covered her right eye and pillows were propped up on either side of her. Tom knew how scary a proposition a car accident was, having had some narrow escapes himself.

Gene saw the twinkle in his eye as he introduced Beulah. She wondered if this could be the real thing. She knew that Tom had been looking. His divorce, initiated by Lillian, was final several years ago.

Gene never knew what to expect from Tom's wry sense of humor, he stepped forward and asked, "How'd it look from the bridge?" At first, Gene was puzzled, but then she laughed. "Well, luckily," she replied, "I didn't get a chance to see."

Gene liked what she saw in Beulah. She listened attentively to Tom, nodding when he spoke, often contributing to the conversation but letting Tom take the lead. This was something he deserved. The whole situation with seven-year-old Christine was still so painful. Gene wondered if Beulah knew about her.

The nurse came in to reposition Gene in the bed. Tom cringed when he saw her wince with the pain of moving. The brother and sister so often exchanged witty comments, their affection for one another evident as they quipped back and forth. Just then, Tom couldn't think of anything clever to say.

After the nurse left, Beulah moved toward the bed and asked Gene if she'd like her to do anything for her. Gene smiled and asked for water. Beulah obliged.

Tom spoke up. "Say, if you don't have any plans once you're out of here, it'd be nice to celebrate St. Patrick's Day with you. We'll be getting married as an enticement for your recovery. See what you can do, okay? That'll give you a couple of weeks to get moving."

With that, Tom signaled to Beulah and the two stepped out into the hall, leaving Gene without a chance for any rebuttal. Tom was pleased to have surprised Gene with his happy news. He hoped for her recovery, though from the looks of it, she'd miss the wedding.

Gene was still in the hospital when Tom and Beulah went ahead and 'tied the knot' in Scottsville on a blustery St. Patrick's Day. Tom was 29 and Beulah was 31. He didn't mind that she was older nor that she was a widow. Both facts showed him that she was someone who'd known sorrow and was strong. He needed that.

Chapter 50
All There Is

Summer 1934

As Maggie stepped into the barn, she saw the last of the kittens skitter away. Every morsel of evening ham and potato table scraps she'd brought earlier were finished, as they were most days. She watched them scamper hither and yon, aware she could count on them to finish up every bit just as their mother before them. How amazing that life has such moments of patterns and promises. You could always count on life, little ones, and new miracles if you but looked for them.

From around a corner near the hayloft ladder, a little gray kitten with a white patch between her eyes watched Maggie as she picked up the bowl to take back for tomorrow's food. What was there about this litter that had Maggie so captivated? She smiled and reached out to this one, bending to pet it.

There'd been barn cats here since before they bought the Lays farm over twenty years ago. It was the year before her twins had been born. It was a dream come true to finally have their own home. And within a year of such tragedy, her littlest twin girl was gone, the boy slower than most and stubborn as they come. She'd coaxed him into his bed at night with a lullaby after she bathed him. She'd rocked him like an infant to settle him down well into his toddler years, not allowing others to care for him. Her daughters chided her when she still washed his hair as a boy of nine and ten. "He's too dependent on you, Ma. Leave him to us and we'll help him grow up properly," Veronica or Genevieve would say. She knew they were right, but the pull of the little lad, like this little kitten peeking 'round the corner, left her helpless. She'd relent and tend to him.

And now, a young man, Donnell was still dependent, often whimpering after he'd come in at night from his radio haven, having nipped too much hooch from wherever he got it, staggering to his bed. He was more than twenty-one, the age for a man, yet his childlike ways persisted. Maggie sighed as she looked about the barn, hoping to see the hayloft filled, the floors tidied, the rafters cleared. Instead, his simple chores were all unattended.

As she made her way back to the house, she peeked into his radio barn and saw Donnell tinkering, ears attentive to every buzz and sound. He was focused as he turned knobs, oblivious to her arrival. How she wished she could turn this interest of his into a worthwhile skill. How she wished he could be dependable help for his brother Bernard, whose own spirit was faltering month after month as the wheat crop threatened to diminish.

Maggie stepped out unnoticed and looked down the northern boundary of their land. The trees Bernard had planted were a testament to continued life. She took a deep breath and sighed, her belief in hope grounding her. "Every season has its own beauty," she remembered her mother saying. Hope, she'd been taught as a young child in Ireland, would see them through if they just held on. Hope did see them through. In the worst of the hunger years, she and her brothers and sisters always had enough. Hard work and hope for the winning combination.

As she carried the emptied scraps bowl back, another bit of counsel rang in her ear, her father's "Waste not, want not," even when his own hunger over the years was far more desperate than any she had ever known. He'd be pleased she was still listening and heeding his words these many years later.

In the most recent letter from her sister Julia, who'd chosen to stay on in the family home in Ireland, she read of the new Irish constitution, the election of Douglas Hyde to the ceremonial office of President, while Eamon de Valera would hold the role of Taoiseach, the first use of an Irish word to designate his position of chief or leader. It all seemed so distant to her, these clever words and special documents. She'd remembered the excitement she'd felt as a young woman, new to America, when the American papers told of Douglas Hyde becoming President of the Gaelic League and being hailed for his attempt to save the Irish language from extinction. She felt so proud to have her homeland written about here, in powerful America, everyone's dream.

Now Maggie wondered if any of it meant a tinker's dam to Julia. Did holding on to the native language matter that much? She'd lost touch with so much from Ireland. Her sister Molly, her husband Paddy, their baby Eugene, daughter Mary and sons Jerome and John were all gone to their eternal reward. Their daughter Margaret was the only survivor, a young woman who carried on brilliantly, tending to the family graves in Calvary Cemetery.

When Maggie's parents, Jeremiah and Margaret, died, followed by her brothers Tims and Michael, Julia, the only one left in Ireland, soldiered on. Maggie thought of her often, trying to take a page from her book. Finally, with the deaths of their sister and brother, Jeremiah and Lizzie, Julia and Maggie became the sole survivors of the Jeremiah Donegans of Ahadallane. Together, they held the memories of the hunger days and the sorrows that came with emigration. Hope had been their anchor and held them together now, half a world away from each other. Maggie treasured the connection she still had with Julia.

She wondered if it would ever matter to those yet to come that there had been an Irish homestead and as well as an American farm or that her children and grandchildren born in America could prosper and were free to build lives to be proud of. She smiled to herself, thinking of her own brood.

Hugh's widow, June, visited less frequently as the years went by, and Jerome's Rachel found love again, marrying Emory Horton, a man well-regarded in his community. Vic and Margaret's loss of two children found them resiliently adding two more, Billy, already nine, and Elizabeth, called Betty, like her aunt before her, now five. Loring and Peggy had six children, including Maureen and another Billy. The adage was true, for time does indeed heal old wounds as it brings forth new life.

Maggie thought of her daughter Betty, who had become a full-fledged Sister of St. Joseph, taking her first vows, then final vows in a moving ceremony. The Motherhouse chapel glowed as the sounds of the hymns were lifted to the heavens. Betty, now Sister Leo Xavier, taught elementary school at Sacred Heart in Rochester while finishing her studies at Nazareth Normal School. Her newest adventure found her at her alma mater, Nazareth Academy, as a teacher of freshman. Awards and accolades for her teaching and for her singing followed her. It was satisfying to be her mother.

As Maggie began to pull open the back door of the house to step into the kitchen, out of the corner of her eye, she saw a flash shoot by. She looked back and saw the same little kitten with a white patch. She let the door close and bent down, the bowl still in her hand. The kitten came up around the step, its pink nose sniffing, padding on the tiniest of paws. Gently, Maggie put the bowl down. Ever so gingerly, the kitten came near to the bowl and put his paw and nose in and licked the sides.

Here's one, Maggie thought, who has had to scrap for its fair share. In these many litters over the years, how many kittens didn't survive? She stood slowly, leaving the bowl. She knew just where to find a little more food.

As she added a handful of leftover rice to the bowl, Maggie waited for the little one to sniff and nibble. Her thoughts continued about loss. She'd lost three, the other nine still finding their way. She knew she had to learn to let them fight their own battles and learn their own lessons, as her own mother had done for her when she left for America, gifting Maggie with her accordion so there would always be music. She'd wept so in leaving her home, even though it was what she wanted. Her heart ached as she remembered. She could never love her mother more.

Luckily, Gene's auto accident had been no worse, the news of it having sent convulsions of fear through her. When Maggie and Bernard visited St. Jerome's hospital in Batavia, she was able to breathe easier, assured that her bright-eyed daughter would survive, her wit still intact. "Couldn't get rid of me that easily," Gene had quipped.

Though Gene was laid up and out of work longer than she would have liked, she had managed the hour-long trip home within a few weeks for an Easter visit, Veronica and Freddie chauffeuring her. They joined Josephine and Betty along with the newlyweds, Tom and Beulah.

Maggie sighed as she listened to them all. Endless love. That's what she had known. Soon enough, she would be seventy years on this planet. Her John would be gone for almost ten years. As she stooped to take up the bowl and shoo the kitten back to the barn, she paused and let in wondrous waves of gratitude. This life she'd been given, with its mix of sorrows and joys, she knew, was all there was. And it was quite enough.

Chapter 51
The Daughters

May 29, 1937

Josephine sat in the front parlor watching the squirrels play in the tree in the next-door neighbor's front yard. The chase and tag antics gave her a sense of glee as she watched them dart up and down the tree branches, sometimes hanging on a shaky limb, capturing her with their sense of risk and competence. How fortunate she felt to be sitting still on this spring day, the sun's warmth washing over her. It had been too long since she'd been 'off duty,' this visit a tonic.

Within a few years, she'd be forty and while she loved her work at Lenox Hill Hospital, she was tempted to join several others in becoming private duty nurses, a job that offered more forgiving hours and a guaranteed pay increase. Over this Decoration Day weekend, she would talk with her mother about it.

The trees and gardens at the Tollis family home had been a source of comfort since they'd become neighbors. The gifts of fresh produce from their garden and their friendliness were both well-received and appreciated. The father, Ignatius, managed a greenhouse before moving to Lima, and his sons, Pete and Franklin, worked with him now at the Moses Nursery up the road. While her husband and boys were off at work, Carmela tended their plentiful fruits and vegetables along with the rose bushes and flowering shrubs that filled the yard.

Maggie joined Josephine in the front parlor, bringing tea for them both. Joyful news had come from Loring and Peggy the previous weekend - the birth of a beautiful baby girl after three boys. She was a blessing to them all, born early in the morning von the same Sunday as Jack's First Communion. Maggie told Josephine of the delight she discovered when she'd gone up to help out once the baby had been born.

"Ah, if you could imagine it, herself, dear Peggy, nursing that beautiful, dark-haired baby girl, tuckered out as you'd expect, smiling and drowsy all at once. And then didn't I spy, nearby, as sweet as could be, the little white suit and brown shoes all laid out in readiness for Jack's First Communion."

Maggie went on about the First Communion, how she attended in Peggy's stead, shepherding Margaret Mary, Bobby, and Loring Jr. to a pew as their father delivered Jack to his front-row seat. She told with the glee of little Jack on his way down the aisle, waving as if he were a celebrity, announcing, "Our new baby is a girl, a tiny little girl." No amount of shushing could contain his excitement. Josephine could picture it all and imagined her mother taking charge as needed. Who could have expected the baby would come on the very day of her brother's First Communion?

It was the new baby's baptism that drew Josephine home and held center stage. St. Rose of Lima Church had been decked out with glorious spring flowers, soft pink roses from the Tollis Family, and a bouquet of tulips from the Moses Nursery. There were even some freshly cut pale lavender lilacs from Sister Betty and the companion sister who had traveled from Sacred Heart Cathedral School in Rochester.

Josephine was pleased that Gene and Veronica had also come from their respective apartments in Buffalo and Niagara Falls. As the eldest, Josephine always leaned into the responsibility of what was necessary and had signed too many family death certificates for coroners, a task none relished. On this trip, she was so glad to learn from her sisters their thoughts on their mother's well-being. Bernard and Don living with her provided some companionship and support. Maggie seemed content even though much of the meal preparation and housekeeping fell to her. Veronica offered that her occasional weekend visits home would continue. That counted for a lot.

Today, an occasion for celebrating was more than welcome. When the pastor, Father John Ball, came out from the sacristy, wearing the white Alb and Chasuble signifying new life, all those assembled stood. He began the service with the Our Father. Then he motioned to Peggy and Loring to bring the baby forward. The three siblings remained in the pew, Maggie sitting with them. The Godparents, Junior Reynolds, whose father owned the American Hotel and Mary McCoy, a long-time friend, came forward next. At Father's signal, Peggy handed the baby to Mary. Junior stood by, still hoping to start his own family once he found the right woman. Mary held the baby over the pink marble baptismal font, Junior's hand gently placed over the baby's torso.

As Father poured the water three times in the form of a cross on the child's head, he said, "Josetta Ann, I baptize thee, in the name of the Father, and of the Son, and of the Holy Ghost." As if on cue, the infant cooed. After a chuckle, all present joined in the Amen.

Father then anointed the child with Holy Chrism, sealing the baptism. A lighted candle was given to the sponsors to hold while he recited the final baptism prayer. "Parents and godparents, this light has been entrusted to you to be kept burning brightly. May all now go in peace with the light of this child to guide you."

After the service ended, all adjourned to the American Hotel to carry on the celebration, the collection of friends and relatives as comfortable as if they were at home. The Reynolds family greeted every guest as they filed into the hotel dining room. They all settled in with their favorite beverage and eyed the lovely buffet being set out, Peggy with the infant in her white bonnet and christening gown nestled on her lap, shone against Peggy's navy-blue dress and jacket that was adorned by a string of pearls.

Loring tapped on his glass and the talking hushed as Peggy began: "Today, we baptized this little one, Josetta Ann, to honor St. Joseph and Sister Josetta, who has been such a support and friend to me throughout the years. We also honor our dear Josephine, here with us from New York City, where we shared such good times when Loring and I first met. For her days, we have decided this little lass will be called Maureen, another favorite name. While always aware of the importance of these strong women in our family's lives, this given name, Josetta, is a special reminder."

Those assembled applauded, laughter in the air. Josephine was honored to be so acknowledged, treasuring her memories of Loring and Peggy's courtship in New York. She'd been at nursing school when her brother first met Peggy. A perfect fit, she'd thought and she didn't hesitate to tell him so. And here they were now with five children. It also dawned on her that like this little girl, whose birth after three boys was so celebrated, she, too, had been in the same position in her family, the first girl after four boys. Josephine smiled to think of the joy this newest child would bring.

Maggie found herself seated with her four daughters, Josephine, Veronica, Genevieve and Betty. Betty's companion nun had been seated with the youngsters, a suitable slot for a primary school teacher. Josephine watched Maggie's smiling eyes as her sisters bantered about. They all seemed happy to see each other, with chatter bright and breezy.

Each of her daughters had a special place in Maggie's heart. It dawned on her, as they celebrated the birth of a tenth grandchild, that each of these grandchildren had been her sons' children. Would Maggie's daughters ever bear children, she wondered?

Josephine's dedication to her nursing profession and reaching age forty didn't leave much room for childbearing, though romance had been something her friend Petie was ever encouraging, having introduced her to a handsome man named Fletcher. While she enjoyed his company and attention, Josephine savored her alone time, too. After a long workday, she was content not to have to answer to anyone. She enjoyed her Galena-Kerrigan cousins and all Loretta and Jack Fennelly's children, as well as her many nieces and nephews. It was enough for now.

Veronica, on the other hand, had settled into her relationship with Freddie, who was significantly older and was a good man and a wealthy one. He often accompanied her for weekend jaunts to Lima when she came. She was excelling as a teacher, her time at Pacific Avenue school in Niagara Falls with her visits home bringing stories of students' priceless comments and excellent work. She was still producing plays and creating skits and presentations to the delight of all.

Genevieve told of various suitors she'd had, but none seemed to have captured her as yet. Her independent spirit was strong, a Donegan trait. She was just turning thirty and her work as secretary to the head of B.F.Goodrich was challenging and fulfilling for now.

Maggie was pleased Betty had done some travel before entering the convent, visiting Josephine in New York City and Veronica in Niagara Falls. With no apparent regrets, Betty's talents were recognized as a soloist for radio broadcasts, glee club performances and her recorded rendition of Danny Boy.

All her daughters knew that Maggie's early years had been swallowed by the excitement of emigration from her home in Ahadallane, Ireland, to living in New York City. They heard about her work as a house servant, meeting and marrying John, having their first child, then moving upstate to a farm and bearing eleven more children. She often said she had a satisfying life, her marriage something that completed her. So far, it seemed, her daughters were on different paths.

After the solemnities and the cake, Josephine signaled to her sisters to meet out on the porch of the hotel. With nods to this one and that one, they all exited and gathered. Josephine began by saying, "With Ma in her mid-sixties, we've no idea how many more years we'll have her. She seems pleased to have all these children about. And she seems peaceful," she added. "If a need arises, I know I'm at a distance from you all for her care, but I want you to know I'll be here in a flash if you need me."

The sisters looked at each other, the reality of their mother's well-being not having been addressed out loud before. Betty spoke first. "Josephine, it's your medical knowledge we'll trade on. We can handle the care but will want to know it's the right care."

Veronica and Gene nodded in assent. "We've got some mighty skills among us," Veronica said. "Together, we'll stay for as long as she needs us. Agreed?" Josephine smiled inwardly as she nodded. With all her belief in the power of women, she'd just experienced it. Glad indeed she was to be a daughter with these sisters.

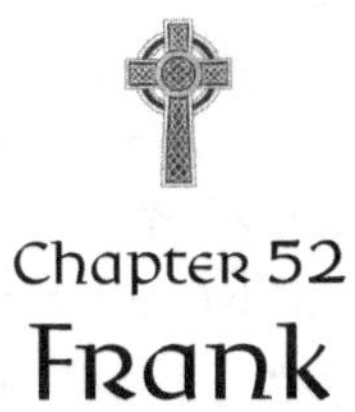

Chapter 52
Frank

September 1937

Genevieve stood at the railing near the bow of the cruise boat, the skyline of her adopted city shining in the setting sun. Glad to be alone, she felt the pull of the stars, the vastness of the night. She was glad for her navy-blue jacket around her shoulders as the breeze off Lake Erie picked up. She'd worn a matching navy skirt and sweater with white trim, a nautical theme seeming appropriate for this adventure.

The event was the Erie County Republican dinner cruise, and she was here with Alfie George, the doctor she'd been dating. She was new to the social group of three other doctors and their wives, glad to slip away momentarily to see the sunset.

Politics didn't interest Gene. The rancor and passion that fueled them seemed so deeply misplaced, opposing one another rather than building something together. Her Aunt Julia's letters from Ireland told of a similar situation there - the War of Independence followed immediately by an Irish Civil War, with more young men losing their lives needlessly. It didn't make sense.

Just a few weeks ago, Julia had sent word of a new Irish Constitution designed and orchestrated by Eamon de Valera, the recently appointed Taoiseach, that made way for input from Archbishop Charles McQuaid, assuring Ireland's continuation as a Catholic country. Gene wondered if that could be good.

Tonight however, she turned her attention to the starry sky over Buffalo, the deep blue/black filled with constellations, the Big Dipper right overhead. She looked for the handle of the Little Dipper, glad for the clarity the darkness brought. She loved these moments, like the nights at home on the farm, where the skies became their own world.

Earlier at dinner, she'd listened while Alfie and the others waxed forth about the great Republican party, diminishing Roosevelt. She remembered Roosevelt's inauguration for his second term this past January and the 20th amendment deliberately shortening the "lame duck" period that formerly lasted until March 4th. Roosevelt had recommend a lot to him as far as Gene was concerned. "We've nothing to fear but fear itself," was one of her favorite quotes of his. True in so many instances.

Gene sighed deeply. She was thrilled to be on this cruise, seeing a whole new Buffalo, the reflection of its buildings shimmering in the water. During her five years here, she'd begun to fall for the city, and this evening was worth it for the skyline alone. It was magical, she thought, fixing her gaze on City Hall built in 1931 that was still receiving rave reviews. She'd taken a tour when she first arrived in Buffalo, impressed with the frieze work on the facades which she learned was Art Deco style. She was taken, too, with what she was told was the practical design that featured 1,520 windows from the first to the 25th floor. They all opened inward, making window washers unnecessary. She'd washed enough windows in her day to appreciate the savings.

Gene understood anew, as the cruise boat drew closer to the dock, why City Hall, its 32 floors gleaming, was a source of such pride. The 1929 Rand Building, who some said had been the inspiration for the Empire State Building in New York City and Buffalo's 1912 Electric Tower, with its white terra cotta exterior, elegant octagonal tower and illuminated spire, was also extraordinary. The same firm also built the Statler Hotel and the

Buffalo Athletic Club in Niagara Square. However, it was this Art Deco structure, built by John W. Cowper Company, that stole the show, City Hall the undisputed prince of the skyline.

The dark came quickly, as it always seems to. As she thought of going back to the table and Alfie, Gene felt a presence next

to her at the railing and looked over to see Frank, the fellow she'd been introduced to earlier in the evening by her attorney, Eldred O'Shea.

"It's a beautiful sight, isn't it?" he asked, his voice gentle, his question sincere. "I never tire of it."

"I've never seen it from the water," Gene said, "It really is dazzling. You must be a Buffalo native," she surmised. Then added, "Oh, you're Eldred's law school classmate."

Eldred had been recommended for the lawsuit after her automobile accident a few years ago. He had represented her and Gerry and Rose Busch very successfully, their hospital expenses reimbursed with something additional for pain and suffering. Gene's settlement had been the largest, her injuries keeping her in St. Jerome's hospital for several weeks. The accident had been a little more than three years ago and despite the doctor's warning that she might not walk or be able to have children, she felt fine. On October 2nd she would celebrate her thirtieth birthday, and she planned to drink a toast to that doctor's mistaken prediction.

She found Frank easy to talk with. His dark eyes and gentle voice were attractive. He asked about her satisfaction with Eldred's service and talked of his fondness for Eldred and their mutual goal of working for justice. Admirable, she thought.

Gene told Frank of a humorous interaction she had with Eldred after the lawsuit had been settled. "I asked him if I were ever injured in an accident while my sister was driving, could I sue her?" She paused. Frank was attentive as she continued. "You know Eldred well enough, Frank, so you know that he takes time before answering, right?" Frank smiled and nodded his head. "Well, after I asked the question, he took a long pause, his baby blue eyes focused on me, and said, 'If you were able.'"

Frank's laughter told her how much they both appreciated Eldred.

Gene was glad for this interlude with Frank. If she were to compare him to Alfie, which she thought she shouldn't, she'd

say he was more peaceful, less full of himself. Alfie was a good man, yet there was something missing in him that she couldn't quite name. She and Frank chatted for a few more minutes, then Frank pointed to the skyline. "There's the Electric Tower where I go to work every day." As Gene looked around, she noticed that Alfie and his group had moved inside. She realized she'd better find Alfie, but not before she learned a bit more.

"Frank, are you and Eldred here with a group?"

"Well, Eldred's in private practice but for tonight he has joined me and the A. T. O'Neill party, the office I work for." Gene recognized the name. A.T. was a prominent Buffalo attorney and the vice president in charge of the Western Division of Niagara Mohawk Power Corporation.

As she looked for a graceful exit, Eldred joined them and Gene, greeting him warmly, said she'd better get back to her group. Leave Frank wanting more, she thought as she walked away, trusting Veronica would fill in any missing details. Eldred had her phone number if Frank wanted it.

Gene slipped into the seat next to Alfie and smiled, ready for some boring conversation, hoping that Frank would call soon.

Chapter 53
Petie

Winter 1939

Josephine stepped out into New York City's below-freezing temperature, pulling her fur collar up around her ears against the blustery winds whipping through the streets. The frigid temperatures of the past days were easing up, but not soon enough. She was scurrying to Lenox Hill Hospital for a 9:00 a.m. consult about her next private duty assignment. As she made her way past other apartment buildings toward Park Avenue, she sighed with relief that she and her roommates had found such a good living situation. Their 1910 building on East 79th Street was a sought-after location, close to the hospital and other attractions, Central Park being Josephine's favorite.

Forty-two-year-old Margaret Wagner, short, blonde, and living apart from her Merchant Marine husband and Anna

Meier, almost fifty, single, tall, intelligent, and strong, had become the perfect companions for this new phase of Josephine's life. Each of them sought relief from the rigors of hospital nursing by becoming private duty nurses. Both women were German born, their competence and compassion a well-known contributing factor to the fine reputation of the hospital, the 1918 name change from the German Hospital, a sign of the times.

Though it was physically less demanding, Josephine knew that not every nurse was suited for taking on private duty work. Being able to communicate clearly, and instilling confidence in patients were essential skills, but tact and diplomacy were also needed. Josephine was confident she'd mastered such skills, having been the 'charge' nurse over many years, supervising student nurses who were the mainstay of the hospital. This new work brought Josephine a welcome breath of fresh air and allowed her time to explore life beyond the hospital walls.

Her plan for this afternoon included time at the nearby Frick Museum on East 70th Street, where she'd become fascinated with a world outside her own, art transporting her to times gone by, providing her a window into the splendor and talent of the Old Masters of Europe. With the help of her friend Petie, she discovered Fragonard's *Progress of Love*, four panels of the four ages of love. She enjoyed learning about the intrigue surrounding these works at the Frick after J.P. Morgan's death, when they were purchased. *The Pursuit and the Meeting* she'd identified with, her own flirtatious encounters with "Fletcher", bordering on something more. It was Petie who pointed out that Josephine's own Progress of Love seemed stalled, the panels depicting *Lover Crowned* and *Love Letters* escaping her as yet.

Petie, tall, svelte and blonde with a ready smile, a recently 'capped' R.N. had competence exuding from her. Josephine had known few who could assess a situation as well and as efficiently or who were as adept and lively, with such a zest for life. Their companionship was a tonic, their visits to museums and the theater exhilarating. Petie's artistic insights complemented Josephine's penchant toward poetry, a richness she hadn't known she'd missed.

At lunch today, Josephine was eager to tell Petie of her recent trip home for Gene and Frank's wedding in Buffalo. They'd arranged to meet at the Heidelberg on 2nd Street, German food a favorite for them both. Glad to be free of the snowy Buffalo weather, she breathed in the warmth and scent of sauerkraut and wiener schnitzel filling the air inside the Heidleberg. Petie arrived promptly, always on time, always a story, laughter, her trademark.

"Just down the street, I saw a poster for an East River Cruise. When the weather lets up, let's plan a day, what do you say?" Petie blurted out as she sat across from Josephine and took off her scarf and hat, pushing her blonde hair back into place.

"Sounds good for warmer weather. I've had my fill of this cold. Even the train ride to Buffalo was frigid, with tons of snow everywhere."

"Ah, but the wedding. Was it wonderful? Do tell." Josephine motioned to the waitress for menus as she began.

"Gene has always been a happy sort of gal, but I've never seen her so ecstatic. She looked gorgeous," Josephine said as she dug into her purse and produced a photograph.

Genevieve and Frank
at Park Lane Hotel in Buffalo,
New York - January 28, 1939

"This photograph was a gift to all the family members."
"Can you imagine?" Petie said as she studied the picture.

"How unconventionally beautiful she is in a suit and hat, no wedding gown or veil. The silver color is stunning."

"She was radiant and so was Veronica who wore a beige skirt and jacket with a colorful blouse and bowtie that blended nicely, a shade lighter than Gene's muted silver," Josephine said as she took the picture back from Petie. "I loved the fur inset on Gene's jacket. Her gardenia was the perfect complement."

As they ordered their meals, Sauerbraten for Josephine and Beef Goulash for Petie, they chatted on about the whole event.

"They were married in what they call the New Cathedral on Delaware Avenue. It's a gorgeous structure, with a white marble exterior imported from Italy. The priest was a gem, Father Garvey. Not stuffy at all."

Petie smiled as she added cream to her coffee, and asked, "How was the breakfast at that posh place you told me about?"

"Oh," Josephine said, as their amazing meals arrived, "the Park Lane. It was perfect. A nine a.m. wedding needed something afterwards. The family and wedding party were all assembled at this long table. I got to sit at the end and observe. I love doing that. Frank and Gene were in the center, with Eldred and Veronica on either side. Frank's father, a small man with a rich Italian accent, was seated opposite me and next to my mother. She sounded more Irish than I've heard her in a long while. It was quite the scene."

"There was a reception after that, right? You stayed right at the Park Lane? I remember those insert cards from the invitation. They were so classy."

"Yes, there was a reception after breakfast from two to four. The breakfast seemed endless, but Gene seemed pleased. Of course, Eldred was there, and several couples from Frank's work. One fellow named Harry Forehead was there, bald as a cucumber."

"Your train ride was cold, yes?"

"I took a lap robe with me that made all the difference. Our hotel was lovely and warm. Veron and I shared a room. Mother had one of her own. Tom and Bernard drove up for the day, a challenging drive in that snow. Don chose not to come and that was probably for the best since the weather was so uncertain. Leaving Lima at the crack of dawn, they barely made it on time."

Josephine paused and took a sip of her coffee, excited to be able to share all these details with a friend who listened so well.

"Gene knew that neither Loring and Peggy nor Vic and Margaret could make it, their children requiring attention. It was also, too bad Betty couldn't manage to find a way. She so loves a party. But at least she did get to see Frank over the Christmas holiday at Mother's. He's quite the charmer. Veronica told me he sang to Betty. And she sang, too. That's all she needed. She thinks he's swell."

Petie finished her next forkful of goulash and then asked, "Did you ever find out why Gene and Frank chose January for their wedding? Buffalo isn't noted for its mild winters."

"Yes. Well, they started dating that fall of the Republican cruise. Frank's mother had been ill with diabetes for quite some time and was doctoring for the better part of the next year. Her death came in September, so there was no reason to wait any longer."

Petie said as she finished her last bite. "It must be nice to have such a big family, Josephine."

Josephine nodded, then paused and looked over at Petie. "It's a comfort and a sorrow. So many to love and so many to lose," she said.

"Tell me, did you get your next patient assignment this morning?" Petie asked.

Josephine's pensive look shifted. "I did," she beamed.

"It's an older widow who lives alone in her own apartment overlooking the river. She has heart disease and, from what I understand, is a charming person. I could use that about now. I'm not getting any younger."

After the waitress brought the bill, which they split down the middle, Josephine asked, "Petie, will you start doing private duty someday?"

Petie slid her money toward Josephine and said, "Right now, I love what I'm doing. The excitement of the variety of patients is stimulating. But private duty is not out of the question. It certainly seems to suit you so far."

"Yes, I love it. You know, I'm turning forty this summer.

Save a spot for me on your roster. One never knows."

As they reached the door, Josephine said, "I'm off to the Frick. If you were on private duty, you could join me. Think about it."

They hugged and parted ways, Josephine grateful for this friendship that warmed her despite the cold. It was like having a sister nearby.

Chapter 54
Bernard's Hope

Spring 1940

Bernard sat atop the tractor in the back forty acres, the day spilling wonder all around him. Bright yellow sunlight flooded the fields, his favorite, and bluest of skies above. The moist, dark soil yielded easily as he plowed it into readiness for planting. He gazed over the fields, eyeing the massive cream-colored barn, with the garage and hen house painted the same color. A picket fence separated them from the yard where the laundry was hung to dry.

The green shingled farmhouse stood solidly facing the road with two horse chestnut trees towering above the porch that was home to a glider and two splendid rocking chairs. Bernard took joy in the stand of trees he'd finally planted just north of the house. In years to come they'd provide a handsome boundary to this land, he thought.

All of this was his father's legacy, he thought. A simple man from Ireland who lived to own forty acres of land and father a dozen children. He'd been a proud man and a fortunate one. A farmer.

Bernard had found pride, too, in being a farmer, having learned what to plant when and how to harvest it. He found it satisfying to live from his own labor, the land supporting him as long as he cared for it. His father had taught him well. For that matter, so had his older brother Loring, who was generous in offering needed advice.

Loring had lost all he had in the stock market crash, a devastating time for so many farmers. Their New York City cousin, John Kerrigan, was unable to help despite his job on

Wall Street. It had become a cautionary tale for Bernard, and he'd learned a lesson he'd not forget. His own nest egg, carefully set aside from the money he earned for his mother and the farm, was finally amounting to something substantial, his financial savvy and conservative investing paying off.

Bernard's three years teaching in the rural schools had been a good start, and one he might have enjoyed for his life's work had he not felt duty-bound to help on the farm. He'd never forget the good teachers he'd had. He counted Sister Teresita among them. Her kindness and encouragement often helped him beyond the academics he'd learned, patience and steadiness serving him well.

He drove the tractor up and down the rows, turning the wheels carefully to line up tightly to the next row, as Tom had taught him; the trick was to start the turn just before you ended the row. As he swung the steering wheel and rounded another row, he thought about Tom, sorry his marriage to Beulah hadn't worked out. If only Tom had the confidence to go with his talents. He'd been glad for Tom's help over the years, his latest assistance during this past harvest. And he was grateful for Tom's connections finding Elmer Wemett, a Lima farmer looking for land to rent.

The time was coming for his mother to cash in on this lucrative land and lease it to farmers able to work it and pay Maggie for its use. It would give her a tidy income and release the boys, mostly Bernard, from the burden of keeping it going.

One good thing about Tom's relationship with Beulah, he'd reported, was that she thought well of his idea to add a side porch onto the house. He launched into his plan to include a screened-in porch with seating for a good number of folks and a chaise lounge for the lucky one who got to sleep outdoors.

Donnell had recently found some work in Honeoye Falls, at the Pitkin Nursery, a job that paid enough that he could be a contributor to the household and be his own boss working in the greenhouses. His farm training and gifted way with flowers helped him to develop prize winning roses, one of his happy successes. He was glad to walk the hour-long journey to Honeoye Falls, sometimes getting rides from passing neighbors.

Veronica did her part from Niagara Falls and sent money when she could from her teacher's salary. Loring and Peggy with their growing family of six stopped by weekly, often bringing fresh vegetables and potatoes. Vic and Margaret occasionally visited with their children, bringing joy worth a bundle.

Gene was currently in no position to help, fully occupied with her first child, a girl named after Frank's mother and herself in the tradition of the day, Mary Jean. Her home was in Buffalo, and Frank was enjoying his success at the electric company.

Ultimately, they all pitched in as they could, Bernard and Tom forming an allegiance of sorts. Bernard remembered their harrowing drive to Gene's wedding. He had thought Gene, a lovely bride. As she said her wedding vows, he found himself far more emotional than he was prepared for. Her eyes gleamed and as she looked at Frank, Bernard felt a pang. Her joy was palpable. It was then he resolved it was time he had a turn at love.

As he brought the tractor around the last row, Bernard paused and looked about him again before he started toward the barn. The shimmering rows sparkled in the sun, the symmetry of his work satisfying. The land was ready for planting and new growth. So was he.

Chapter 55
Remembering

Spring 1940

Maggie settled into a chair at the dining room table, the rainy April afternoon perfect for a cup of tea and time to spend with her green valise. She had been pleased with this little green train case, the survivor of a three-piece set, its clasps still in working order. It had served her well over the years as a place to keep cherished documents and every now and again to peek inside and remember. She pulled out the most recent clippings from the Lima Recorder:

Thursday, May 27th, 1937:

Announcing a daughter born to Mr. and Mrs. Loring F. Donegan of Rochester St.

And as sweet a daughter as one could hope for, little Maureen had been joined by William Eugene a little over a year later.

The next clipping brought yet another smile.

June 17, 1937 Lima Local Bernard P. Donegan, '25, President of Lima High School Alumni Association, announces the annual banquet to be held next Tuesday at 7:30 p.m. in the Town Hall dining room.

How Bernard had fretted over the details and what fine reviews came to him from so many afterward. He was a man about town, capable and talented, there was no doubt. And though she'd miss him, she was pleased that he was now dating a woman who just might become Mrs. Bernard P. Donegan. She knew enough not to ask too much, but she had hopes.

And here, a notice mentioning herself.

Mrs. W.F. Hovey, Mrs. Margaret Donegan, and Mrs. Margaret Boheme attended a retreat from Thursday to Saturday at Sacred Heart Convent in Rochester conducted by the Redemptorist Fathers.

She had enjoyed those days, so glad Betty had alerted her to the opportunity and grateful for Margaret Boehme, who drove each day. Since Betty was missioned at Sacred Heart and was on summer break, it gave Maggie a chance to have lunch with her, a treasured time. Maggie found the talks that the Redemptorist priest gave inspiring, especially enjoying the quiet time for prayer away from the busyness of her life.

She pulled a few more *Lima Recorder* clippings from the pile and saw, tucked below, the packet of holy cards from her sister Molly's family. Her collection of little remembrance prayer cards that held the birth and death dates were tied with purple ribbon. She lifted them out and gently untied them, knowing that each card offered prayers and blessings:

Mary Healy Dec. 5, 1896, infant girl
Eugene Healy 1910, infant boy
Jerome Healy, April 24, 1914, son
Patrick Healy, November 7, 1914, husband
John W. Healy, son, April 7, 1917, son

In the midst of all Mollie's grief, she and Maggie also shared the loss of their sister Lizzie, Jeremiah's twin, who died on September 22, 1916. She had been only forty-three, her constitution too weak to fight the pneumonia that most likely took her. And before too long, that same illness took Mollie, her daughter Margaret, caring for her night and day until the end in 1923.

Maggie didn't know how she'd ever get over the loss of Mollie, someone who knew her and loved her like no other, someone who greeted her as she got off the boat from Ireland, someone to share memories of home and their parents with, and especially, someone who meant home to her in America.

Thanks be to God for Mollie's daughter who had attended to so much. Named after her grandmother and her aunt, Margaret

Healy had already added a stone monument for her brother John, in Calvary Cemetery in Queens, and included Aunt Lizzie on the stone, quite near the other Buckleys, the last two deaths just seven months apart.

Maggie sat back in her chair and sipped her tea. Her gaze fell upon the reproduction of Millet's painting of The Angelus on the dining room wall. She was grateful that it had been left by the Lays family when they sold them the house. It was a source of solace and a reminder to Maggie of her key to survival: prayer. She reached down, pulled her rosary from her apron pocket, and fingered the beads as she looked at the couple in the painting, heads bowed, pausing from their fieldwork at the call of the church bell to say the Angelus. How else do we endure? Maggie wondered.

She sighed and smiled as her eye caught a stray article on the table from two years ago stating that Veronica and Genevieve were home for a visit on Easter Sunday. She remembered it. What a grand visit it had been. These two daughters had been women in love and giddy with it. They brought such spirit and laughter with them, encouraging Maggie to do a dance for them, Veronica singing one of her many songs from her years performing under the direction of her teacher, Miss Belle Chapin.

Maggie looked forward to the joy that was still to come, meeting Gene's first child, Mary Jean, born on May 1. The excitement of yet another grandchild held Maggie ever grateful. She'd known overwhelming joy despite her sorrows. She hoped the same for her children.

She tied the ribbon back around the Healy clan cards, remembering the comfort she took from her sister-in-law Annie's 1917 letter about a visit with Mollie:

Mollie was here on Sunday. She stands it all very good. It is like old times when we get together. She is a lovely woman, just as stately as she was thirty years ago.

As she reviewed the clippings, photos, cards, and letters, reading them and remembering, Maggie had a hope that her children would save them and perhaps pass them on to their children and their children's children, lessons of life for each of them to learn and draw strength from. These tales of survival and surrender were important, Maggie thought, for posterity.

Only two years ago, word had come of the death of Maggie's sister-in-law, Annie Donegan's 2nd husband, Bryan Kerrigan. May 10th death marked the loss of the man who brought such strength and love to Annie and the five Galena girls after Hugh Galena's sudden death. He was the man who took on a family of five daughters and added to it three Kerrigan children, John, Catherine and Anna, great assets to them all.

Bryan had outlived Annie by ten years, his children holding him close. He had been living with their son John and daughters Margaret and Frances when he died. The fact that he and Hugh, Annie's first husband, had been friends made his marriage to her even more fitting. What a gift to have another man keep your children safe from harm and give your wife the gifts you'd hoped to.

Next, Maggie gingerly picked up a clipping from the June 21, 1938, *Daily Item* newspaper, knowing it to be a keepsake.

Legion Pays Final Tribute to War Nurse
Miss Elizabeth Galena
Given Honorary Escort
by Harrison Post

American Legion services were conducted last night for Miss Elizabeth Galena by Carle-Anderson Post 559, Harrison, at the home of her sister, Mrs. John J. Fennelly, 19 Coakley Avenue. Miss Galena was one of the few women members of the Post. She served with the Army Nurse Corps in France during the World War...

Many floral tributes and a full attendance of friends testified to the popularity of Miss Galena, who had served as Harrison district nurse for 16 years until her retirement last year. During the past year, Miss Galena was an office nurse for Dr. George C. Menninger of Mamaroneck…

Auntie Vic, as Elizabeth, the oldest Galena daughter, was called by the family, was fifty-four, each year measured by her giving nature. Vic's younger sister, Loretta, had married John J. Fennelly and brought a new generation to Harrison, New York, with Anna Marie, Jim, Mary Elizabeth, and Catherine all adding to the Galena clan. Auntie Vic's noteworthy nursing career made a lasting mark of love on them all.

As Maggie began putting things carefully back into the valise, Bernard and Don came in from their morning work, bringing along the mail from the day. She wondered what news it might carry, what joy or sorrow, what wonder or worry. No matter what, she would leave it with a whisper and a prayer for all yet to be.

Chapter 56
The Perfect Day!

May 1941

Bernard stepped into the kitchen at Loring and Peggy's, just down the road from Maggie's farm. This early day in May boasted a periwinkle blue sky. He put his well-worn straw hat on the hook and took his regular seat near the stove, leaving Margaret Mary and the three older boys, Bobby, Jack, and Junior, in the yard, their laughter following him into the house. The two youngest, Maureen and Billy, were playing with blocks in the dining room, intent on building a fenced-in yard to keep their toy horses corralled.

Peggy smiled and nodded as Bernard began to first whistle and then sing the song that had become his signature since his regular visits with Loring's family began several years ago.

When you come to the end of a perfect day
And you sit alone with your thought
While the chimes ring out with a carol gay
For the joy that the day has brought
Do you think what the end of a perfect day
Can mean to a tired heart
When the sun goes down with a flaming ray
And the dear friends have to part?

With a tumble of their blocks, the children stopped their building and came out and sat at Bernard's feet as he continued.

Well, this is the end of a perfect day
Near the end of a journey, too;
But it leaves a thought that is big and strong
With a wish that is kind and true
For mem'ry has painted this perfect day
With colors that never fade
And we find at the end of a perfect day
The soul of a friend we've made.

The song thrilled Peggy each time Bernard sang it. She looked forward to this ritual they'd begun, his visits a balm for her weary soul. She clasped her hands together, looked at Bernard and said, "Once again, you've made my day a perfect one."

Bernard smiled, his whole face beaming. He reached down and lifted the children onto his knees.

"Horty ride, horty ride," they chanted, another favorite treat they savored. Bernard began to bounce them as he said the nursery rhyme he'd learned as a boy: "This is the way the ladies ride, bumpety, bumpety, bump." He picked up his pace as he continued to recite. "This is the way the gentlemen ride, bumpety, bumpety bump." And finally, he bounced them vigorously as he chanted, "This is the way the farmers ride, bumpety, bumpety bump," as he bounced them higher and higher. The children screamed with delight and hugged Bernard as he lowered them down.

Bernard's own satisfaction matched that of the children. He was keen for these little ones and felt his heart swell to see their smiles. Might he ever have his own little ones? he wondered. Thoughts of Etta came as he remembered meeting her at a

Legion dance a few months ago. Her manner continued to beguile him each time he was with her, which was more and more frequent.

As he stood and reached for his hat, Peggy handed Bernard the shepherd's pie casserole she'd prepared for Maggie, certain that he, Don, and Maggie would enjoy this traditional and nutritious meal of lamb, vegetables, and mashed potato. Peggy had been sending a meal home with Bernard each week without fail as her way of contributing to the family farm. John's death, coupled with the difficulty farmers were facing during this pre-war time, made every bit of help appreciated.

Her children were aware that Maggie, now nearing seventy, had wavering stamina. It was only last year that she'd had gallbladder surgery, a scare for all of them. Veronica continued coming down from Niagara Falls for a weekend each month to see to the household upkeep and give direction to her younger brothers.

"Ma says your pie is the best around," Bernard said, his blue eyes shining. "She's right, you know." He slipped out the door, skirting the children whom he'd love to stop and play with, yet knowing the dinner must get home.

As Bernard walked off down the road, his work with Loring finished for the day, and he was pleased. A perfect day indeed. Their arrangement of sharing chores was working out well, and the family farm was thriving for the time being. Loring was spending several days a month helping Bernard, and Bernard was faithful in returning the favor. He began to whistle his song again, glad always for the opportunity to sing it.

And we find at the end of a perfect day
The soul of a friend we've made.

A friend indeed. Once again, Etta came to mind. Her dark hair, vibrant eyes, and clear complexion were similar to those of his sisters Josephine, Genevieve and Betty. Of the girls, only Veronica had blue eyes and red hair. Etta's industrious personality was also familiar. The second child of seven, her brothers and sisters, like Bernard's siblings, were also dependable workers.

Etta worked at the Stromberg-Carlson factory in Rochester. The company's production of the "farmer's telephone" and its well-known tagline advertisement, "It's cheaper to talk than walk," had helped decrease the isolation of farmers and promoted the safety and efficiency of telephones. Bernard found Etta to be as solid as the company she worked for.

Over the past weeks, Bernard and Etta had continued to meet at occasional dances at the Legion Hall and even had some Sunday afternoon strolls along the creek, one of his favorite spots. She chattered about her work and asked about his family. Her own father, Louis, was a farmer as well. She was younger than Bernard by six years, but he determined that her intelligence was an equal match to his. Her mother, Grace, with her steady gaze from dark brown eyes, had taught Etta well, so when she came to Bernard's home for Sunday dinner, she helped with the preparation of the meal and cleaning the dishes. It was as natural as could be that she shooed the men away, pleasing Maggie with her feminine support.

With World War II active in Europe, Bernard's draft card became his safety valve. It stated him as five feet six and a half inches, with blue eyes, a light complexion, and brown hair. Yet to Bernard, the most important line on the card was the answer to the question that asked for "employer." His answer, "Self-farm," went a long way in preventing him from being drafted. His father's death left Bernard the logical choice for "head of the family".

It was during this time Bernard began to consider being married, the notion often foremost in his mind. By next January, he'd be thirty-six. Being a self-employed, married farmer certainly would secure his status and, more than likely, defer him from active duty.

Bernard happily delivered the shepherd's pie to Maggie's grateful hands and washed up for dinner. As he joined his mother and Don at the table, he said, as an end to his perfect day, "Perhaps I should get married. What do you think?"

Chapter 57
Thank Heavens for Freddie

Spring 1942

Thank heavens for Freddie! As Veronica drove into the crushed stone driveway and pulled her black 1938 Dodge up by the garage, she smiled as she thought of his gift for her fortieth birthday this past February. He brought such joy and excitement to her life, providing a wonderful counterbalance to all the responsibilities that were hers.

Freddie had hoped to surprise her with the trip to Bermuda on her 40th birthday to coordinate with her school winter holiday. It was a trip Veronica had dreamt about ever since Josephine had gone so many years ago. The ship, the Queen of Bermuda, serves Hamilton, the island's capital. Josephine had raved about the St. George's Hotel and beach, the Gibb's Hill Lighthouse, and the Cathedral of the Most Holy Trinity.

Freddie sadly reported that they couldn't go because of a new naval base and reactivation of the air bases that turned Bermuda into a military outpost. "The darn war didn't know we were planning a celebration," Freddie had said.

To mark his promise, he presented her with a rain check: a ten-inch metal airplane replica that was engraved with the name Tiny Pursuit. He'd had it made using ingenuity and his Aero Pattern Works factory. His hope was that a plane would one day carry them to her dream vacation.

As she accepted the gift, realizing his sensitivity and pure intention, she wondered if the dream would ever be fulfilled. This year, she had taken time off to help nurse her mother back to health after gallbladder surgery. Maggie hadn't been gravely ill but definitely needed help. When another time would be available was anyone's guess. She'd hold onto her airplane until then.

Freddie's daughter, Mary Jane, was often a part of their planning. Mary Jane's schooling included Our Lady of Lourdes grammar school and St. Mary's Seminary, a women's business school in Buffalo. She had hoped to work for her father's company as a way to spend more time with him since much of his attention was devoted to his work.

Mary Jane had been raised and nurtured by her father's sisters, Bert and Tilly. Any fears of Veronica taking her father away, while not spoken aloud, were continually being allayed. Veronica had a bevy of friends beyond Freddie and her family responsibilities kept her on the go between Niagara Falls and Lima. For now, all was well.

As Veronica stepped into the dining room, the quiet told her that her mother was resting. She put her things in the small bedroom on the far side of the kitchen and changed into her slippers, the ones she left tucked under the bed.

As she straightened up the buffet, she noted a handful of pictures from Bernard's December 31st wedding. How lovely a couple they were. The pictures of Sister Betty and Etta looked almost like they were blood sisters, except for Betty's religious habit with its starched headdress and crucifix. They were standing out in a blanket of snow in the front yard under the horse chestnut trees, smiles filling their faces. In the next photo, Bernard and Etta were with Etta's brother Melvin and his wife Edith, their witnesses. A photo with just Maggie and Bernard was a telling one, Veronica thought. Neither was smiling, a bittersweet parting. Bernard's presence had been an incomparable solace to Maggie these ten years since John's death.

The newspaper clipping from the Democrat and Chronicle's January 15th edition was tucked into an envelope. Veronica would see to it that it was placed in a frame, the seventh and more than likely, the last of Maggie's brood to be married.

The marriage of Miss Etta Rumsey, daughter of Mr. and Mrs. Louis Rumsey of Honeoye Falls and Bernard Donegan, son of Mrs. Margaret Donegan of Lima, took place Wednesday, December 31, in St. Paul of the Cross rectory. The ceremony was performed by the Rev. William J. Killackey. The couple was attended by Mr. and Mrs. Melvin Rumsey. After a short wedding trip, Mr. and Mrs. Donegan will reside in Lima.

The rectory wedding was on New Year's Eve, a simple event with great dignity and no fanfare.

Bernard was shrewd about many things, money one of them. A marriage before the new year would be financially beneficial and with the December attack of Pearl Harbor, he was certain that marriage would keep him off the rolls of the draft, two wise moves.

Despite both her sister Gene and brother Bernard marrying within a few years of each other, Veronica had no such inclination, nor, it seemed, did Freddie. She was content, her life full to the brim. His obligations were many as well. his daughter's presence in his life very important. Both were satisfied for the time being.

As she did regularly, Veronica brought family news home with her. She was glad to report that Gene was doing well, her next child due in July, but Mary Jean, the firstborn, was still the shining star. It was likely that Bernard and Etta would have children in due course. No doubt the Donegan name would go on.

She wondered if Josephine's beau, Fletcher, had been proposing marriage. Might Josephine be ready? Time will tell.

Chapter 58
Petie in Lima

Josephine at home on the farm

August 1948

Margaret Petersen, known affectionately as "Petie," brought sunshine wherever she went. That's what Josephine told her mother as they arrived home in Lima in early June. Petie would stay with her. She was not to be concerned.

Josephine had said little of her breast cancer to anyone, determined not to trouble others. She'd made peace with her fate, grateful for time to put things in order. She would have time to love them all to the very end now that she was home. Petie's presence would help assure that.

Josephine and Petie's friendship was solid from the start, and their dedication to nursing was mutual. The two had traveled often to the art galleries that glittered in New York City, Petie teaching Josephine things she might never have known; Josephine teaching Petie nursing skills for a lifetime.

Josephine once described the painting in their dining room at home to Petie: a couple portrayed pausing in their fieldwork, a church in the background. Petie easily identified it as a work by Millet titled *The Angelus*. On one of their forays to the Met, Petie showed Josephine Millet's *Calling the Cows Home*. The cowherd sounding his horn at the end of the day was equally evocative. The Metropolitan Museum of Art and the Frick, both short walks from the hospital, found the two learning and laughing weekly. As they navigated the aftermath of the days following the Great Depression, its toll heavy, they found solace in artists who depicted the reality around them.

Edward Hopper's *Tables for Ladies* was one of their favorites. Two women portrayed arranging displays and checking out customers at the cash register. This kind of work was only recently available to women, giving confirmation of the value of their existence. Petie and Josephine identified with the weary workers who, much as they themselves, were bone-tired yet glad for the work. The painting's title told of the recent social innovation; "tables for ladies" advertised to welcome female customers who were now free to dine alone. The victory over the societal norm that women dining alone was scandalous had finally been won.

Petie and Josephine were attracted to the work for equality and the essential rights of women, happy for the vote and ready for more freedoms. The entrance of Eleanor Roosevelt onto the international stage gave them substantial hope amidst the trying times. Eleanor's spirit and openness to all women are something they both prized. They looked to additional women of the day for inspiration and easily found college graduate Frances Perkins, Secretary of Labor; Molly Dewson, an ambassador of Roosevelt's New Deal; and Mary McLeod Bethune, who often stood with Eleanor, was in the "kitchen cabinet" and served as president of the National Council of Negro Women.

The fact that both their parents had emigrated, Petie's from Norway and Sweden and Josephine's from Ireland, gave them empathy for the plight of others and more respect for differences.

It was one of the many bonds these two 'soulmates' possessed. They shared their life stories and had much fun in their years together. Dancing was one of Petie's many passions, along with art. Josephine was vehement about the role of women, bringing rich, philosophical discussions that occupied much of their time together.

On one occasion, Josephine declared, "No man should have domain over a woman. With four older brothers, I learned quickly enough that women can be far more clever and more efficient. Equality isn't just a nicety. It's a necessity."

In Lima, Petie settled into the upper bedroom at the Donegan farmstead, glad for this private space apart and time to absorb what was happening. She could tell by the look in her eyes that Maggie was frightened. She hoped she might provide comfort for her as well as Josephine. They all seemed accepting of Petie and her assistance, helping where and when they could, wishing none of this had to be. Veronica had given over her first-floor bedroom to Josephine and returned to the little room next to Petie on the second floor. They had talked into the night on Petie's first evening, sharing recent events and reminiscing about visits they'd had in the past.

"Do you remember the night we went to the "Ritz-Carlton?" Petie asked.

"I'll never forget it," Veronica replied, her eyes alight with the memory. "Gene was with me, and it was on that same trip we met Josephine's beau, Fletcher, and her patient who adored her. What was her name?"

"There were so many that adored her, but I know who you mean. She was well-to-do and quite smitten with the care Josephine delivered."

"How is Fletcher taking the news? She certainly didn't lead him on at all once she knew, did she?"

Her mention of Fletcher led Petie back to the night Josephine had told him of her diagnosis and her plan to return home to Lima. The three of them had supper at the restaurant on the corner, a familiar and cozy spot. Josephine had asked Petie to join them. She told of remembering Fletcher's clear blue eyes clouding over as he listened to Josephine, their marriage plans melting away.

"The advantages of being in the medical field helped her make her decisions. She knows what's coming and what might have been," Petie told Veronica. Their talk slowed and sleep took over. Another day to be addressed soon enough.

As the sun rose, its red steaks vibrant across the fields, Josephine was there to see it. She slipped out the door and stood feasting on the sky as ribbons of pinks, reds and yellows colored it. She was glad to be alone in these moments so she could capture and savor them. She was determined each day to remember something significant about this idyllic place she had called home these many years. She would be forty-three in August. She'd had such a good life. Even her choice to leave work and come home for her last days was not difficult and so much easier once Petie agreed to accompany her. She felt beyond blessed despite the breast cancer. So many didn't know what would take them. She did. Was it faith, she wondered, that helped her keep her equilibrium so steady?

She knew her mother's faith had seen her through so many difficult times; the death of Baby Rose, Don's limitations, Hugh and Jerome's deaths and her dear husband's. Yet somehow, Maggie didn't act mournful. Her twinkle, while diminished in certain moments, still shone when she did her Irish jig for them as they gathered around the piano. She still wore her ancient laced-up shoes and raised her skirt as she kicked up her heels, bringing applause from all.

Josephine turned from the sunrise and looked back at the little farmhouse that had held so many of them over the years.

She glanced at Bernard's trees on the northern edge of their land. He'd made his mark in so many ways. Just then, she saw Petie slip out the door. She waited for her. They walked hand in hand silently for a while. The sun rose over the creek's bank and lit up the fields that were filled with the spent corn stalks of the season.

"How are you feeling?" Petie asked as she moved ahead in the field. "Glad you're home?" Josephine had been Petie's mentor from the moment they met. She recognized wisdom and peace and trusted her guidance. Though Josephine was fourteen years older, their friendship made them peers.

Josephine spoke softly at first, "Glad to be home?" she repeated. "Yes, for as long as I will be. How am I feeling? I'm glad you're here with me to administer opium and morphine. Sorry to say, but I think I'm going to need it. I don't want to frighten Mother or any of them if I can help it."

Petie nodded, understanding what they had agreed to when she talked about coming to Lima; this family was big enough to help each other out, but Josephine was independent enough not to want to interrupt their lives one iota.

Petie pulled a husk off a spent stalk of corn and began to fold it in halves until it was tiny. "I'll do my best," she said as she let go of the husk, knowing her job was just beginning.

At breakfast, Veronica served up the eggs and pancakes, something Josephine had been in charge of in the past. They talked of Bernard and Etta, the new baby due in February. Then Veronica, who often saw Gene and Frank, announced that Gene would have their third baby this month, little John a year old in July and Mary Jean two in May.

"She's trying to catch up, I guess, since she got such a late start," Maggie said and chuckled. She had her own start at age 18 when Hugh was born, quite ahead of Gene's age of 33 when Mary Jean, when Gene was 33 was born, her third child at 35.

Josephine's illness was not spoken of, and everyone was doing what they could to assure her comfort. The chaise lounge they had purchased for the side porch for Maggie's comfort last year now became Josephine's spot, visits from her brothers and their families made comfortable. Chairs were pulled around to seat those who visited, and Petie was always mindful of entertaining the children who came. Loring and Peggy's children were, as Josephine said, "as handsome and talented as their parents." The girls, Maureen, aged 5 and Margaret Mary, at 15, led them all in singing songs from school and the boys, Bob, Jack, Loring Jr. and Billy, even did a bit of an Irish Jig to please their grandmother.

Petie told the children tales of her native Canadian province of Saskatchewan, where women had earned the right to vote in 1916 and where she had learned to ice skate in her own backyard. She told of cold winters and playing hockey day in and day out.

The evenings passed pleasantly, Father Ball, a frequent visitor. "I saw the lights on and thought I'd say hello," he would tell them. His news of the parish and the solace of his attentive presence were a comfort. Petie never tired of the parade of people and watched carefully to be certain that Josephine wasn't overtaxed. The medications, dispensed carefully by Doc Coburn and saved for Josephine's comfort, were used as needed.

Soon came the news on August 18th of the birth of James Michael Osta, a curly, dark-haired child who made number three. Unlike John Francis, named after his grandfather and father, no traditional naming rights seemed to be in place for this newest boy. He'd be his own person.

With Petie in Lima to help take care of, Veronica was able to go off to Buffalo and use some of her remaining summer holiday to give Frank a hand; Gene was recuperating for two weeks in Children's Hospital. During John's birth the previous July, Frank and Gene had arranged for some help to come in daily. Gene had discovered when she got home that her golf clubs had been taken along with some sterling silver.

"Luckily," Gene said to Veronica when she visited her at the hospital, "your presence will save us from any further pilfering. Of course, you're certainly welcome to use my golf clubs."

August 21st found many of the family together as they celebrated Josephine's 43rd birthday, the bittersweet moment accompanied by yellow cake with chocolate frosting, a family favorite, decorated with a tiny nurse's cap and seven candles in two rows, 4 + 3.

A few weeks later, just ten days before his 38th birthday, word came through that Tom was to report for duty on September 11th to Lincoln Army Airfield in Nebraska. The memory of his presence at Josephine's 43rd birthday party made it all the more special. He'd be gone for his September 21st birthday and so would Josephine, the medications bringing her comfort to an end.

Following the evening calling hours and the Mass the next day, Father Ball read the words of committal at the graveside as they all came together in the cemetery.

"May Josephine's soul and the souls of all the faithful departed, through the mercy of God, rest in peace. Amen."

It was just then a rainbow appeared in the sky.

Chapter 59
M. M. Josephine

Autumn 1942

"I named her Margaret Mary Josephine, after me and Mary and Joseph," Maggie said to Petie, this gift of a woman who'd brought them such support during Josephine's final days.

"This precious girl was such a gift after the birth of the four boys. Every single day of her life, she brought joy and healing. She held my hand and heart after the loss of Baby Rose. She was only fifteen and she somehow knew how to help." Maggie looked into Petie's eyes as she continued. "She had quiet ways, softness, and strength. I wasn't surprised at all that she wanted to be a nurse. She was one before she even studied."

Petie listened as Maggie reminisced, feeling privileged to be here, to be able to hear this mother whose heart was breaking yet again. They were sitting in the front parlor where the coffin had been two days earlier. The furniture had been put back in place, and the chairs straightened. The piano music for Red Sails in the Sunset was on the rack, one of Josephine's favorites. Petie remembered her joy at her first hearing the song. They'd gone together to the Broadway production of Provincetown Follies that featured the song.

Maggie filled both their teacups. Her blue eyes were ringed with red, yet her voice was remarkably strong. "When her two older brothers died, I felt my heart was outside my body, the pain barely containable. It had been a dozen years since the baby's loss. When Hugh died and then Jerome, not even two years later," she paused, "do you know what she told me? I'll never forget it. We were walking in the cornfield. She never tired of the farm and the fields. She took my hand as we walked along,

Jerome's burial just past Hugh's grave, finally with an engraved stone she'd seen too. She looked up in the direction of the creek, a place we all enjoyed.

"'Mother,' she said. Josephine always said Mother rather than Ma, saying it with such respect." Maggie paused and dabbed her eyes with her apron as she spoke. 'Mother, we were loaned those two men who loved the life you gave them so much. They were both good, loving men. You can't ask more than that.'"

Petie watched Maggie's eyes smile as she sipped her tea. "Imagine, Petie, this young woman with such wisdom and good sense. At the time, she wasn't even thirty years old. Oh, how deeply I will miss her. How very deeply." Tears streamed down her cheeks. Petie sat in silence.

Within a few days, Petie said her goodbyes to Josephine's family, her own heartbreaking. She'd been treated to an insider view of the family she heard so much about over the years, the people who loved her friend Josephine so well. She'd met the parish priest, Father Ball and Doc Kober, who'd helped her keep Josephine as pain-free as they could. Gratefully, the opium, morphine, and aspirin, administered in careful doses as needed, had been sufficient. She'd watched as Josephine tolerated so much. Now, it was over.

Petie knew by their many kindnesses, a special nod, a gentle touch, a cup of tea at the right time, that she had been appreciated by them all, her presence bringing peace as she nursed Josephine. Moments such as these were the reason she chose nursing. People such as these were the reason she believed. Petie suspected that Josephine knew precisely what she was doing by asking Petie to be with her in Lima. Besides bringing support to the family, she was giving Petie some solace, a family with whom she could share this love and this loss.

Petie learned what a rock Josephine had been for them all, handling the details of her two brothers' deaths, her father's death and now her own. She'd even seen to the purchase and engraving of the rose granite stone that would stand in St. Rose Cemetery for years to come with the names of the John and Margaret Donegan family as they came home to Lima. The headstones for Hugh and Jerome were in close proximity. The large family stone, its distinctive color standing out, would remind them that they were family and they were home. Soon enough, just under her parents' names, the stone would read:

M.M.Josephine
1898-1942.

Rest in peace, dear friend, rest in peace.

Chapter 60
America

September 1945

Maggie set off for church, trusting the walk would do her good. It had become routine to walk the mile up Rochester Street on her own, though a generous ride had been offered by Loring and the others when they could give it. She'd been known to take the pony and trap during her younger days. These days, with her Don the only one still living with her, the walk felt freeing, away from his chatter and the worry of what would become of him.

She knew that Veronica and the others talked of his limitations. He was simple, no doubt about that, but he wasn't simple-minded. She'd cared for him and had seen him develop, watched his way with plants, reviving the most lost-looking ones with his patience. His love of radios that took him around the world made her marvel. If she could keep him from the drink, as they had tried to keep her own brother Tims from it, he'd be all right. She was certain of it. Ah, but Sunday morning was not a time she needed to worry. Though he had no interest in going to church, this surviving twin was happily working in the garden and that gave her this freedom.

Traffic was always light on Sunday mornings. As she started off, she nodded to her neighbor, Mrs. Tollis, as she tended her lush gardens. The roses were in such plenty they fell over one another, their heads drooping in the crisp fall air, the last roses of summer. Their blood-red color and prominent thorns seemed to proclaim their majesty among the fading daisies and clusters of Black-eyed Susan.

Maggie felt a new freedom with the end of the war. The evil that crossed the world during these past years rivaled her memories of the Irish troubles, senseless deaths to attain freedoms that were God-given. She was glad to learn of Hitler's suicide, trusting he'd earned his own fate. She knew the tortured soul of her boy Hugh had led him to end his life and couldn't imagine what Hitler's soul was like. The atomic bomb that had finally ended it all frightened her. What would life be like for all of us now? Freedom, yes, but at what price?

Three of her sons had spent time in the United States Army. She prayed her grandsons wouldn't have to.

She passed 'The Stand' on the right with its white-hot dogs and ice cream cones. Simpler days would come, for sure, when they would all enjoy life's pleasures again. Her grandchildren, growing in number, would one day bring a new order to the country and that was worth something. Her own citizenship gave her an authority that, up until recently, she had lacked. How could she preach loyalty and allegiance to others before she pledged her own?

Several years ago, she had donned her best coat, the black one with the beaver collar and her small velvet hat and went off with Josephine to the Geneseo Courthouse on a blustery Monday morning, one day before St. Patrick's Day. Good luck, Josephine had declared. When she stepped inside the courthouse, whose grandeur had been created by architect Claude Bragdon, her mind was flooded with her first memory of America, standing on the deck of the S.S. Etruria, seeing the new Statue of Liberty come into view.

She remembered how her heart ached for Ireland, for home, for her mother, her father. How could she ever imagine she would abandon her loyalty to Ireland, to Ahadallane, to all she knew and pledge a new loyalty to America? Yet fifty-one years later, she had made a petition for naturalization. Within another three years, in 1942, she signed her name to an oath of allegiance declaring to "absolutely and entirely renounce and abjure all allegiance and fidelity to any foreign prince, potentate, state, or sovereignty" of whom or which she had heretofore been a subject or citizen. . . so help her God.

Her Certificate of Citizenship with her attached photograph in her favorite black dress with the fitted bodice and tuxedo lace collar would be preserved for her grandchildren. They would learn what she had done so that they might prosper. They would learn that she could love her homeland with all her heart and yet give allegiance to the country that her children and grandchildren would call home.

Maggie sighed at the memory of it all. She neared the four corners of Lima, the American Hotel prominently standing on the southeast corner, the American flag proudly displayed. Within a few months, Tom would be returning from the Army Air Corps where, like his older brother Hugh, he made his mark as a competent soldier, his time in the motor division commendable. When he finally did arrive home, he'd find a new nephew, Bernie Junior, Etta and Bernard's boy. He'd also find out that Gene and Frank brought their number of children to five, adding a boy named Thomas, honoring Gene's affection for her older brother, and a girl named Elizabeth, named after Gene's younger sister. She'd be running out of names soon, Maggie mused.

She slipped into her pew on the front right, blessed herself and pulled out her black rosary beads that had been her mother's, carried with Maggie from Ireland. Another loyalty not forgotten.

Chapter 61
Maggie's Lima

September 1945

Maggie stepped out of St. Rose Church into the cool September air, the Sunday Mass having provided a familiar comfort. The Latin words soothed her soul, the priest reverently bowing and kneeling as the ritual progressed, the organ playing the Kyrie and Agnus Dei, the congregation saying the prayers in unison. Father Ball's sermon was short enough to let them all out early into the sunshine of the autumn day.

When her neighbor, Pete Tollis, offered Maggie a ride home, she declined, saying, "Many thanks, but it's good to keep these legs moving a bit." In her seventh decade, Maggie was proud to have some vigor left. She waved him on and began her walk home.

She was just past St. Brendan's Hall, recalling the arrival of the Sisters of St. Joseph's arrival in 1875 under Father

FitzSimons. She glanced up at the familiar spire and cross, and it suddenly came to her. She was happy. She was at home here in this town. It was as comfortable as her childhood town of Ahadallane, that she left at age 16.

The countryside was so like home, with greens that rivaled her Irish homeland. Lima had been a welcome relief from the crowded tenements, streets filled with garbage, the horrid stench and the fetid air of New York. Here, she could breathe.

As she began to cross Main Street at the four corners, Maggie looked left toward Avon and then to the right toward Canandaigua. On her immediate right was the American Hotel, a fine place for a good meal and comradery, and even a drink, though it was a 'gentleman's only' bar for so long, she'd become used to sitting in the front dining room. She wouldn't stop today despite her fondness for the Reynolds family, who owned and operated this establishment. This would not be a time to chat with Aretha, who would be bustling at this Sunday lunchtime. Besides, Maggie was happy to continue her walk and to carry on her reverie of thanksgiving.

Maggie recalled her arrival in America in 1888 at Castle Garden. The Mission of Our Lady of the Rosary was to be her saving grace. Charlotte Grace O'Brien, a Protestant woman, daughter of William Smith O'Brien, who had been key in so many of the Irish freedom struggles, had made connections and saw to it that young Irish immigrant girls would be kept safe. Father Riordan, the Director of the Mission, had even visited her townland on a tour in Ireland, an historic moment, this man full of compassion and care. His untimely death might have diverted her, but her sister Mary had been there to see to her safety. It was a memorable beginning.

As Maggie crossed Main Street, she gazed up at the majestic spire of the Presbyterian Church and moved on down the road, nearing the corner grocery store. For how many years has she depended on this store to fill in with just what was needed for supper, providing a sweet or two at the right moment? The children had favorite candies that often accompanied the grocery list: Dots, Boston Baked beans, Snickers and Milky Way bars. Veronica had been a dependable errand runner, never dawdling for too long as the boys often did. Sweet, those memories.

Maggie's gaze shifted. She glanced up College Street and saw the stately building of Genesee Wesleyan Seminary. She still felt pride that Hugh had attended this school, receiving his eighth- grade certificate there, which she kept with her important papers. The Seminary brought stature to Lima, one of the earliest co-educational institutions in the country, at a time when education for women was almost unheard of. She was so glad her girls had been able to pursue education in their chosen fields. That the Seminary closed its doors just a few years ago, after such a prestigious run, was still sad.

Thankfully, the National Youth Administration New Deal program championed by Eleanor Roosevelt and announced by President Roosevelt occurred toward the end of the campus's life. One of the work centers provided vocational training to young people located on the campus, which was a final contribution to the rich life on College Street in Lima.

As Maggie passed the Slattery's home, she remembered their early days, Tom purchasing his farm just before they purchased theirs. He had lent moral support to John, his wife Catherine, an Altar and Rosary Society member, along with Maggie. Together, they kept up with the news of the day, their daughter, like Veronica, becoming a dedicated teacher.

As she neared home, Maggie felt her heart expand as she viewed their farmland. The fields were pristine, the sun covering them with a glorious sheen. She'd known from her childhood days how precious farmland was. She remembered her Da, describing the rotted potato, the devastation to the land. Yet he talked more about survival than he did loss, telling how they cleared the death, planted again and somehow survived. It was a lesson she never forgot.

So, when she and John came to New York State to seek farmland, they both knew its value. They had escaped to a new land and a new hope. This land would be their dream with a start on Clay Road, the Keenan farm. John worked the fields, and his children learned its importance. By the time ten of their twelve children were born, they had scrimped and saved enough to buy this forty-acre farm on Rochester Road. It had been a fair price and the continuation of a dream for Maggie and John, by then in their forties. Their children, aged 24 down to age 2, filled the house with new life and special moments. Like her father, Maggie had known losses, but also, like her father, she thought more of survival.

Maggie stood in front of their house, her house. Heartache mixed with gratitude filled her. The stately trees on the northern boundary of the property, Bernard's trees, swayed in the afternoon breeze, birds calling and carrying on, the azure blue sky coloring the landscape. The little green farmhouse, its inviting porch with its white rocking chairs and green glider called to her. She answered by walking down the trimmed walkway, and settling into a rocker, blessed to be at home in her Lima.

Chapter 62
The Picnic

Saturday, August 13, 1949

Gene packed up her six children for what was becoming an annual trip from their Buffalo home to the farm in Lima to celebrate Maggie's August 15th birthday. Donald Mark was already two years old. Veronica had orchestrated a picnic this year and had invited all eighteen grandchildren and three great-grandchildren to celebrate Maggie's 75th birthday.

The party Veronica planned, with Betty's promise to help, would be the kind her mother enjoyed, keeping the bulk of the activities outdoors; games that included badminton, horseshoes and croquet; a cookout menu with hot dogs, hamburgers, potato salad, corn on the cob, coleslaw, baked beans, and deviled eggs. Dessert called for yellow cake with chocolate frosting, as well as cupcakes. Beverages included lemonade, iced tea and the ever-popular Coca-Cola, which debuted originally as a temperance drink, its popularity remaining high. Rochester's Genesee Beer, proudly brewed since 1878, made the party complete for the adults.

Gene was always pleased whenever her children could spend time with their grandmother. They'd never known their Grandfather John, his death preceding Gene's marriage; nor did they know Frank's mother Mary Barocco, also gone before their marriage. This opportunity for them to spend time with an elder was important to Gene, who hadn't known any ancestors; all her grandparents were in Ireland, so having her own children experience elders was priceless.

Frank became accustomed to and actually enjoyed these outings to see Grandmother Donegan. He had never met his own grandparents, who lived in a town in Italy called Osta, his father not telling much about them. Frank found Maggie fascinating and she appreciated the attention.

As the family arrived to a warm and sincere welcome, Veronica saw to it that Gene and Frank's children would have places to sleep, making the trip an adventure for all. The daybed in the front parlor folded out to become a special spot for four-year-old Betty Anne and her nine-year-old sister Mary Jean. The three boys, John, 8, Jim, 7, Tom, 5, slept upstairs in a double bed in the big room across from Don's bedroom, their parents nearby in the two little rooms, each with a twin bed. Little Donald Mark was tucked into a small trundle bed in Veronica's room and happily napped like a top.

The weather cooperated for the adventure. Gene, never fond of humidity, found the day unusually pleasant for mid-August, comfortable with even a slight breeze. They arrived mid-day, the older children scampering off to the yard to check out the hen house, climb to the hayloft and run off some energy. Later, Betty would shepherd them to the front porch, a favorite spot where they invented their own games, sang songs, and rocked in the big white chairs or went back and forth on the glider. Keeping the day amenable to Grandmother so that she could enjoy the children was the goal. So far, so good.

As the afternoon wore on, other families began to arrive, all dressed in their summer best. Vic's Ruth, the oldest grandchild, arrived with her husband Larry Delaney and their two children, Lawrence and Mary Kay, and two dozen deviled eggs, which Larry transported with care. Vic's two other children, Billy, just out of the service and daughter Betty, who was about to graduate from high school, completed the group.

Rachel, Emory Horton, and Cecilia arrived next. Cecilia's joy was contagious as she introduced her husband, Wes Payne and her little boy, Terry.

Within the half-hour, Loring and Peggy arrived with six children and a big potato salad. Margaret Mary, wearing a smart-looking navy-blue dress with white trim, was already twenty-two and a brand-new college graduate. Maggie remembered that little dolly of a child amazed that she was now getting an apartment on her own. Her brothers came as well: Bob, who was courting Mary Ann from Mount Morris, Jack, and Loring Jr. The youngest, Maureen, 12, along with Billy, 11, ready for games.

Cousins Bernie and Mary Lou, aged six and three, were taken in hand by Sister Betty, who couldn't resist bringing them together with the Osta children. While she held Ruth's four-month-old Mary Kay close, she showed Etta, who brought an array of condiments along with a beautifully arranged coleslaw, where to place the food on a buffet table set up in the dining room. The rest of the family found one another, and great conversation flowed.

Gene saw Mary Jean following Maureen into the yard and knew they would be like two peas in a pod. The boys had taken out marbles and were huddled over a bare spot in the stone driveway.

"Well, I think this is working out okay, don't you?" Gene asked Veronica as she came out to the yard. "I can't believe there are so many. How did Mother ever manage all of this?"

"Well, you're doing a fine job of it yourself. You and I learned how to do this as small children, as I recall." Veronica surveyed the scene, watching the older children looking out for the younger ones. "Isn't it wonderful that even great-grandchildren are here? It's been a long while since Mother has seen Cecelia, and I don't think she's ever met her son Terry. He's adorable."

Gene nodded in agreement and added, "I'm glad Betty has been good to her word. She's got the younger children playing Tiddlywinks on the front porch. They seem to be loving it. And she sure loves holding Ruth's little, Mary Kay. It must be hard for her at times. Maybe I should suggest we trade places occasionally. I could stand a rest."

Veronica chuckled as Tom came over with Maxine. His discharge from the army seemed to have given him a new lease on life. He had landed a job at Wickwire, a solid family-owned manufacturing company in Buffalo that specialized in steel and strapping wire. It was a company he hoped to be with for a long while, especially with a new baby on the way.

Gene greeted Maxine and Tom, who lived not too far from them in Buffalo. Maxine, her due date of October showing, noted that Gene had slimmed down since her last baby. "How's it feel not to be pregnant?" she asked. "I'm wishing it were time already."

Gene remembered her first pregnancy nine years ago. She encouraged Maxine by saying, "The end result is worth the effort. Most of the time." With that, three children came racing past, just barely missing them as they charged for the ball.

"See what I mean?"

Rachel and Emory joined Tom and Maxine, as did Loring and Peggy. No one ventured any comment on the job Truman was doing in his second term of office, nor that he signed an order ending segregation in the U.S. military. They had long ago been schooled by Maggie to leave any talk of politics at the door. "There's always bound to be differences of opinion and that can be good. Just not at a family gathering," she had said. Instead, they took advantage of the camaraderie and spoke about the great turnout of family for Maggie's party.

"It's so good to have all the grandchildren here, including the one awaiting arrival soon," Veronica said, looking at Max.

"Our last count was eighteen. Once these grandchildren start getting married, as Ruth and Celia have, there'll be no end to this clan."

The meal went off as planned, the children scarfing up everything. They perched on the porches, steps and on blankets put out in the lawn. The adults pitched in, making sure the children all got what they wanted. Little Mark awoke from his nap in time to get his hot dog cut into pieces alongside some potato salad and a deviled egg. He looked around as Maxine presented his plate and asked, "Is there dessert, too?"

With his question, the answer came. Those assembled gathered around Maggie, who was seated in one of her lawn chairs, a host of little ones from two to five sitting at her feet. Betty generously nestled the four-month-old Mary Kay on Maggie's lap. The older ones waited expectantly before starting their games again, their parents prompting them, with a glance, to stay put.

Maggie looked about her, first at Jerome's Rachel, then to Loring, Vic, Bernard, and Tom, as well as Genevieve, all of whom had ventured into marriage and created these children who were here today, children who were all a part of her.

She blinked her eyes at the thought of it and bent to kiss little Mary Kay. Then she looked up and said, "In Ireland, my birthday was a feast day called Lady's Day. That was the day the Blessed Mother got to go to Heaven. I almost thought I was in heaven, seeing you all here. 'Tis an honor you've all given me all this day. And isn't it time we should have our cake?"

With that and shouts of "Hooray," Maxine and Etta handed out cupcakes while Betty, Veronica and Gene served the layer cake, the chocolate frosting dripping as they cut it. Betty lifted Mary Kay from Maggie's lap and Veronica presented Maggie with her slice of cake.

Soon enough, as the little ones were wrapped up for home, the older ones helped pick up everything, and the Osta children got ready to settle into bed. After Maggie said her good-byes and thank yous, she took her rosary to her bedroom, happy to give praise for what had been a perfect picnic party.

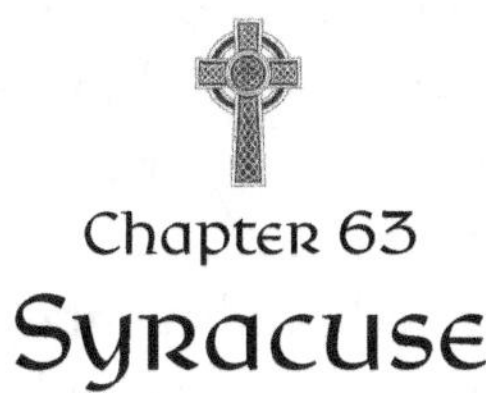

Chapter 63
Syracuse

Late Fall 1950

Gene looked out the kitchen window at the side lawn where the children were playing ball. As she put the dishes in the brand new General Electric dishwasher, a part of the GE kitchen that came with this new house, Gene smiled. The kitchen, the likes of which Gene had never imagined, came with a big refrigerator, electric stove with double ovens, and dishwasher. Such luxury. Frank's company, Niagara Mohawk Power Corporation, had made the arrangements as part of his job offer. Gene had never lived so spaciously in all her life.

This new home at 119 Ruskin Avenue, Syracuse, New York, was a 1900s Victorian, three-story, seven-bedroom house of yellow clapboards and green trim standing among twenty or so other homes on an elm tree-lined street.

Gene remembered the feeling of being overwhelmed when Frank came into the kitchen of their Blantyre Road home in Buffalo with news of his promotion. A transfer to Syracuse? Oh no. When he posed the question of moving, Gene knew a negative reply wasn't in the cards. She had fantasized for a moment what a "no" answer might mean. They could stay put in their three-bedroom house on their sweet street off Hertel and Starin in St. Rose of Lima parish, where they had lived almost ten years with neighbors who had become friends. Yet she knew what this promotion would mean for Frank's future, for their future.

Frank was to act as associate counsel for the newly founded Niagara Mohawk Power Corporation just as he had for Buffalo's Niagara and Eastern Power Company. With the promotion, he would also take on the role as head of the Employee Relations department. It was a great move for his career, but still a move. Gene felt every bit of it.

She took a deep breath and mentally rattled off what was about to transpire. Their youngest child was due in early June. Seven children under the age of ten would be in a new house with new schools, new neighbors, new doctors, grocery stores, and Lord knows what else. What's more, Gene would be leaving her sister Veronica, whose proximity to Niagara Falls had been such a comfort, as had her help as a babysitter. She'd also be leaving her brother Tom, his wife Maxine and their new baby boy, Mickey, who lived in Buffalo now and was becoming an important part of family events and celebrations.

Inevitably, Gene's imagined 'no' turned into 'yes' and the family's August move occurred in time for the September start of school in Syracuse. She marveled at herself for accomplishing it all. Packing up a two-month-old child was a major accomplishment in and of itself.

On the August day when the huge moving van arrived in Buffalo, 10-year-old Mary Jean was saying her good-byes to Gary Becker, her best friend, five-year-old Betty Anne, who was running up and down the ramp on the truck, making sure her books and dolly were settled safely. The three boys checked to make sure their blue Rollfast bicycles were secure, trying for one more ride before they were packed away. The three-year-old Mark and two-month-old Kathleen were kept in tow and with an overnight stop in Lima on their way to Syracuse, the children all received extra attention from Grandmother and Veronica.

Gene had never even seen the Syracuse house in person; her ability to go house-hunting was hampered by caring for the children. She wondered who would ever move into a house with seven children, never having laid eyes on it. But here she was.

The house was splendid, its front entryway and tiled vestibule, reception hall and front window with benches on either side topped off by an oak-spindled staircase leading to the second floor.

Gene arranged the furniture and directed the movers, finding places for everything. The piano in the reception hall fit under the stairway like it was meant to be there, music in her household as important as it had been in her youth. The old maple dining room table fit between the window seats and overlooked the front porch.

A highlight of the new house was the oak-paneled dining room with its handsome oak ceiling beams. It had a bonus sunroom behind French doors. Between the kitchen and the dining room, the children discovered a butler's pantry with glass cupboards and ample storage bins. A swinging door made passage easy when carrying dishes and fun for games of chase until they were curtailed.

Gene was already imagining holiday meals at the huge oak dining room table that had moved with them, thanks to Buffalo friends Ethel and Harry Forehead, who were downsizing. A matching buffet and China cabinet were more than sufficient for dishes and glassware. She could finally unbox the crystal glasses, a wedding gift from Josephine, whom she thought of frequently.

The GE kitchen was really the heart of this house. A modern look, gray and white Formica countertops, a matching six-foot-long table with a Formica surface, blue upholstered benches on either side and a matching 'babytenda' for Kathleen, made it something right out of Better Homes and Garden magazine. The fluorescent lighting and large picture window completed the look.

With the dishwasher now filled, Gene closed the cover, twisted the dial to ON, and sat down on the blue bench to let the time-saving device, as the advertisements described it, do her work. At least this part of it.

She thought back to their Buffalo times. Some of their ten years on Blantyre Road had been tainted with war, rationing, blackouts and fear. She had lost her sister Josephine and, very recently, her brother Bernard, a deeper sorrow than she could have imagined. He'd been the world to her as they grew up, handsome, smart, and kind. She was in awe of her mother's ability to go on with all the heartaches she had suffered. Gene could only pray to have half her courage, for that is what it took. Courage to go on, trusting the pain of loss would lessen and joy would return in some measure.

As milder breezes began to fill the valley that was Syracuse, school started, the five oldest children enrolled at Most Holy Rosary, a kindergarten through twelfth-grade school only a few blocks away. With Kathleen and Mark still taking a morning nap, the quiet time in this great 'castle' of a house was delightfully serene.

Soon, Veronica would be coming to visit for Gene's October 2nd birthday. It would be so good to hear her reactions to these newfangled gadgets and appliances, including her new Ironrite, the mechanized rollers that accomplished ironing while sitting, its mahogany case fitting as part of the furniture. With uniform blouses and shirts to be ironed weekly for five children, being able to sit made the chore so much more doable.

The new television Frank received as a parting gift from his department in Buffalo was already a bonus. The children were hooked on Howdy Doody, Menasha the Magnificent, and all were treated to Perry Como on Saturday nights just after bath time.

The 1950s, Gene hoped, would serve as a new beginning in a new city. The next-door neighbors, Polly and Jack McAllister and their three children, along with the Hoffmann family of nine across the street, had the possibility of friendships for years to come.

The on-going threat of nuclear holocaust that filled the headlines would not fill her children's lives if Gene could help it. She was grateful for their nightly prayer ritual, Frank always including special ones for peace.

Chapter 64
Lima Christmas

Christmas 1950

Maggie heard the church bells and smiled. She would be going to Christmas Eve Mass with Veronica, glad for the stamina she still had to celebrate this wondrous holiday. Oh, it had its sadness; there was no mistake about it. But she wasn't about yesterday. She was about tomorrows, and she was grateful for each day she'd been given.

She thought back on her own childhood times in Ireland, the reverence for the birth of the Savior, something she'd been taught early on. She'd even played a part in a Christmas pageant as the Blessed Mother. She had held the infant child and laid it ever so carefully in the cradle, never dreaming she'd end up with a dozen of her own.

Maggie remembered the mincemeat pies, the scones, the brown bread, and the candles in the windows, lighting a way of welcome for the Holy Family as they sought safe harbor at an inn. She loved the sound of the Irish greeting exchanged by friends and neighbors, Nollaig Shona Duit! A Happy Christmas indeed.

A special childhood memory she cherished was seeing the fairies dancing in the fields from her window. It had always helped her believe in a world beyond our own. Even though the adults couldn't see, Maggie knew what she saw, and the sight brought deep comfort.

Veronica had come home from Niagara Falls amid a blustery snowstorm on Saturday, her Dodge coup holding the road well enough to ensure her safe arrival. She brought with her the Christmas treasures she'd been given by her fourth graders: perfumes, bracelets, and trinkets of all kinds, including hand-made cards.

"Look at this one, Mother," she said, holding a construction paper replica of a Christmas tree with crayon-drawn ornaments. Carefully written on the back, the message Merry Christmas was accompanied by the signatures of all the children, displaying their best Palmer Penmanship method.

"I imagine you must get a good bit of satisfaction from these kindnesses," Maggie said, her own pleasure at seeing Veronica's joy bringing a fulfillment of its own.

She'd watched Veronica over the years of her teaching career, getting accolades for her leadership in directing plays, helping youngsters gain confidence in navigating the world as they played the lead in The Christmas Carol, singing solo songs in concerts, or reciting poems they had written. Veronica was thrilled to talk of them, her blue eyes shining as she recalled their successes.

"That little red-haired Bobby Martin that I've been telling you about was cute as a button in our Christmas pageant this year," Veronica said this afternoon over tea. "He had on a shepherd's costume and held his staff just so and stepped forward as we'd practiced. His shoelace must have gotten tangled in his costume, and he tripped up toward the infant's crib and without missing a beat, said, 'Sorry, baby Jesus, I didn't mean to frighten you.' Can you imagine the ability to ad-lib like that? The audience roared with laughter, and he even took a bow."

Maggie was tickled to think that the simplest stories were such a joy for Veronica. She felt proud of this daughter who'd seen her through so much and still had the sense of living fully and laughing often. "Thanks be to God," Maggie thought as she laced her shoes and galoshes in readiness for the outing to Mass. Donnell wouldn't be going with them tonight but would hopefully be home when they returned. Etta and her two children would be there, she hoped, and Loring and Peggy with their six, and Bob's new wife Mary Ann possibly. Their August 26th wedding still brought smiles.

The snow of the day before had let up and Veronica drove with great ease, pulling the car up in front of the church, very near to where John had often delivered Maggie in the pony and cart. Once inside, out of the cold, they settled into the family pew. Maggie pulled the fur collar of her Schiaparelli Persian wool cape around her, feeling the warmth of the genuine curly lamb wool surrounding her. Bernard had presented it to her a good many years ago at Christmas. It was a kind of a parting gift as he married Etta and moved to his own home. Its expense surprised her, but she'd known he had a good way with money and a great success in the furrier trade. She ached with the wish he could be here now to round out this holiday celebration.

His April death hadn't startled her. She saw the swelling in his face and hands and knew he'd been suffering over the past year. On his Sunday visits with the children, he never complained. She'd worried that this horrific, hereditary disease would surface somewhere, never suspecting that Bernard would be felled by it.

She'd worried from time to time about Tom, whose wanderlust combined with his drinking could come to no good end. For now, he seemed to be managing, all right, his marriage to Maxine and the birth of his little boy, Mickey, a steadying force. Donnell's immaturity, coupled with the drink, could be his nemesis. But Bernard.

She'd put great hope in him. Over the past years, he faithfully stayed on the farm, though she knew he'd had other dreams. He'd helped and advised her like his father might have, with a common sense that was unparalleled. Loring had a similar sense, but Bernard had been available when needed. His talent, his productivity, his success and now his wife and young children all pointed to his ability to escape from the clutches of this devastating illness. Yet despite all the combined efforts of prayer, good care, and medicine, he was gone in a matter of months, the hospitalization expenses wiping out much of his savings.

Nephritis, they'd said. There was no coming back.

Bernard had chosen a fighter and a clever woman as his wife. With little or no complaint, Etta made her way and scraped by, gathering goods through sales, providing more than sufficient for her two children. She continued work she'd once known at Stromberg Carlton. A strong and sensitive woman, her seven-year-old Bernie Jr. carried on like a little soldier, helping as much as he could with farm chores, feeding the animals and raking the barnyard, his four-year-old sister Mary Lou, trailing close behind.

This past June, after the weight of Bernard's death, new life helped lighten the intensity of loss with the arrival of Gene's daughter, Kathleen. She might just be the last of her brood, Maggie thought.

Gene, nearly forty-three years old, more than likely wouldn't be having another child. Her hands were full as it was, now with seven children aged ten and under. Their regular visits to the farm were memorable, these well-behaved children taking turns entertaining her with artwork from school, songs they'd learned and poems they recited. Mary Jean, the oldest, had already learned to play the piano quite well, just as Maggie's daughters had years before.

As the gathered church congregation sang Silent Night, Maggie came back from her reverie, the church lights dimmed, candlelight taking over. It was magical.

Eight grandchildren from Lima were nestled with their parents, sitting in the rows just behind Maggie and Veronica. As the celebration of the Mass ended, one of the altar servers tip-toed up to the crib ever so carefully and spread a blanket on it in readiness for the birth of the infant.

Veronica leaned over to Maggie and whispered, "Sure, that's not Bobby Martin."

Maggie chuckled as they stood and sang Hark the Herald Angels Sing, and soon enough, they were on their way into the night and home to continue to prepare for the next day's dinner when many more would gather to celebrate a Lima Christmas at home.

Chapter 65
Grandchildren

Autumn 1951

Maggie bent down on the stoop to fill the water bowl outside the kitchen door, the cats very grateful recipients. As she poured from her pitcher, she felt a twinge that took her breath away. After twelve births and a lifetime of hard work, she was used to pain. But this was different. It couldn't be related to her gallbladder. That pain that rivaled childbirth was removed several years ago. She straightened up and decided to fix herself some tea and sit down for a bit. Her chores could wait.

An hour hadn't passed when there was a knock at the door. She didn't get up but rather called out, "Come in," to be surprised by her granddaughter, Margaret Mary, stepping into the dining room from the side porch door that opened into it. Maggie was grateful for this most familiar guest. Less familiar visitors used the front porch, which would necessitate Maggie going to the door. Today, she was glad not to get up.

"Good morning, Grandmother. I hope I'm not interrupting," the young woman said. Maggie watched as dressed in a polka dot blouse with a matching navy-blue skirt and blazer, she stepped in and glanced around the room, her red hair pulled back in a ponytail, her gaze stopping on the painting of the Angelus, just behind the chair where Maggie was sitting. They all loved this painting, Maggie thought.

Margaret Mary continued, "Mother sent me down with these potatoes from Dad. He's just now dug them, and she thought you'd enjoy some for your supper. There will be more in the coming weeks." With that, she put the bag on the table, careful not to muss the lace tablecloth. She wondered what the occasion was for the lace tablecloth until she recalled that Grandmother felt every day was an occasion. "Every season has its own beauty," was one of her frequent sayings.

Maggie sat forward, glad the stabbing pain had subsided. "Well, your mother's kindness never falters. I will enjoy them this very day. Now, if you can, would you like to share a cup of tea? There are cups on the sideboard and I've a pot of freshly brewed tea right here, if you please."

The young woman's blue eyes brightened. "I'd love to stay for a visit if I'm not disturbing you. I just came up from Rochester for an overnight to give Mother a hand, though Maureen, imagine - my baby sister already fourteen - has become a great one for helping. She and mother have cleared the extra bedrooms now that the three boys have left."

"'Tis grand as you say. Your father and mother are raising a fine family and I suspect you'll do the same one day."

Margaret Mary filled her cup and settled down across from her grandmother.

"You know, Margaret Mary, I never imagined by my eightieth year that I'd still be here and there would be all these children with their children having children. Where has the time gone?" Maggie glanced toward the window that fronted the road, her eyes distant, then turned back to Margaret Mary. "Why, Cecilia's little Terry is already 5 years old. Do you remember her from the birthday picnic? I wouldn't be surprised if Cecelia had another child soon."

Margaret Mary sipped her tea and replied, "I do remember Cecilia. She came right up to me and asked how I liked having red hair. Hers was as bright a red as mine. I must confess, I told her I loved it once I'd grown up a bit. She smiled." She tossed her head and pushed back her red locks.

Maggie smiled and nodded. A chatterbox this one is, she thought, and before her thought was finished, Margaret Mary continued.

"You know Bob's baby boy is the first grandchild for our family," she said, holding her teacup with her pinky extended. "His middle name is after his father, my brother Bob, and his first name is Charles, after Mary Ann's stepfather, Charles Brady. Did you know Mr. Brady was Mary Ann's stepfather?" She took another sip of tea, her eyes shining, seeming so proud to be giving juicy news to her grandmother. "When she was a wee one, my mother told me, her father, Olin Wheelock, died. Her mother, Anna Swede, alone with a small child, was blessed by one Charles Brady, who adopted both Mary Ann and Myron. Isn't it wonderful? Best of all is that Charles Robert is my first nephew."

Maggie filled her teacup, smiling at the innocence of this young woman. "How old are ye now?" she asked, knowing full well this one had turned twenty-four last January but interested to hear her reply.

"Why, Grandmother, you know I'll be a quarter century after the new year. And I've already been teaching for two years. I absolutely love it. The children are like sponges, soaking up all that's being taught."

Maggie smiled again. This young, red-headed beauty seemed to be taking the world by storm. She was already studying for her master's degree in elementary education, certain she had found her niche. She had majored in languages as an undergraduate, with French as her major. That gave Maggie to believe she had enough wanderlust in her to keep her days fascinating.

Maggie remembered her own longings for adventure as a youngster in Ireland. Her desire to come to America wouldn't leave her, and she never regretted the move. Now, she was listening to her children's children share their dreams.

"At Brighton Elementary Twelve Corners School, I'm part of a program to teach conversational French to more students. C'est tellement excitant," Margaret Mary said.

"Well, what about the new baby boy? Isn't that excitant?" Maggie asked, a twinkle in her eye.

"Oh, mais oui!" exclaimed Margaret Mary, as she asked, 'Parlez vous francais?"

"Un peu," Maggie replied, having raised enough children who studied French at one time or another to have learned 'a little'.

"Are you excited to have another great-grandchild?" Margaret Mary asked. "Does this make number 4?" Without waiting for an answer, she went on. "Mary Ann and Bob are over the moon with this baby. He's just perfect, Grandmother."

Maggie suddenly felt weary. Charmed as she was by this grandchild, she felt she'd extended herself enough for this afternoon, so she excused herself, telling her young guest she'd look forward to another visit next time she was in town. Fortunately, Margaret Mary, taking the hint, put the teacups on the sideboard and with a glance around the dining room, exited quietly.

As Maggie settled down for her afternoon rest, she thought about this newest great-grandchild, Charles Robert, the start of another whole line of children as her grandchildren married and started their own families. There was nothing like a few more babies to cuddle. Nothing like it in all this world.

Over the years, she'd been blessed with twenty-four grandchildren, including Tom's Christine and little Marjorie, Jack, and Harold, the three who had died young. Thoughts of her own Baby Rose, never far, flashed back. She turned her mind to the living as she'd learned to do all these years. There was nothing, she thought, like the whole brood of them in all this world, one more special than the next.

Maggie heaved a sigh of contentment, thoughts of famine days far away now. She knew that this little 'lay me down' would be just what the doctor ordered.

Chapter 66
Oldest Daughter

Spring 1953

Veronica knew what her future was. No one had to tell her. With Josephine's death, she'd become the oldest daughter.

It was Josephine who contacted the doctors, explained the medicines, and oversaw the recovery from their father's heart condition. She cared for Maggie during her gallbladder troubles and all the various aches and pains in between. She'd been ever- present to help after Baby Rose's death, only fifteen years old, yet knowing what was needed. Her choice of nursing as a career was a natural fit. Her helping role as she signed the death certificates of her two older brothers and then her father, each event separated by only two years, became invaluable gifts she gave to them all. It was also Josephine who saw to Maggie's citizenship papers. How could Veronica possibly fill those shoes as the oldest daughter, she wondered.

Bernard's death became Veronica's first foray into the complex world of loss and legal documentation. He'd died at Strong Memorial Hospital, his extended illness offering little hope. Nephritis was nasty. It could easily go unnoticed and then be too late to treat. The backache, the bloating, the tiredness and even the memory concerns all piled up, and soon Bernard was gone.

Bernard's widow, Etta, had signed his death certificate, but Veronica was the one who helped arrange the calling hours, the funeral Mass, and the reception afterward. Father Ball was on hand to counsel and console just as he'd been so many times before. Etta had seen to it that the children were baptized and enrolled at St. Rose school, a promise she'd made at their wedding, a Catholic prerequisite for their marriage.

Veronica became a frequent visitor to the Egan Road farm, taking groceries and treats for the children. Etta, her brown hair curled and combed back, was gracious yet reluctant to take too much help, so she often prepared something to send home to Maggie in return. The children, Bernie Junior and Mary Lou were precious, each staying close by when Veronica visited. Bernard had scrimped and saved over the years for their farm, but hospital costs had eaten up much of what he'd squirreled away. It was a worry how the family would survive.

Money wasn't plentiful for any of them. Veronica's teacher salary helped with her own housing, with enough extra to bring her mother milk money, newspaper change and pay the taxes. Her burgundy Plymouth sedan carried her many weekends to Lima to help her mother with household chores. She noted with concern, on each trip, that Maggie sat more frequently in-between meal preparation, dishes, and gardening tasks. Loring stepped in as he could to care for the acreage, but there came a time when the fields lay fallow and that pleased no one. Veronica and Loring had agreed that getting someone to rent the acreage was the next best thing. Maggie was reluctantly amenable. It wasn't charity. It was business.

Elmer Wemett, a Lima High graduate and neighboring farmer, became a tenant who couldn't have proved more suited to the fields, keeping them sown and reaped, allowing Maggie the sense of pride that so often accompanied farming families. He was like clockwork, arriving as the weather permitted on Tuesday and Wednesday mornings to reap or sow as the season dictated. He even kept the barn in order, the barn cats multiplying undisturbed.

Veronica's drive to Lima took her through luscious terrain along Route 5 through Clarence, Pembroke, Batavia, Stafford, LeRoy, Caledonia, and Avon. She never tired of seeing the farm fields when they were planted, enjoying the sight of corn, beans, wheat and hay, the neat rows rivaling her brother Tom's, whose precision in planting seemed unparalleled. His precision in many things was great. He and his wife Maxine, with her vibrant eyes and ruddy complexion, were raising a fine youngster, Mickey, whose visits to the farm were thrilling for Maggie and Veronica, both of whom reveled in children and their fascination with the farm. Veronica smiled as she remembered Maggie's pronouncement after Mickey's or Gene's children visited.

"The trouble with young people in these cities is that they're getting too far away from their roots. A little fresh air and a walk in the fields would make them all the better for this life."

As Veronica drove through Caledonia, she always looked to see Eldred and Marie O'Shea's house on Avon Road. Set back twenty feet or so, it looked like a picture book illustration, with its window boxes and stone front, a big oak tree shading the yard. It was Eldred, who had started his law practice in Caledonia, who helped Gene after her car accident in Batavia almost ten years ago. The fact that Eldred was the best man in their wedding said much about the longstanding friendship.

Veronica had helped Gene and Frank as each of their seven children was born, taking care of them at their Blantyre Road home in Buffalo as often as she could arrange. The first three babies were born in close succession: May 1940, July 1941, and August 1942. She had great admiration for Gene, who handled the births like she'd been born to it. Her mother's children had been plenty, but almost always with at least a two-year span between them. At 32, Gene's age was considered advanced for childbearing. Maybe it was their reasoning for so many close together, but then so could the unquestioned church regulation on contraception. Close as she was to Gene, Veronica never asked her about it.

The oldest child, Mary Jean, named after Frank's mother and Gene, with an adjusted spelling, resembled Frank's family with dark hair and almond brown eyes. Veronica was pleased to be her godmother, happy to spoil her as often as she could. Eldred and Marie were John's godparents; Jim's were Irma Hendriks, Gene's classmate and friend from Rochester, and Jimmy Gleason, another Lima friend. Veronica had been most delighted when Freddie was asked to be Tom's godfather, an acknowledgment of the special place he held in their lives.

When Veronica started 'keeping company' with Freddie, she was pleased with the relationship. Her interest in travel and adventure was fed by Freddie's stories of his travels before they met, including places that she'd never even thought of visiting. Buenos Aires, Havana, and San Juan were never high on her list, but Bermuda, South Hampton and Liverpool, England, Le Havre and Halifax held great interest.

They were finally able to arrange their February trip aboard the SS Queen of Bermuda to celebrate both their birthdays. Hers on the 14th came with appropriate Valentine's Day chocolates and a bouquet of fragrant (and expensive) roses; his on the 16th with a romantic lobster dinner in the dining room of the recently opened four-hundred-room Castle Harbour Hotel.

For Veronica, the fact that Freddie became Commodore of the Buffalo Launch Club two years prior to their trip, added magic and romance. Freddie's dark hair and chocolate brown eyes complemented his alluring look when attired in his uniform. Boastful never, he was generous and inviting always.

Those early years had been like a fairy tale for Veronica: school days filled with fourth graders she adored, plays she directed and friends she made. Evenings and weekends were filled with Freddie, Frank, Gene and their children, who were growing up so fast, and her great roommates. Veronica's two favorites, while she lived at luxury apartments minutes from the Falls, The Jefferson, were Mary Tubbs and Emeline Engel. Emeline proved to be a long-time friend, her father owning a local gin mill in Wayland, New York, not unsimilar to the American Hotel in Lima. She was a great pal, no more in a hurry to marry than Veronica was. Together, they enjoyed the blessings of being single and childless rather than bemoaning it. Over the years of teaching together and moving about Niagara Falls, Veronica was glad their friendship continued, even with Freddie in her life. Her most recent move to Cayuga Drive School from Pacific Avenue School added more stories to share. One day, she hoped to invite Emeline to visit her in Lima when the time seemed right.

Right now, she was worried about her mother's health and missing Josephine, who could so deftly allay fears and get to the root of the problem, if there was one. Maggie had been living with just Don for some time now. She fixed meals and saw to the laundry without much difficulty, but any gardening seemed beyond her stamina these days. Thankfully, Veronica loved it, often staying Sundays after Mass to clear just one more patch of weeds or plant one more row of geraniums before heading back to Niagara Falls.

Don had seemed peaceful with his life, his own gardening skills applied to the wild rose bush out by the barn when he wasn't working for the Moses Nursery up the road. He kept it trimmed, producing the fragrant roses that frequently filled vases for the dinner table. Maggie saw to it that he had three meals a day and Veronica knew that she was thankful for her visits, bringing needed groceries and more.

Veronica doubted that Maggie knew much of the burden placed on her oldest living daughter. She was just glad things were working out as well as they were for the moment, Freddie's support a great part of her ease.

Chapter 67
Great-Grandchildren

Early Autumn 1953

As summer faded and the earth cooled, Maggie's thoughts turned to her great-grandchildren. The most recent birth of Pamela, Cecilia's second child, was a tonic, a child as fair and lovely as any, her blue eyes shining with light. Maggie met her for the first time at a family picnic at Mendon Ponds, organized by Loring and Peggy. This park was a favorite place John had enjoyed throughout the years, its famous glacial Devil's Bathtub always worth a viewing in any season.

Having had her own first child at the age of eighteen, Maggie had never given thought to grandchildren let alone great-grandchildren. Her own Buckleys were nearly all dead except for her sister Mary's daughter Margaret, who had tended the graves in Calvary Cemetery so faithfully.

Of late, and from all indications, it seemed to Maggie that the Donegans would live on, both her and Annie's broods making sure. It was Ruth, her oldest grandchild, who blessed them with her first great-grandchild, Lawrence William Delaney. And then Cecilia gave birth to the second great-grandchild, Terry. Mary Kay Delaney came in short order, followed by Bob and Mary Ann's boys, Chuckie and Jimmy.

With six great-grandchildren already, Maggie conjectured there would be more to come to carry on the amazing family story that had started so long ago in another country. She hoped these children and their children's children would continue to learn of their past and feel proud. She certainly did.

As she sat on the porch this autumn day, Maggie noted the spent peonies that lined the driveway, their glory days for now over. She knew her own days were fading and thus she savored each one all the more.

Out of the corner of her eye, she spied a new kitten on the stoop, mewing like it had lost its way. She didn't dare bend and scoop it up, fearing she might frighten it. Also, she feared that if she bent down, she might not get up. Ah, she thought, the vagaries of age. She got up and noted the empty food bowl. She'd look for some scraps for this newest little one.

As she went to the kitchen, she mused that she'd lived her years always active and free of significant aches and pains, except for the occasional creaks from her neck and back. But of late, she felt the tightness in her chest and shallowness of her breath, seeming to make the doctor's earlier prediction of heart failure true. Was it the power of suggestion? She wouldn't chance it too much in order to find the answer.

She sorely missed her Josephine, who would be a comfort these days, her gentleness and knowledge a balm for her when she'd suffered from gallbladder. Veronica, Genevieve, and Betty all chimed in with their advice, offering their best. Loring's Peggy was also on hand, as were her Lima granddaughters, Margaret, Mary and Maureen. She felt safe and blessed.

Just as she pondered what to do for the kitten, Maggie looked up to see Ruth at the porch door with her children Larry and Mary Kay, bringing a lovely addition to her day.

She'd tend to the kitten after supper. For now, she would be lifted by these great-grandchildren, the promise of tomorrow.

Chapter 68
Mother's Day

May 9, 1954

Maggie switched on the light. As the shadows disappeared and the yellow light filled the room, she felt her heart slow its beat. No one was in the room. She knew that now. It had been a dream. A vivid dream.

She had been with Bernard and Josephine. They were sitting with her, telling stories of their younger days, stories she cherished. Bernard, his health returned, his eyes sparkling, told tales of his teaching days and special moments of success when students understood the lesson. One had exclaimed, "Ah Ha!".

Josephine chimed in with patients who recovered under her watchful care. Her dark hair shone as she told how she'd administered medicines on time and encouraged patients to breathe deeply and envision their health. It often worked, she said. They each encircled Maggie in a dance, twirling her in her chair and singing an Irish lullaby to her:

Hear the wind blow love,
Hear the wind blow,
Lean your head over and hear the wind blow
Oh, winds of the night,
May your fury be crossed,
May no one who's dear to our island be lost.
Blow the winds gently, calm be the foam,
Shine the light brightly and guide them back home
On the wings of an angel.

Then they were gone.

Maggie shivered and reached for the glass of water at her bedside. She sipped slowly. These nightly visits had comfort and sorrow mixed into them. Her sister Molly was a frequent visitor and so was Baby Rose, sweet as ever, but she often slipped through Maggie's fingers as she had so long ago. Maggie lay down again, her long white hair surrounding her head on the pillow. She picked up her rosary beads and felt the coolness of them bring calm. Tomorrow would be a new day.

The new day did dawn with sun sweeping the fields. As Maggie lit the kettle for the tea, Don stumbled in, eyes still sleepy. "It's your big day, isn't it?" he said. "Betty's the big cheese at the breakfast, right?" Maggie smiled and nodded, glad that Don had paid attention and remembered.

The St. Rose Mother's Day breakfast sponsored by the Catholic Daughters Association would follow the Mass. Her daughter Betty - Sister Leo Xavier - would be the guest speaker coming from De Sales school in Geneva, where she taught music. Maggie felt pleased and even a bit jittery. Betty's colleague and friend, Sister Edwarda, would be driving. She imagined they'd be there in plenty of time, their morning prayers starting at 6:00 a.m., Betty had told her.

Maggie's morning prayers sometimes started then, too, but of late, she found herself drifting off during the first decade of her beads. It wasn't a bother to her, for Don was never too impatient for his breakfast, porridge his favorite. And she enjoyed the extra sleep.

Once up, milk for the cat's bowl had become a routine, the mother cat and kittens circling around Maggie's feet, trusting she would care for them. As she stood on the outdoor stoop, she noted a red sky lighting the day. Red sky at night, sailors delight. Red sky in the morning, sailors take warning, she recited aloud to no one. She'd heard it said so many times at Cork Harbour as a child. These days, she was glad to be on solid ground in Lima, with no sailors worrying for the winds. She resolved not to let any foul weather spoil this day.

Her seventeen-year-old granddaughter Maureen, Loring's younger daughter, arrived promptly at 9:15 to take her to the 9:30 Mass prior to the breakfast event at Lima Town Hall. Maureen was to be the pianist for the event. Like her older sister Margaret Mary, Maureen played by ear. The talent these two girls exhibited had amazed her. She didn't attribute any of it to herself, though she did love music. She smiled as she thought of her mother's accordion, which she often played for the children as her mother had played for her. She'd encouraged each of them, the girls and boys, to play an instrument, to sing and to laugh. Music was one of the best gifts she could give them.

As she pulled her 'next to best' dress over her head, Maggie felt a shiver. Her dream came again, reminding her of so many losses. But she mustn't think of that today, for this would be a day of great gains and celebration. After all, it was Mother's Day.

The altar was bedecked with roses, the sun shining through the stained glass, giving a regal glow as the Mass was said. The congregation of mostly women responded in unison to the prayers. Maggie loved the sounds of the Latin, the same words she'd learned as a child. As they neared the end, she listened for Ite Missa Est, Go the Mass is ended. As the response, Deo Gratias, Thanks be to God, was said, Maggie felt a chuckle. Depending on who gave the sermon, she supposed, there might be quite a bit of gratitude. Today, with the breakfast to follow in the Town Hall, there was certainly much to be grateful for.

Maureen drove the car onto the stone driveway, Maggie happy to be home from an exhilarating morning. The Mass had been fine, Father Ball didn't drone on too long and was even a bit humorous. "Today, we honor mothers. None of us would be here without them."

The breakfast was well prepared and served beautifully, and Maggie was proud to watch Betty take center stage, her habit pressed and perfectly in place, her veil falling over her shoulders just so. Her remarks had been clever and her nod to Maggie, "a woman who has loved and lost," was so simply stated it held Maggie's heart. She was glad to be able to leave the church without too much ado once Maureen played the closing "Hail Holy Queen" hymn.

Somehow, today, Maggie felt like a Queen. Hadn't the Blessed Virgin about whom they sang lost her only son? And hadn't Maggie, even though she lost three sons, been blessed with four others? Despite the sorrows and the woes that often came with being a mother, the whole of today was filled with a richness and beauty that lifted her higher than she'd felt in a long time.

The refrain of the song reverberated in her mind, *"Hail Mother of Mercy and of Love, Oh, Maria."* Grateful indeed.

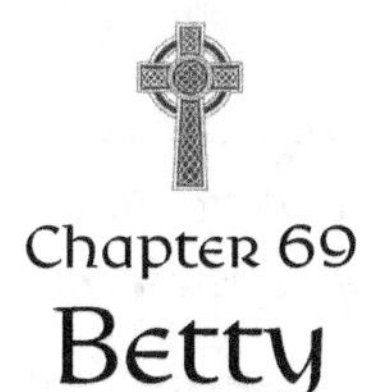

Chapter 69
Betty

August 26, 1954

Betty lifted the lid that covered the keyboard of the mahogany piano, remembering their old square piano, this spinet such an improvement. She spied some favorite music: How are Things in Glocca Morra, the popular song from the musical Finian's Rainbow. The lyrics and the melody often transported her, and she was ready for the ride. "I hear a bird, a Londonderry bird..."

She played the song with abandon, the third verse bringing with it a feeling of nostalgia.

> *How are things in Glocca Morra?*
> *Is that willow tree still weeping there?*
> *Does that laddie with the twinklin' eye,*
> *Come whistling by?*
> *And does he walk away*
> *Sad and dreamy there not to see me there?*
> *So I ask each weepin' willow*

and each brook along the way,
and each lass that comes a-sighin' too ra lay
How are things in Glocca Mora this fine day?

Betty's memories of the spring brook that ran beyond their fields were glorious childhood ones. The fields were hers to walk through, the trees to wander under, and the brook to sit by and dream.

While happy in her chosen vocation, thoughts of those early years often came, as did the memories of the laddies who caught her eye. Don Driscoll was one laddie with whom she often sang duets, his eyes shining and an easy smile gleaming. She was glad to have known bits of flirtatiousness before she entered the convent, her two years at Nazareth College helping her become more certain. A stolen kiss here and there, out on a walk with a boy, helped her know some of what she'd be missing.

Ultimately, the romance she desired she found in the church. It was this "higher calling" to religious life her mother had prepared her for since a young child, admiring so greatly all the Sisters who lived and worked in the parish. Sister Hermine was a favorite, her delicate ways nurturing the youngest of the children. Sister Teresita's gentleness and wisdom stayed with her, too. Sister Lucinda, her mother often said, was like her name, hard as nails. Betty resolved to be more like Hermine.

As she played another favorite, *Red Sails in the Sunset*, Betty's mind drifted back to Baby Rose's birth and death and though she was only three at the time, her images of her mother cradling the baby and rocking, rocking, rocking, then holding Betty were vivid. She remembered tears falling on her dolly.

The presence of prayer seemed everywhere in Betty's upbringing, her mother's devotion to the Rosary foremost. Each night after supper, those who were home gathered for a recitation of a decade of the Rosary near the homemade shrine in the dining room, its holy water font almost always filled. She also recalled so many novenas to Baby Rose's patron saint, St. Rose of Lima, all playing a part in her destiny.

This afternoon, Betty continued her reverie, happy no one else was around. The music continued to hold her, like *Believe Me if All Those Endearing Young Charms*, and of course her favorite, *Danny Boy*. How blessed she'd been to record the song, something to keep for the next generations. The silver record was distinctive; Nazareth College gifted it to her as they aired her song on the radio. There were no royalties or prizes, just honor, which, as a Sister, she tried to accept humbly. A treasured memory.

Tonight, her faithful companion, Sister Edwarda, would be back to take Betty up to St. Rose Convent since her mother's house would be full. The Osta children were 'landing' on the farm, and tonight they'd all gather 'round the piano for a bit of a song fest, Gene and Frank grateful for the time together with Maggie, Veronica, and any others who might stop by. Loring's son Jack's wedding was the occasion, his marriage almost exactly four years after Bob and Mary Ann's, two boys, Chuckie and Jimmy, welcome additions.

This past month, Betty had been reassigned to St. Agnes Convent School in Rochester to teach grades 6 and 7. She had previously been Principal of this same school when it was still St. Agnes School for Girls. She held favorite memories of her times with Sister St. Catherine, a Sullivan from Geneva, a fine family, her father had said.

Over the last few summers, Betty had been selected to attend the University of Rochester, where she studied for her Master's Degree in Education and Guidance. She loved learning her Master's Thesis in Guidance, part of her on-the-job training while at DeSales. Summers had been filled with studies, the rest of the year with students. She enjoyed the sprawling campus of the University and the lure of academia, glad to be a part of it all. This newest assignment, to teach younger students again, was not something she was looking forward to, but then, wasn't that what her vow of obedience was about?

After a final rendition of *Danny Boy*, Betty closed the piano and went into the dining room. She stood in front of the mirror over the buffet, examining herself. At age forty-three, her skin was still smooth, no wrinkles, the white linen of the coronet framing her face, a black veil strategically pinned in place covering her hair. She straightened her head and thought about the number of times she'd assembled this headpiece, her rimless glasses covering green eyes beneath dark eyebrows. The gabardine material of the habit was durable and washable, a practical consideration for long-time wear. The cloth 'bib' hooked around her neck and placed over her breast concealed any feminine shapeliness. Betty smiled as she touched the rosary beads that were hung from a cord around her waist. It was Baby Rose's brief life that set off the chain of prayers that gave Betty the first glimpses of her vocation.

The sound of Veronica's car tires on the crushed stone driveway pulled Betty from her reverie. Her mother and Veronica came in the door, bringing bags of food to prepare for the arrival of the family of nine, all of them spending the night. A hot dog roast was the fare for this evening, Frank offering to grill. Maggie's classic potato salad was a must, along with beans, sliced tomato, and deviled eggs. Betty had readied the tableware and plates and moved things about to make way for the seven generally well-behaved children, ranging in age from four to fourteen.

As the children came to the front room, Betty learned from Tom that he was the only one allowed to touch his Godfather Freddie's silver model airplane, a gift to Veronica with special words etched on the wing. Betty Anne would probably organize a game of skunk or some other activity for Mark and Kathleen. The three older ones, Mary Jean, John, and Jim, would be about the farm, in and out of the barn and pumping water to their heart's content with the white pump handle on the cement slab just beyond the porch. The front porch game that the oldest boy, John, invented was watching for cars on the busy Rochester

Road, and when one neared, running to hide on the porch. It seemed to please them all. The porch chairs and glider gave them all space to sing their songs and carry on.

Que Sera Sera, whatever will be will be,
The future's not ours to see.
Que Sera Sera.

Betty would not soon forget the event during another August visit six years ago that taught them all a lesson. As the story was pieced together, told, and retold, it took on its own life. It all started with the discovery of the metal holder that hung on the door frame by the stove to hold Diamond Kitchen matches. The two boys, John and Jim, ages six and seven, needed no prompting to snitch a few. And what better place to take them than to the hayloft. They could try them out there to see if they worked. You could strike them anywhere. Once they'd seen a little bit of hay burn, they'd blow it out, no one the wiser. That was the thinking of six and seven-year-olds, if they thought at all.

Mary Jean, age 8, was along for the adventure. Up, up, up they climbed into the hay loft. Jim and John got the matches to work just fine, but hay burned much faster than they realized. Mary Jean called for help and the three of them, unable to contain the flames, climbed down. The fire spread across the far wall. Within minutes, Don alerted Veronica, Genevieve, and Betty. Maggie's accounting of the event was classic.

"The three older children were sent to the front porch and told sternly by their father to stay put. Gene, in her high heels and apron, had started her own bucket brigade; she and Veronica carrying pails of water to the barn. The younger children, Tom and Betty Anne, were kept in the kitchen and allowed to look from the windows as the firetruck came and the firemen unfurled their hoses, handily extinguishing the flames." Betty remembered remarking how dangerous this could have been. Her mother, having lived through so much more, simply said, "The children have learned an important lesson."

In the end, with the children subdued, their parents chagrined, the damage contained, and no injuries except to the damp hay in the barn, which would soon dry, the story became a part of family lore for years to come.

On this night, Betty counted heads and scurried about as the children were fed, serving food, and clearing places. She noted what a young lady Mary Jean had become, now a teenager. She favored her father's family with olive skin, shiny dark hair, and a radiant smile. At fourteen, she had inherited the gift of the keys. Betty asked her help in starting the evening's entertainment and Mary Jean started off by playing her spring recital piece, Chopin's Nocturne Opus 9 No. 2.

To applause from all assembled, Mary Jean bowed, and Betty initiated a great singsong, playing some of the favorites, including How are Things in Glocca Morra. As a finale, Mary Jean accompanied Frank as he dedicated the next song to Betty. They all sang together as Betty tiptoed out, waving to all.

Too-ra-loo-ra-loo-ral
Too-ra-loo-ra-li
Too-ra-loo-ra-loo-ral
That's an Irish lullaby

Betty was glad to see her mother take advantage of the song as she bid her own good night, wisely saving her energy for the wedding tomorrow. Betty's ride, Sister Edwarda, awaited to take her up to St. Rose Convent, her heart full, knowing these were the best of times.

Chapter 70
Julia

Fall 1959

Maggie let Julia's letters from Ireland rest in her lap. She was sitting on the side porch, the September sun scattering its light over the hillside, the growing season over.

During her whole life, there had always been Julia, her older sister. The one, as children, they nicknamed "Julia Rulia" because she was so proper about everything. Maggie could hear her admonitions to this day:

"You should always bless yourself before and after your breakfast, Maggie, if you're to have a good day."

"You should never leave your clothes on the bed stand. They'll wrinkle and be a disgrace when you wear them again."

"I wouldn't be caught dead leaving church before saying my rosary. What would people think?"

Their oldest sister Mary, tender and loving Mary, had settled in America several years before and Maggie was left under the guiding hand of Julia, the next oldest sister. Thankfully, her mother's presence was strong and loving. It wasn't that Julia was mean, but oh, the joy she lacked! Dour was the word, Maggie thought. No matter how many times Maggie invited her, she found reasons not to come to America. Yet she didn't seem to find much happiness staying in Ireland either.

Whenever Maggie reread Julia's letters, her punctuation and grammar not perfect and her contrary spirit showing through.

Ahadallane January 21, 1925

Dear Sister Maggie

Just a few lines to you and family it seems to me you are very busy all the time. My advice to you is not to kill yourself as I can read from your letters how interested you are about them.(?) Sure enough its true about the young people now, as I guess there is a craze for dance all over the world have they not dancing halls all over the country now and coming far and near to them with Motorcars and Horse and traps, no notice to call me at eleven o'clock to know could they get stables…

…all the snapshots were very ancient looking I thought I could get some nice ones for a stand frame as I got Michael and Tims and Father Riordan and Lizzie enlarged that all were dead when I got them done. They are life size and framed.

Well, the weather is terrible here rain all the time the land around is like a bog with water its no wonder for the past 2 years rain all the time. I send on some papers. I can keep you supplied with them as I get the Weekly every week and all the daily news is in that if you want any other paper name it and I will post it.

Love to husband and children Your fond sister Julia.

Their mother, Margaret Riordan Buckley, had died in 1913 in Ireland, the same year Maggie and John had moved to their new house on Rochester Road in Lima. For a time, her brothers Tims and Michael and sister Julia were on their own in Ireland, staying in the family homestead, their father's death not long after Maggie had emigrated. The twins, Lizzie and Jeremiah, had come to America just after Maggie. So it was that Jeremiah and Margaret's children had split into two groups, three in Ireland and four in America.

Before too long, Tims and Michael were also gone, their deaths leaving Julia on her own. Maggie had tried more than once to encourage Julia to come to America, her replies very "Julia like".

Ahadalane Sept 9th 1925

Dear Sister

Just a few lines to say I am over the Binding.

You tell me I am not send you any news but I am a very poor hand at writing now as I have very stiff fingers owing to all the rough work I have done.

Well Maggie you want to know if I will go to live with you, well darling you know how very hard it is to break up a home you was raised in not I must say that I ever eat much idle bread but still I never wanted for anything T. God

I am most sure children would have great fun at me, their old Green Horn Auntie.

Dear Sister don't worry over me at all if there was anything serious the matter with me of course you would be the first to hear it and you could come and take farm lock stock block and all and do what you like with it there are only the two of us left now…

Remember me to husband and family and tell little Don to pray for me.

Believe me to remain your fond Sister Julia.

Though Julia entreated Maggie not to worry, there were times when she did worry. So much responsibility was left on Julia and over the years, Maggie could do nothing to help. She ultimately came to believe that worry did no good. It only robbed you of the present moment and gave no help to resolve the problem. She didn't recommend it at all.

Maggie picked up the most recent letter in her lap and re-read some of it. It was from the neighbor, Julia Crean, who had taken Julia into her home in the last days.

Donoughmore, Cork December 4, 1952

"…Julia is carrying on the poor dear. She was anointed last night though the Priest was in and out. He thought there was no immediate danger until now. I was terrified until she got the Last Sacrament lest she may go at night, still the Priest lives next door. She had the doctor too since I wrote last. She is very easy now. All

the talk is gone. Looking for horses and all the old work. I had a friend of hers here about a fortnight ago. A God-son of hers and the 1st thing she asked him was did he see the horses that went astray. Oh! He said that's posted up in the Creamery and they'll be found." All that's gone now, God help us all. This young man (Jimmy Buckley) is a friend of your mother's as well and Julia likes the whole family. He told me he'll be here with me if the worst should come. I'll have plenty help, don't forget. We are near everything and near the people who are all anxious to help. Kitty, (the niece and myself) are carrying on well T.G. Those others would only be more trouble to me. I'll write soon again and let you know everything. I'm busy as I've to keep a watch on Julia all the time.

Julia's friend, J. Crean

Maggie could picture the scene, Julia Crean seeing to Julia as the last days approached, her home up the hill in Stuake, in their parish of Donoughmore, close to the church and the cemetery where more than likely Maggie's parents and brothers had been buried. She'd never been back to see any of them. More's the pity, she thought.

It was just after Christmas that word came in a post from the priest of Julia's December 19th death. She remembered fighting back tears, for she was off to the Catholic Daughters luncheon and couldn't take time now to blubber. Once home, she read the letter more carefully, amazed by the fact that once the property that included a house and barn and sufficient acreage was sold, a check would be sent to Maggie.

The poor dear, Maggie thought, her heart aching for this loss. Julia, for all her grumbling and bitterness, had managed everything at the end with grace, including the sale of their home, seeing to it that any proceeds would come to Maggie at a time when Maggie could use the assistance for her own farm's upkeep.

Maggie listened to the bird songs with the background of road traffic and how Julia would have something to say about that. 'Wouldn't they know better than to put a road so close to God's beautiful creatures?" Maggie remembered their girlhood days, picking blackberries, traipsing through the fields back and forth to school, Julia always cautioning Maggie to slow down. "Ladies don't rush; they stroll," Julia would say. Maggie had long ago learned not to argue with her. Julia generally had the last word on any subject, as she even did now.

When Maggie left for America, it was Julia who had given her an envelope she wasn't too open until she was onboard the ship. Enclosed were ten shillings and a letter Maggie had memorized on the voyage. She first read the letter as the ship pulled away from the harbor at Cobh.

Dear Maggie, you know I'll miss you and will pray for you. I enclose this small donation for your safe passage with hopes that you remember I remain forever your fond sister Julia.

Of all the good-bye gifts and parcels, Maggie was surprised at how deeply this one touched her.

For all her faults and scoldings, Julia was a good and true sister and friend. Now, she was gone forever. And now, Maggie was the last of the Jeremiah Buckleys of Ahadalane, Ireland.

Chapter 71
Visits

Autumn 1960

Maggie pursed her lips, wondering who might accompany her in tonight's dreams. Each of her children had been there at one time or another. First to come was Baby Rose, whom she held close to her heart as the others arrived. Hugh and Jerome, her red-headed boys who carried her looks, were next. Then her dear John wandered in, his field cap in place, followed by dark-haired Josephine with Bernard. They all laughed and danced and sang to her. It made sleeping so attractive, she didn't mind napping so much.

Doc Kober had told her it was her heart that was giving out. Congestive heart failure, he called it. Her heart had borne its share of sorrows, she knew, but ah, she wouldn't ever forget the joys, so many still filling her days. Never did she think she'd live well into her eighties, every moment a treasure.

Veronica and Genevieve had helped to orchestrate fine meals and even entertainment when Maggie, in her waking moments, was up to it. As the days warmed up, they sat on the side porch, she in the bouncy chair that had been a gift for her birthday several years ago. Its metal frame, padded seat and solid spring construction let her touch her feet to the floor and, with a little tap, give herself a lovely ride up and down, like the horsey rides she'd given each of the children when they were small. Like the ones she'd been given by her brothers Michael and Tims when she was small. Full circle times were upon her.

Maggie had always loved the comings and goings of the children, some of their visits long enough for them to recite a little poem, perform a song or even a short dance. How she enjoyed seeing them grow into such fine youngsters. She trusted that the shy ones, who held back from performing anything, would find their way eventually.

Besides the children, one of her treasured visitors was the priest, Father Ball. He'd become a Monsignor of late and was still the same dear man who knew of Maggie's woes and had tended to her losses. If the lights were on, he would stop by at night to see who was with her and how Maggie was faring. He had also visited during the days when Petie was there, nursing Josephine as the breast cancer had its own way.

"Isn't it a scourge, Maggie," he'd said. "A nurse needing a nurse. Thanks be to God she has such a friend in Petie." Indeed, a friend she was. None truer, Maggie thought.

Of her twelve children, the surviving seven, Loring, Victor, Tom and Don, Veronica, Genevieve, and Betty, filled her days with enough joy and love to hold her. Over the years, her losses had taught her to fret less. If she could teach the young ones anything, it would be to worry less or not at all. Worry never helped change anything. It only robbed you of the moment in front of you. She'd told her children her belief many times. And now, with so few moments left, she believed it all the more.

Since John's death, with Betty off to the convent and Gene eventually starting a family of her own, Veronica had been an ever-present comfort. Her weekend visits to Lima from Niagara Falls once or twice a month seemed enough for Maggie to keep up with the groceries and the gardening. Maggie was watchful for signs of overwork or impatience in Veronica or any of the others who helped her. She never for an instant wanted to be a burden, praying that would not happen. She knew how easily family members could become resentful. She had only to think of her sister Julia Rulia as an example of someone who was bitter, though Julia would never admit it.

Besides the groceries and the gardening, Maggie found that the gabbing was important, too. Veronica's classroom stories, her times with Freddy, and her travels with her chums gave them plenty to chatter about. Maggie filled in with what she'd learned from church friends and from occasional visits with neighbors. A laugh was always included, Maggie careful not to let it be at anyone else's expense, at least not most of the time.

"Do you remember that day three of you girls were at a Sunday Mass with me for one occasion or another? I don't think any of us will soon forget it."

Veronica knew immediately which event Maggie was recalling. "I do," she said. "It was the Sunday after a Saturday dinner celebration at the church hall. Father Ball had stopped in and we had a grand visit with him, his warmth so natural."

She continued as she watched her mother's reaction, a smile crossing her lips. "Early the next morning, there he was in his full vestments, processing down the aisle, looking from left to right as he blessed us all with holy water, nodding and smiling as usual. Except, instead of the ceremonial biretta that was part of his Mass attire, he still had his Homburg hat on. It was a picture so absurd that it must have brought to mind the likes of Abbott and Costello and caused giggles throughout the congregation."

"You and Gene were the worst," Maggie added. I'm glad Betty wasn't with us or it might have been even more disastrous."

"Did anyone ever talk about it afterward?" Veronica asked. "At the Catholic Daughter's meeting, we all had a good laugh.

They said that one of the altar servers was able to hand Father Ball the biretta when he returned to the altar. Other than red cheeks, he went right on."

Maggie so enjoyed the laughter. Her children knew how to appreciate humor and filled the house with it.

Veronica once asked, "Do you remember the time Mrs. Doran was here, Mother? You and she had a wonderful conversation. It was just a few weeks after her son Don had died. Her daughters Betty and Mary had come along with her and Gene was home for the weekend."

"I do remember," Maggie said. "We'd had a lovely visit and when she stood at the door to say good night, she said, 'Well, I had a better time than I thought.' Her daughters were aghast until we all burst out laughing."

It was, after all was said and done, an understandable comment. Maggie, too, had known such feelings but had kept them to herself.

Maggie's August 15th birthday had always been a special time each year with visits from many of the young people. She loved seeing so many redheads, four of the six of Loring and Peggy's children displaying the family trait. She watched as the children came into the front parlor to visit, twitching their hands or swinging their feet as they chatted about school and friends and pets. If the age was right, they might even tell of boyfriends or girlfriends. She'd been pleased that Maureen often stopped by with a beau at Maggie's New Year's Open House. This year it had been Austin Stewart for Maggie to meet, perhaps even approve of.

Though her physical pace had slowed, her walking and breathing a bit labored, Maggie could easily follow conversations. She loved learning the jargon of the day and noted the changes in attire. The laced-up shoes of her day were long gone. Shawls, long skirts, and dresses were replaced by sweaters, slacks, and tops. She learned that "I dig it, man," had nothing to do with men farming. She particularly enjoyed "Put an egg in your shoe and beat it."

She noted so many milestones in her dear *Lima Recorder, the Avon Herald, Caledonia Advertiser, and Canandaigua Daily Messenger,* all carrying stories of the day. For her most recent birthday, Betty had given her a black leather scrapbook filled with clippings about herself, her children, grandchildren and even some great- grandchildren. She read and was reminded, with great satisfaction, of her brood.

First off, she noted that Margaret Mary never missed a beat on sharing her adventures, of which there were many. Maggie imagined that her latest European travels would provide stories for years to come. Articles that told of the singing and acting that each of her girls had done also told of the boys who displayed their own prowess, academically, athletically, and some with service in the military.

Maggie was especially glad to remember that Loring's son Jack, who had become quite the fellow, was a paratrooper in Alaska for the huge Army-Air Force "Operation Warm Wind." He'd also been a part of "Operation Long Haul, the largest airlift of men in history.

From her bouncy chair, Maggie was delighted to think that these young folks were making history, the future of the world in good hands.

When her children were young, she'd been proud when they became known for academic and career successes. As adults, they continued to achieve. Veronica was a teacher; Genevieve had landed a job just out of Rochester Business Institute as secretary to the Superintendent of Nurses at Strong Memorial Hospital. She especially remembered the time when Josephine was visiting and helped Dr. Kober treat two Auburn men who were unconscious and badly injured in a car crash.

As she turned the pages, she saw the clipping that Jerome's widow, Rachel, had remarried a man named Emory Horton and was finding her way with her surviving daughter, Cecelia. Surviving heartache was a family trait, it seemed, Maggie mused as she kept reading.

Happily, articles noted when Betty had made her final vows and Don had gone off to Fort Dix for a time.

Maggie's own visits back and forth to New York City were written about over the years, reminding her of the joy the Galena/Kerrigans had provided.

When she read about her newly installed hardwood floors, she laughed out loud. It was an accomplishment that didn't need to be publicized, but then it was an accomplishment in this old house and a great improvement.

Maggie was pleased at being appointed Chaplain of the American Legion Auxiliary; also, her committee work at the National Catholic Rural Life Conference was noted. Being a Catholic Daughters Trustee, attending retreats, and even having surgery for a gallbladder attack all made it into the Recorder.

Whew, she thought. What a review of her life. She wondered if anyone would ever read these articles. Well, it would be alright if they did, for they painted an ordinary life full of extraordinary blessings.

Chapter 72
Clippings

Autumn 1960

Maggie awoke from her rest, eager to continue perusing the black leather scrapbook. She was mesmerized. Betty had somehow found time to collect clippings of the day from the local papers about so many of her children and grandchildren and insert them into a book, preserving them for all time. Or at least for some time. How long could these little triangular- shaped corners that held the clippings stay in place, she wondered. For now, they did the trick, the pleasure of remembering hers.

She settled herself at the dining room table with a pot of tea, ready for her journey through time. Veronica was due soon; her weekend travel home was always an elixir for Maggie's spirits. As Don wandered through the dining room, he paused near her chair to look at the book.

"Lots of stories for you," he said, his familiar small frame leaning against her chair. He'd been the smallest of all the boys, the result of being a twin. At only five feet four inches, he was adamant that it didn't bother him. "I can do lots more than some of those tall fellas, fitting into some tight spaces, getting under lots of plants at work when I need to." He watched as Maggie turned to the first page of the scrapbook. "There's a few in there about me, Betty told me last week."

"I imagine there are," Maggie said as she turned a page and read one of the clippings.

June 15, 1922,

A little play, "What's in the Basket?" convulsed the audience with laughter when Don Donegan proved to be the "bear" in the basket, and he also showed that he is quite a singer.

"You've always been quite a comedian, even at eight years old. A handsome one, at that." Maggie said, smiling up at his hazel green eyes. "And it seems you were off with the CCC to Mississippi from Camp Dix in no time. Here's the article from 1935. You were just twenty-one."

She was so glad for his luck in becoming part of the Civilian Conservation Corps. It was a good way for him to get an established trade. He'd only been only sixteen when his father died, not yet skilled at any trade. His time first at Fort Dix and then in Mississippi was a chance to get some training while giving some service. He'd even sent money home every week.

"It was hot work, I'll tell you that," Don said.

Maggie remembered when he came home that he'd grown a bit taller and found a few pals in town. A good experience all around. He'd even landed a job in the nursery at the Tollis' Florist. Maggie sighed as he went off to the garage, his favorite spot, to tinker with his radio collection, Philco tube radios his primary interest. She'd done her best for him, she told herself, hoping it was enough.

As she turned back to the start of the scrapbook, she saw that Betty had listed the names of all the children, along with their birthdates, including five with death dates. Never could she have known she would live through such anguish. Nor that she would find solace despite it. Yet she had.

Hugh Michael born NYC 1890,
died in Lima 1926

Jerome Joseph born W. Bloomfield 1892,
died Rochester 1928.

Loring Francis born Lima 1894

John Victor born Lima 1896

Margaret Mary Josephine born Lima 1899,
died in Lima 1942

Veronica Genevieve born Lima 1901

Michael Thomas born Lima 1904

Bernard Paul born Lima 1906,
died Rochester 1950

Genevieve Juliet born Lima 1907

Elizabeth Adona born Lima 1911

Donnell Gervase born Lima 1914

Rose Agnes born Lima 1914,
died Lima 1914

Maggie breathed deeply into the knowledge that hers had been a good life, her children's accomplishments, her own travels and adventures worth celebrating. The fact that she had borne twelve children, all of them special, still seemed a bit unbelievable. She recalled her mother's response when asked if she'd had a favorite. "Yes, all of them. Each one has such favorite qualities." Maggie understood that well.

Betty had been a studious one, continuing her studies in the convent, achieving a Bachelor of Arts degree in 1938 and more amazing to Maggie, ten years later, earning a Master's degree from the University of Rochester. Maggie marveled at her determination and dedication, studying in the summers in- between teaching assignments and even becoming a school Principal. She remembered the stationery box that contained her seventy-page thesis.

Organization and Practice of Guidance in Secondary Schools by Sister Leo Xavier Donegan.

Submitted in Partial Fulfillment of the Requirements for the Degree Master of Education.

"Throughout the world, the United Nations Educational, Scientific, and Cultural Organization is proclaiming the power of education as an international force for peace."

This newly established United Nations had captured the attention of a nation, and now her daughter was quoting from it. Maggie, with her eighth-grade education, smiled inwardly. Never could she have imagined such a life and outcomes for a daughter of hers.

If she took a long view, she had to admit that her four oldest boys, despite the early deaths of her oldest two, had managed quite well. Hugh with a motor company in Columbus, Ohio, at a young age; his wife June a gem of a woman; Jerome and Rachel had two children, known throughout the area as an accomplished farmer, meat dealer, and fur buyer; Loring had married Peggy Keough, from New York City who brought out the best in him. The father of six, a seasoned farmer and fur buyer of renown, he led the way for his younger brothers. Vic, with his wife Margaret Owen, became the father of five, two dying as children, his love of cars sustaining his success as a car salesman in Avon.

Her next four were equally accomplished: Josephine, a well-regarded nurse in New York City; Veronica, a popular teacher in Niagara Falls; Tom, father of two, a sought-after carpenter; and Bernard, with his wife Etta, father of two, successful businessman and farmer, who became Maggie's savior, staying on the farm when she was in such great need after John's death.

And finally, there were Genevieve, her only married daughter, mother of seven with her husband Frank, and a sharp businesswoman; Betty, a Sister of St. Joseph and her spiritual support; Donnell, her baby boy forever; Baby Rose tucked safely into a special corner of her heart since she became an angel at four days old. Maggie sipped her tea, a smile crossing her face.

Just then, Veronica arrived, groceries and packages in hand. She'd arrived from Niagara Falls after her week's work, ready for a change of scene. Maggie knew it wasn't a rest, for she'd watch Veronica bustle about the house, putting things in order, fluffing pillows, straightening rugs and chairs to be just so, after she fixed a dinner for them all. Tonight's fare was from Tom Wahl's in Avon, where Veronica occasionally stopped for a treat. When the restaurant first opened, Veronica and Maggie had gone for a car ride, a real treat for Maggie. But of late, eating at home was far simpler and Maggie enjoyed the fish fry and frosty root beer that it was noted for just as well at home, while Veronica filled her in on the news of the week.

Tonight, it was Maggie who filled Veronica in, sharing with her the clippings that kept her spellbound. Before Veronica even was able to clear the table for dinner, Maggie asked, "Do you know our trip to Gene's was written up in the newspaper? Read it aloud, will you?

Maggie slid the book over to Veronica, who adjusted her glasses and read:

Lima Recorder. September 7, 1950.

Mr. and Mrs. Frank Osta, who moved recently from Buffalo to Syracuse, were visited last Thursday (August 31st) by her mother, Mrs. M. Donegan of Lima, and her sisters, Miss Veronica Donegan, Niagara Falls; Sister Leo Xavier, Geneva; and her brother, L. F. Donegan, wife and son, Billy of Lima. All made the trip in L.F. Donegan's car.

"It's remarkable that Gene had just moved in with all those children and we landed on her like that. Loring was so insistent that we all go. Six of us in one car. Oh, my stars!"

"All I can say is that I was certainly younger then," Maggie said. Veronica slid the book back to Maggie and said, "Mother, the other remarkable thing is that it was just a week after Bob and Mary Ann's wedding in Mt. Morris. What a party time that was. We were all a bit younger."

The mother and daughter poured more tea, content to share such fond memories.

Chapter 73
What They Knew of Her

Spring 1961

Maggie put the last scraps of the potato skins in the pot and took them out to the back room, adding them to the compost pile. She was tired, but no more than usual. She'd fixed a dinner of potato and ham with a bit of salad for Don and herself. Earlier, she'd spent time tidying the front rooms, straightening the few antimacassars she'd been given by Julia for the chair arms and backs. She remembered her mother teaching her the intricate stitches for tatting and how pleased she was with the result of these lacy protectors. Her oldest sister, Mary, had never shown much interest in needlework, while Julia seemed to do it perfectly, of course. Maggie regretted never bringing any of her own handiwork from Ireland, but in America, you could buy all you ever needed or wanted, she'd been told. Now, it was hand- made tatting she wanted and regretfully had left behind so many years before.

As she straightened the front parlor and slid one of the children's favorites, the Skunk dice game, in place on the lower shelf of the walnut table, she thought of its center drawer holding the playing cards. She loved her game of forty-five and only wished she still had the energy to teach it to all the grandchildren. Her own children hadn't been interested; Canasta and Bridge the craze for them. Occasionally, she did wonder what these younger children thought of her. Just an old lady with strange ways, she guessed.

Maggie's own grandmother, Gran, they called her, had been a bit of a curiosity to her, having lived with them for a time. She was stern sometimes, telling them all to sit up straight and chew their food carefully and, at other times, soft as a lamb, wrapping one or another of them in her arms. Maggie remembered Gran saying her beads, thrilled when she taught Maggie to do the same. She'd only been ten when Gran died. She remembered the people and the prayers filling her house. There'd been tears and laughter and plenty of food.

Maggie's favorite memory was talking to Gran after she'd gone with the angels. When she had asked her mother after Gran died if Gran was in heaven yet, her Ma told her she'd know when Gran said her special goodbye. Maggie sighed. And then she waited, sitting near the candle at Gran's bedside, its brightness lighting the room. The proper treatment for death had been attended to, the cloth covering the mirror, the window left open and the lit candles. She waited, closing her eyes, and was saying the prayer that Gran had taught her, "Hail Mary, full of grace…" when she heard Gran's voice. "Blessed art thou amongst women…" She opened her eyes to find light shining around Gran. She looked to see if others saw what she did. No one stirred. Then she heard Gran's voice again. "Now and at the hour of our death. Amen." She'd never forgotten that moment nor had she ever shared it with anyone. It was hers for a lifetime whenever she needed it.

Maybe, she thought, as she made her way to the front room, just maybe, one of the little ones would carry her faith forward as she had carried Grans. Maybe they would know the peace that came with such love and faith. Just maybe.

A knock on the door startled her. It was after seven and twilight had lit the sky over the fields. Seldom did she have evening visitors on a weekday. Veronica was not due until the weekend. Her curiosity was heightened. She turned on the porch light and, when she opened the front door, was pleased to discover Father Ball. He usually appeared when the lights were on and a crowd was on hand. Tonight was different. There was just Maggie and Don and no extra lights.

"I'll be apologizing in advance, Maggie, for this evening's intrusion, but might I come in for a brief visit?"

Maggie opened the door wider and stepped aside to make room for him to enter. "Well, you're surely welcome, Father. I'm delighted to see you. Don's gone off to his radios, so it's a fine time for a visit. Come right in. It's just in time, you are, for a cup of tea or something a bit stronger if you'd like."

"Ah, a cup of tea with a drop of whiskey in it would be a perfect end to a busy day," the priest said as he settled himself at the table.

As Maggie busied herself getting the teacups and pulling the whiskey bottle out from its hiding spot in the back of the cupboard so Don wouldn't find it, she set the flame under the kettle and brought out the teacups and the whiskey bottle.

"We'll have some fine tea in no time," she said as she straightened the lace tablecloth, another reminder of special needlework, this one a gift sent by Julia.

"You've had a busy day, Father. Is everything all right now?" "Well, it's your health that's my first concern, Maggie. What's the doctor telling you these days?"

Maggie smiled and waved her hand. "I'm taking it as easy as I can, Father, so you needn't worry. I can't say I'm as fit as a fiddle, for I'm not. But I can say that I've had a wonderful life and each day going forward is a blessing. And you're one of mine."

With that, the whistle on the teakettle sounded off and Maggie stepped away. Father Ball sat quietly and upon her return with the tray, she noted him eyeing this familiar dining room where he'd spent so many pleasant times. The favorite Millet painting, the Angelus, that he'd spoken so fondly of, the desk tucked in the corner by the north window with the black telephone on top, the handsome Windsor chair next to the end of the buffet. He often commented on the little homemade shrine that was in front of the south window, putting him in mind of Sister Betty, who was doing great things lately; her reputation for singing continued even in the convent. All

Maggie's girls had been musical; even Josephine, God rest her soul, and Father Ball knew them all.

As Maggie returned and put down the tray with its tea cozy covered teapot, cream and sugar and some spoons as well, she nodded to him, feeling comfort in his presence. She adjusted the candlesticks on the table to accommodate the tray, returned to the kitchen and brought back a plate of cookies, some favorite shortbreads she'd made just the other day. Then she sat and poured their tea, handing Father Ball the whiskey bottle to add his own touch. When he'd finished, she capped the bottle and returned it to the cupboard. "Just say if you'd like some more later, Father. I keep it well hidden to avoid temptation for Donnell. I know over the years you've understood."

Father Ball smiled at Maggie, admiring her nurturing ways. "I do understand, Maggie, and commend you for your perseverance. It's paid off handsomely, for you've raised a fine family indeed. And it's that "paying off" I'd like to talk with you about."

Maggie put down her teacup and looked at the priest.

Whatever could he mean, she wondered.

"Maggie," he continued, "remember when the money came from Ireland after your sister Julia died and you were able to pay the taxes on all your acreage?"

Maggie nodded and the priest continued, "There's good news to share. The property up by the stand on the west side of the road is becoming most desirable. A fella came to see me today to ask if I knew who owned it. He knows of a company that would like to build on it, Maggie. They'll pay handsomely, he says, to build affordable housing for this little town of ours. The issue of 'right of way' is something that needs to be resolved. But once that's straightened out, you'll have something very valuable to leave to your children after all and enough to have Donnell be cared for if it comes to that."

Maggie remembered bemoaning her financial plight to Father Ball over the thirty years since John's death. She'd told him of her desire to be able to leave something for the children, especially Veronica, and he'd remembered. The consolation in his knowing was worth it, of having someone with whom to share the weight that came with the hope for something better.

Though they'd never spoken of it, Maggie sensed that Veronica would be on hand for Don. She'd seen her 'manage' him when he'd been 'in his cups.' She knew how to cajole without antagonizing, an art form Maggie had learned from her own father when he dealt with her brother Tims. Now, to think that the worries of money wouldn't be something Veronica would be saddled with. She felt a deep contentment and, with it, exhaustion.

"Well, Maggie, it's sure to be a load off your mind to have a way through for the next generation. You've done your best; I can testify to that for certain."

With that, Father Ball took his leave, putting his teacup and saucer on the sideboard and picking up his hat that he'd left on the chair as he came in. Maggie giggled silently as she watched him don his hat, remembering the Sunday he kept his Homburg in place. As she saw him to the door and watched him go down the walkway, she felt a wave of gratitude for his counsel and caring. Leaving the cups together on the kitchen sink, she made her way to her bedroom, eager to rest in the arms of Morpheus, knowing tomorrow would be another day, one with fewer worries than today.

Chapter 74
The Youngest Granddaughter

June 15, 1961

Gene put her finger to her lips, nodding to her youngest daughter, Kathleen. "Grandmother might be resting, so we'll tip- toe in," she said. With that, she opened the door into the dining room, her eleven-year-old tiptoeing behind. They'd driven down from Syracuse to spend these special days in Lima. Veronica was beside herself with the chores of ending the school year for her fourth graders, so many programs and details to attend to. Gene had shepherded her seven children through June programs enough to know the season was full of busyness and anxiety. Add to that Maggie's precarious condition, and Gene didn't hesitate to offer help. Kathleen's good grades meant she could slip out of school a bit early and go with Gene. Happily, Mary Jean, at age 21, could get a meal for Tom, Betty Anne, and Mark, each at home since they still had final exams to complete. John and Jim were old enough to be on their own, though food may draw them to dinner with the younger ones.

There was no telling how long Maggie would hang on, but it was clear she needed help with her "basic needs," as Veronica described it. "She's still in command, but she's not steady on her feet, and I don't dare count on her to even make her beloved pot of tea."

Gene didn't need to know much more. She'd been raised in this 1890s house that had seen them through so many rough times. Every home improvement, from getting electricity and replacing the gas lamps in each of the rooms to getting an electric wringer for the washer and an electric stove to replace the wood fired AGA, all seemed miraculous. As she entered the dining room, she felt a warmth and familiarity that comforted her. She was glad to have her youngest with her. Even if Kathleen seemed too young to absorb the importance of this visit, it was a comfort to think she might.

Gene guessed right. Maggie was sound asleep. She peeked into her bedroom to see her mouth open, gentle snoring sounds emanating from her. She returned to Kathleen and led her up the attic stairs to the little front bedroom whose rectangular windows looked over the driveway. It was here the powder blue Victorian glass lamp resided on the stand next to the twin bed. Gene would sleep in the room next to this one and listen for Grandmother in the night. Veronica had given her fair warning.

It was Monday afternoon.

Maggie's diagnosis of congestive heart failure was less of a shock than it might have been, each of the children watching her slow down over the last months. They shared their observations after their visits, always out of Maggie's earshot. Where she once would go to the barn on her own, she'd wait by the porch door for the kittens to come to her. Don took over the task of picking the peonies, one of Maggie's favorite summertime joys. Don's work in the nursery taught him a few tricks of the trade. The old wife's tale of peony blossoms being opened by ants was one he dismissed as he cut the stems at an angle, shook them, and rinsed them with water from the pump.

Maggie was proud of his skill and grateful for any help he gave. She'd grown to depend on him more and more as the days wore on, tying her shoes one of the first helps. Bending over was no longer something she took for granted, nor was lifting the tea kettle. When the grandchildren came to visit, she invited them to fix the tea as if they were doing her a favor.

"Ruth," she'd say, "wouldn't ye like to fix us a nice cup of tea. The fixings and the cups are all on the table and the kettle will boil in just a few minutes." And then, when Ruth returned with the teapot and teacups, Maggie would exclaim, "Aren't you the clever one!"

All through her life, Maggie had gained from giving. Her childhood days were filled with helping her Ma and often doing the bidding of her sister Mary or being bossed about by Julia, sometimes more than she could bear. Yet somehow, it served her well, knowing not to pass bossy behavior on to her girls, who seemed kind and uncomplaining in their giving.

It was the receiving that Maggie found difficult. She'd been the one 'in charge' all her years in America. Now she knew she needed to be cared for. Being gracious was the goal that too often eluded her, and her tongue spoiled her intention.

"Did the kettle stand for a while? This tea's just lukewarm." "I might make some soup, if I find some strength, to remind you how I taught you." Oh, how she'd wished she could leave well enough alone. She found herself more and more cross with her own behavior, turning to her rosary for comfort and consolation.

Her girls may have guessed she wasn't happy with this development of needing help. She could hear them into the night planning how to get more 'hands-on deck' to handle the chores.

The farm work had been in the competent hands of neighbor and friend Elmer Wemett, who saw to the fields with mastery, Don not needing to lift a spade. The twenty-seven acres were cared for with precision that made Maggie proud, Elmer even paying for the corn and wheat he planted. A win-win situation. The additional acreage up the road soon would be taken care of by someone else, a worry lifted.

Household chores and meals were seen to by Veronica when she was home on most weekends, but the weekdays were a challenge. That's when Peggy and Loring's girls might have been a help, but both Margaret Mary and Maureen had gone off to Syracuse, teaching jobs calling to them. Betty was mostly unavailable as well, except for an occasional Saturday visit. Even though she was now at the new St. Agnes High School on East

River Road, which was handier for a visit to Lima when she could get the time and a ride.

Peggy herself often sent Loring down with an extra this or that, a casserole, or some sliced ham and potato or even some apple pie, the fruit fresh from her tree. These kindnesses were returned favors for the days when Peggy was swamped with babies and household chores and Maggie would send a homemade loaf of bread, biscuits or a soup at just the right time. They had a cordial and loving relationship that pleased Maggie very much.

Gene stepped into the kitchen and opened the refrigerator. She could see Veronica's handiwork in the little glass-covered dishes with fruits or vegetables. She had told her of the prepared meal she'd left for tonight's dinner, a favorite for Kathleen. Macaroni and cheese. A side salad would be just right, along with some sliced bread and butter. Don would take his dinner at 5 p.m. in the kitchen, Veronica had said, and then he'd be off to his radio world for the evening.

Kathleen appeared at the kitchen doorway, looking a bit lost. She'd not been the only child in this old house in the past, usually accompanied by a family full of companions.

"Would you be able to play a tune or two for Grandmother?" asked Gene. "She'll probably be waking up as I get dinner started. I'll bet she'd enjoy that."

So, the days went by, Kathleen helping with food preparation, occasionally peeking into the slim metal cupboard that had all the little juice glasses. Gene saw her eyes light up when she discovered the plastic pear shaped dishes, ones she remembered from earlier trips. "These are so cool," she exclaimed, her mother pleased that she was settling in. Her evening concerts were a diversion for them, the songs familiar and challenging for Kathleen, who stepped up to the task. She even sang along as she played, a true Donegan trait.

"I hear a bird, a Londonderry bird," she crooned and played through to the title, *"How are Things in Glocca Morra? How's the weather there?"*

Gene was thrilled that she'd given her girls the same advantage she'd been given as a child. Her piano and voice lessons with Belle Chapin had been a highlight of her youth, each of her sisters also Belle's students. Their performances were always remarkable, her memories of them bringing a smile. She watched her mother enjoying yet another generation as the songs continued: *Harbor Lights, Red Sails in the Sunset* and the classic An Irish Lullaby. *Too ra loo ra loo ra…*

Gene was aware that these days were as significant for this youngest daughter as they were for her. She had taken care of her younger sister Betty and brother Don and now her own seven children, but she'd never really taken care of her mother and felt a little skittish to be doing so. Helping her dress and undress each day was unfamiliar. Kathleen helped with her shoes and stockings and carried on great chatter as she did. It eased them all.

Veronica finally arrived late Friday afternoon, tired from her year's end with all the children, the closing play she directed a great success. Her two-part Christmas Operetta, The Red Candles had been well-received earlier, and this closing year-end student play, while exhausting, had been equally successful. She was pleased to see newspaper clippings of her efforts and happily brought them home for storage in the green valise.

The 93rd Street School Parent-Teacher Association sponsored the programs under the direction of Miss Veronica Donegan, her colleagues and faculty friends.

Maggie sat in her chair in the front parlor as Veronica and Gene prepared dinner and Kathleen continued her serenade. "Here's the one I played for my recital, Grandmother," she said proudly and played Percy *Grainger's Country Gardens* with a smart beat. Maggie glanced about as this youngest of her grandchildren entertained, happy for this moment.

Later that evening, Gene and Veronica helped Maggie walk into the kitchen, where they assisted her in bathing and pampered her with powders and lotions. Kathleen watched from the doorway as they brushed her white hair, still thick and pretty. She spoke of her childhood days, of St. Lachteen, Donoughmore's patron saint, and the holy wells in the hillside where they'd see their own reflections at the water's edge.

"It was a simple time and simple faith," she said softly. Maggie looked radiant as they each went in to say goodnight. Her blue eyes were peaceful and her hair shining. She wore a pink nightdress that brought a glow to her pink cheeks.

There would be more to hear from this lovely woman, Gene thought as she pulled the bedcovers up and bent to kiss her mother's forehead. At least, she hoped there would be.

Chapter 75
Until You Come to Me

July 15, 1961

Gene had read the Lima recorder article to Maggie during her week's visit.

Mrs. Frank M. Osta of Syracuse is spending the week with her mother, Mrs. Margaret Donegan of Rochester St. Mrs. Donegan's many friends sent their best wishes for a speedy recovery.

Maggie smiled when she heard it. Soon enough, they'd be reading her death notice, she thought. She'd been known to many, whether through trading in the village, or the Catholic Daughters, school programs or children she'd met through her own children. She'd lived long enough to know a good number of them and was pleased that she'd been hospitable to whoever was presented to her. Why wouldn't she be? She'd been carried by so many who helped her through sorrows and sadness during her nearly seventy years in this town to somehow find strength again. She'd found the good in all she met. There was no point in doing otherwise.

Over these last few days, she had felt herself drifting in and out. She'd awaken from what she knew was a dream but seemed so real. At one time or another, they were all there: the twins, Jeremiah and Lizzie. Then Mary and Julia, Tims and Michael… all making an appearance in her dreams. Even Gran floated in, smiling just so. Then the treasures of her beloved John, Baby Rose, Hugh, Jerome, Josephine and Bernard also appeared. She could almost touch them.

Then they'd be gone, and she'd be in her rocking chair in the parlor, hearing Gene and Veronica as they were 'tending to her.' They'd converse about this one or that one –'gossiping'– something Maggie had no time for. She remembered the priest and the story of feathers in the pillow, once spread they couldn't be collected again. This small town was no place for such trivial time-taking traps. She'd prefer to "call a spade a spade" and be done with it. She'd done just that last night when she said to Veronica, "That other girl's been drinking. I can smell it." She realized, once she had said it, that the 'other girl' was her daughter Gene. Veronica didn't look left nor right, simply said. "Oh?"

Maggie knew of the 'drink'. She'd lived with it since childhood with her brother Tims, bright and handsome, taken by the drink. As she'd grown, she enjoyed a drink herself, but it didn't rule her like it did some because she knew when it got hold of you, it didn't let go easily. So, often, she simply said the truth out loud, even to the priest if it was called for, and to whomever else she felt needed to hear it. It freed both her and the listener of gossip and innuendo.

She looked around the parlor, the piano such a central part of their time together. Across the way, in the front parlor, there now stood a television. Aside from Perry Como, she hadn't found much of interest. Her daughters had encouraged her to watch it, and she knew it would be a part of their lives for years to come. It needn't be a part of hers.

They were good women, her girls. Josephine, Veronica, Genevieve, and Betty. She wasn't surprised that Betty had stayed so close to her over the years. She'd held her tight when Baby Rose had gone. Betty never quite let go, even when she went into the Convent. She'd come home on her vacation once she was allowed visits. She'd fuss about as a way of helping, changing this thing or that thing, trying to improve things. Maggie let her be, understanding her ways.

Gene had done well enough with her own brood of seven, all of them seeming to be on the right track. She knew she'd not see what would become of them, but she'd had enough of a glimpse to know they'd be just fine. Bernard's two children,

Bernie Jr. and Mary Lou would be fine as well, with her praying for them every day.

Maggie had been pleased that Josephine and Veronica, never having borne children, were both strong women and highly regarded in their professions. Josephine's stories and friendships with patients and Veronica's teaching adventures had given them both a fine disposition. Get a job that you can't wait to put your feet on the floor for in the morning, she had told her children. It seemed to have been good advice.

While being a grandmother to nineteen grandchildren was quite a responsibility, sixteen great-grandchildren felt monumental. They'd all brought such joy over the years. Loring and Peggy's six children and their love for Lima paralleled Maggie's. Billy with his vegetable stand, Jack with his ESSO gas station and Bob and Loring Jr. all making their way as salesmen just fine. Vic's daughter Ruth was a prize, loved by all. And her brother and sister, Billy and Betty, were great, proud Donegans.

All of a sudden, Maggie felt weary, just thinking of them all, glad for their visits when they occurred yet often craving rest. She loved mostly from afar but never let them forget she loved them, always saying a kind word and giving a compliment. That was the most important lesson they could learn and pass on. Love.

Maggie closed her eyes and could see her mother clear as day. How she'd loved being in her presence. Whether helping hang the wash or watching her tend the hearth, she knew something special was there that would never go away.

"Would you like some tea, Mother?" Veronica asked as she approached Maggie's chair. Maggie had dozed off yet again.

"You know what I'd like, dear Veronica. I would like very much to go to bed now, if you'd be good enough to help me."

More dreaming was what she was after. She missed them all.

It was Saturday night. Veronica peeked into her mother's room as dinner hour approached. She hesitated to awaken Maggie yet knew she wouldn't want to miss Betty's visit. Veronica indicated to Betty to go on in. Just yesterday, Doc Kober had been in and said rest and comfort were the medicine now. Betty's visit would be a comfort.

After a few minutes passed, Betty emerged, smiling, her eyes tear-stained. "She wanted me to sing Danny Boy and I couldn't get a note out."

"Well, let's both go and serenade her now," Veronica said.

Softly, the two sisters, standing side by side, sang to their mother the last verse of Danny Boy. Maggie's breathing was shallow, her eyes fluttering as they sang.

> *"For you will bend and*
> *tell me that you love me,*
> *And I shall sleep in peace*
> *until you come to me!"*

They tiptoed out, eyes damp.

Sunday morning, Dr. William H. Kober attended Maggie for his last visit. He certified her death at 5:00 a.m. just before sunrise on July 16, 1961.

Epilogue

Lima Recorder

July 20, 1961

Mrs. Margaret Donegan

Funeral services were held yesterday, Wednesday, from the O'Connell Funeral Home and St. Rose Church, Lima, for Mrs. Margaret A. Donegan of Lima, who died Sunday, July 16, 1961, at her home after an illness of about five weeks. Burial was in St. Rose Cemetery. Mrs. Donegan was born in Ireland on Aug. 15, 1874, and came as a child with her family to New York City, then to Lima. She was predeceased several years ago by her husband, John. She was a member of St. Rose Church and the Catholic Daughters of America. Surviving are three daughters, Miss Veronica Donegan of Niagara Falls, Mrs. Frank Osta of Syracuse, Sister Leo Xavier of Sisters of St. Joseph, Rochester; four sons, Loring of Lima, Victor of Mumford. Thomas of Buffalo, Donald of Lima; 19 grandchildren; 16 great-grandchildren; several nieces and nephews.

They were all in attendance: Her seven surviving children, Loring, Victor, Veronica, Genevieve, Tom, Betty, and Don. Spouses, grandchildren and great-grandchildren also assembled. Even two of John's New York City nieces came, Margaret and Bertie. They stayed at the farmhouse, up in the little side room. Betty Doran opened her tourist home to the Osta family as she had done before; this time, Gene and Frank stayed there as well.

The wake had been at Jimmy O'Connell's, as all the family wakes had been. The tiny funeral home on Main Street had lines out the door. Aretha and Junior Reynolds, Catherine Sullivan, the Hogans, Betty and Mary Doran and more stood and waited to pay their respects. Maggie had known them all indeed. At 7 p.m. they gathered and said a rosary together and Gene and Frank's Kathleen said the final Amen. At the American Hotel, after the calling hours, the drink flowed freely with calls from the older Irish of Sláinte, the word for health, as they raised glasses on high.

The young ones, in their early twenties, were coming of age. Cousins meeting cousins, the children of Gene and Loring getting reacquainted since their last meeting eleven years earlier at Bernard's funeral when they were all in "knee pants." Vic and Margaret and their three children, Ruth, Billy, and Betty and all their children, clung to one another as the prayers were said. Etta and her two, Bernie and Mary Lou, looked wide-eyed and sad.

The next morning, the high Mass was one for the books, with the Ave Maria sung by the choir and other familiar hymns resounding to the rafters as the congregation raised their voices on high. Monsignor Ball officiated, a man who knew Maggie's soul so well. The grandsons were pallbearers, strapping young men, some with tear-stained faces. At the graveside, with Margaret Mary in the lead, those assembled sang An Irish Lullaby. They had lost someone of an era now slipping away.

Maggie had brought song and faith and laughter with her from Ireland. They'd all received it, her gift to them. She was on her way to heaven; they knew that for certain. It eased the pain of the loss to hope they would see her again.

It wasn't long before the rest of her children joined Maggie, Victor in 1965 and then her Don in 1966, with Loring, Gene, and Tom following. And finally, with Veronica in 1991 and Betty's Christmas Day death in 1994 the last, all of Maggie's brood were with her in eternity.

A unique love of Ireland and of Lima has united her children, grandchildren and great-grandchildren. While she never taught any lesson directly, many a lesson was learned of love, laughter and lasting devotion.

And wasn't it a granddaughter, taken by those lessons, who penned this story?

Family Tree
John Family

Hugh Michael
19 Nov. 1890 -
19 Nov. 1926

Jerome Joseph
25 July 1892 -
1 Feb. 1928

Bernard Paul
24 Jan. 1906 -
6 April 1950

Margaret Buckley
23 June 1871 -
16 July 1961

Loring Francis
28 July 1894 -
24 Nov. 1974

Genevieve Juliet
2 Oct. 1907 -
7 Mar. 1981

John Victor
24 Nov. 1896 -
8 April 1965

Elizabeth Adona
7 Sept. 1911 -
25 Dec. 1994

John Donegan
10 Oct. 1865 -
3 Dec. 1930

Margaret Mary Josephine
21 Aug. 1899 -
21 Sept. 1942

Donnell Gervase
26 Aug. 1914 -
27 July 1966

Veronica Genevieve
14 Feb. 1901 -
14 Mar. 1991

Rose Agnes
26 Aug. 1914 -
30 Aug. 1940

Michael Thomas
21 Sept. 1904 -
19 Feb. 1983

Family Trees
Anna Family

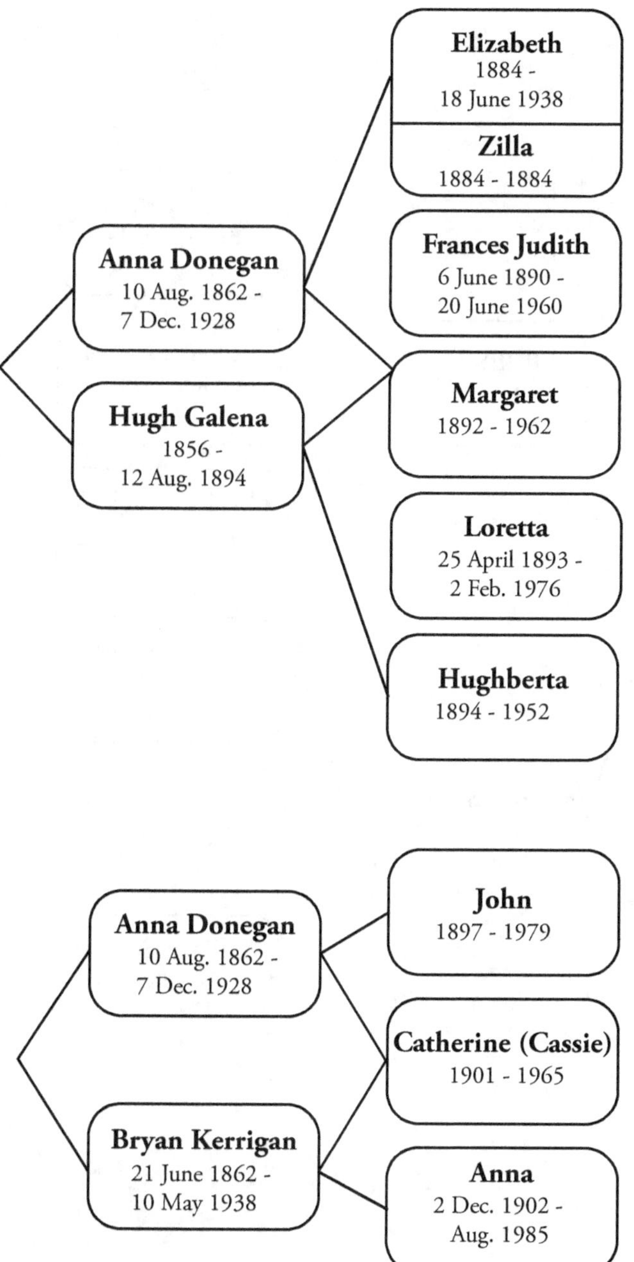

Family Tree
Loring Family

Loring Francis
28 July 1894 -
24 Nov. 1974

Margaret Mary Keogh
11 Jan. 1895 -
May 1973

Margaret Mary
31 Jan. 1927 -
17 Mar. 2021

Robert Francis
28 July 1928 -
1988

John Joseph (Jack)
19 Mar. 1930 -
4 Nov. 2015

Loring Francis Jr (Larry)
25 Nov. 1931 -
28 Feb. 2010

Josetta Ann (Maureen)
23 May 1937 -
20 Jan. 2022

William Eugene
25 Oct. 1938 -
6 Dec. 2014

John Victor Family

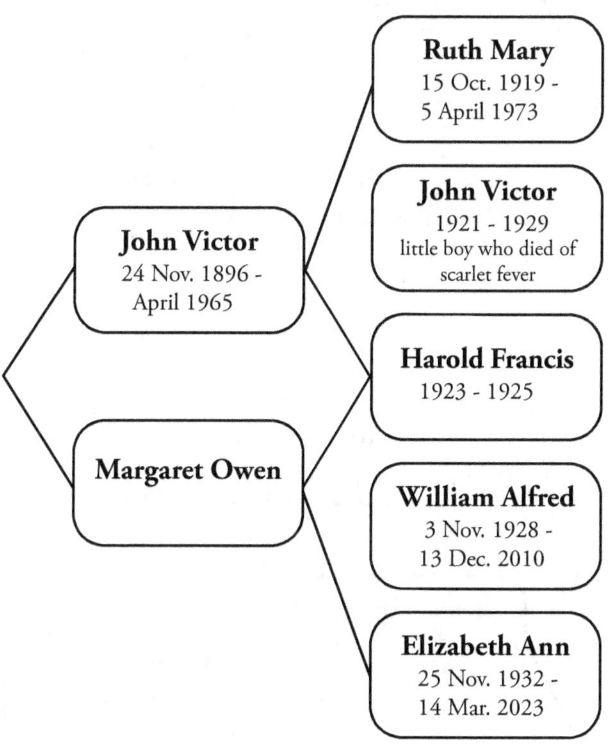

Family Tree
Jerome Family

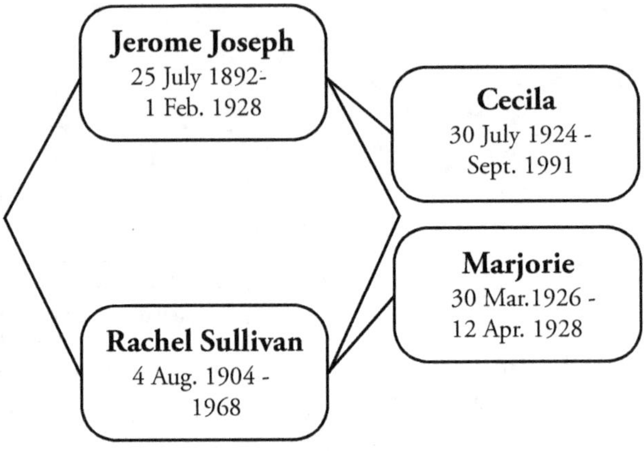

Family Tree
Michael Family

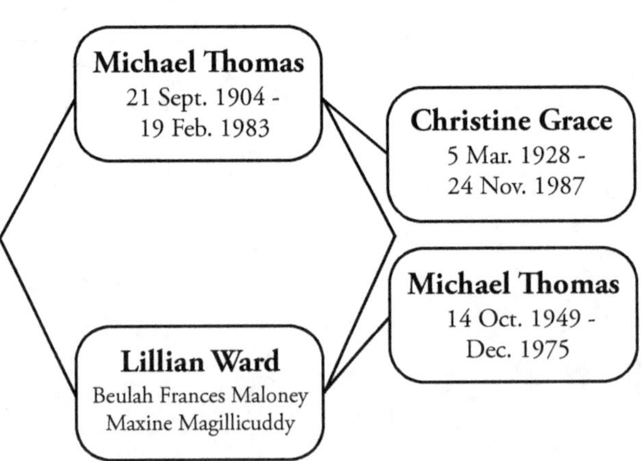

Family Tree
Genevieve Family

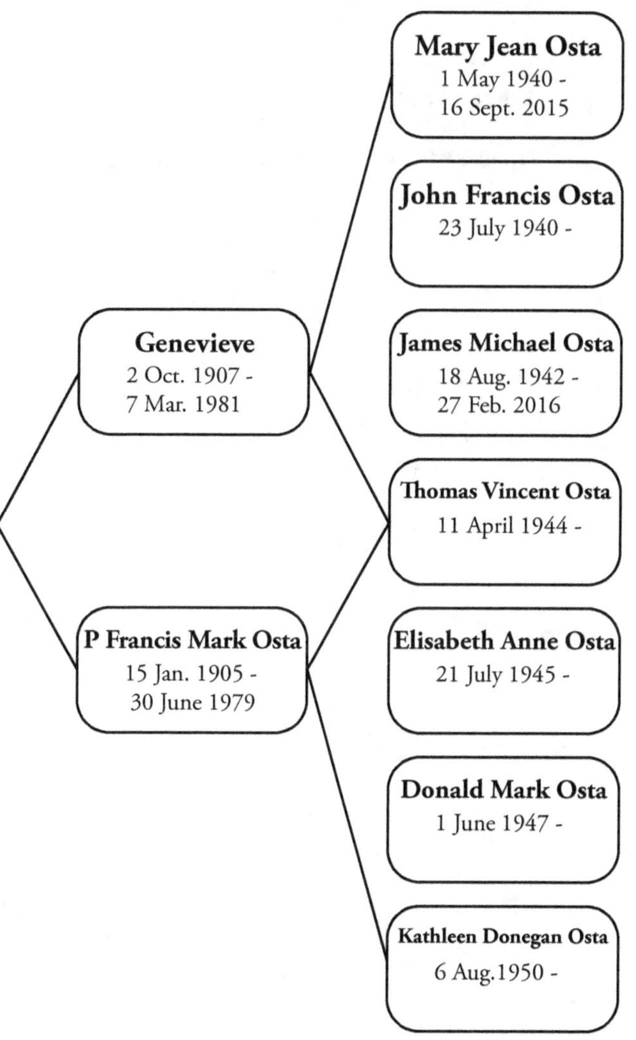

Family Tree
Bernard Family

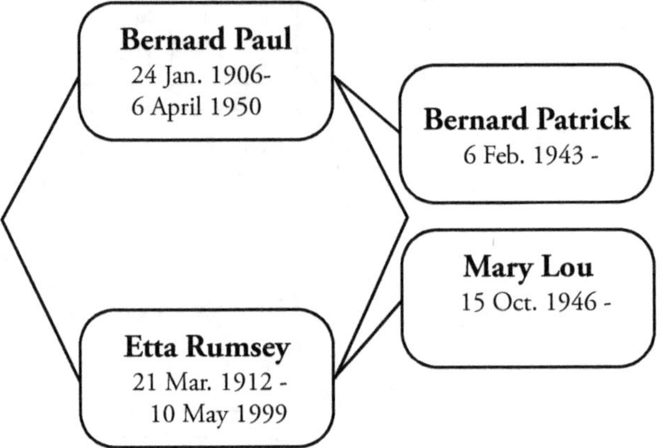

About the Author

Elizabeth Osta's historical novel, *Jeremiah's Hunger*, and her memoir, *Saving Faith: A Memoir of Courage, Conviction and A Calling* which was nominated for the Best of Rochester Award, have been accompanied by critical acclaim. She is a recipient of Florida's Amelia Island Literary Award for Non-Fiction and Rochester, New York's Writers & Books Big Pencil Award. *Maggie's Brood* is her fourth publication. She currently lives near Lima, New York on the Erie Canal in Fairport with her husband Dave Van Arsdale. She is enchanted by twin grandsons.